Dictionary of International Investment and Finance Terms

Series Editor: John O E Clark

Apart from any fair dealing for the purpose of research or private study, or criticism or review, as permitted under the Copyright, Designs and Patents Act 1988, this publication may be reproduced, stored or transmitted, in any form or by any means, only with the prior permission in writing of the publisher, or in the case of reprographic reproduction in accordance with the terms and licences issued by the Copyright Licensing Agency. Enquiries concerning reproduction outside those terms should be addressed to the publisher's agents at the undermentioned address:

Financial World Publishing
IFS House
4-9 Burgate Lane
Canterbury
Kent
CT1 2XJ
United Kingdom

T   01227 818687
F   01227 479641
E   editorial@ifslearning.com
W   www.ifslearning.com

BELFAST EDUCATION AND LIBRARY BOARD	
GENERAL REFERENCE	
C111078862	
Bertrams	23.03.07
368.003 A	£15.00
	G060242

Financial World Publishing publications are published by The Chartered Institute of Bankers, a non-profit making registered educational charity. The Chartered Institute of Bankers believes that the sources of information upon which the book is based are reliable and has made every effort to ensure the complete accuracy of the text. However, neither CIB, the author nor any contributor can accept any legal responsibility whatsoever for consequences that may arise from errors or omissions or any opinion or advice given.

Typeset by Kevin O'Connor

Printed in Spain

© The Chartered Institute of Bankers 2001
ISBN 0-85297-577-5

FINANCIAL
WORLD
Publishing
THE CHARTERED INSTITUTE OF BANKERS

Preface

This book is intended to provide access to the terms of trade finance for students and professionals in the growing world of internatonal trade, and its interaction with banking and the stock exchange. It should also assist private investors and people who read financial journals and the financial pages of daily newspapers. Like its companion volume, the *Dictionary of International Trade Finance*, it does not limit itself merely to well-established terms. It also includes definitions of the everyday jargon, acronyms and newly adopted words (many from the United States) that are now common in national and international financial dealings.

The Dictionary of International Investment and Finance Terms is one of a series of publications complied from The CIB's unique database of dictionary definitions that relate to various aspects of finance and their applications. As a result, some definitions appear in more than one book – as they should to maintain a comprehensive coverage of the subject within a single self-contained volume. The dictionaries in the series published to date include:

Dictionary of International Accounting Terms
0-85297-575-9

Dictionary of International Banking and Finance Terms
0-85297-632-1

Dictionary of International Business Terms
0-85297-574-0

Dictionary of International Insurance and Finance Terms
0-85297-631-3

Dictionary of International Investment and Finance Terms
0-85297-577-5

Dictionary of International Trade Finance
0-85297-576-7

John O E Clark

John O E Clark is a writer and editor who regularly contributes to dictionaries, encyclopedias and other types of information books for publication in Britain and abroad. He specializes in explaining technical subjects to students and other non-experts, and to people whose first language is not necessarily English.

A

A1 In the best condition. In marine insurance, a ship that is well maintained is shown in Lloyd's Register of Shipping as being A1.

ABC agreement In a US brokerage company, an agreement with an employee detailing the rights of the company if it buys a membership of the new York Stock Exchange on his or her behalf.

ABI Abbreviation of *Association of British Insurers*.

ability-to-pay taxation A theory of taxation whereby those who are able to pay more are taxed at a higher rate. It may be applied to luxury goods, for example, which thereby attract a high rate of tax.

above par Normally describing a share that has a market value above denomination or *face value*.

Abu Dhabi United Arab Emirates currency dirham (AWD), divided into 100 fils.

accelerated accrual See *accrual rate*.

accelerated depreciation The practice of depreciating an *asset* at a rate greater than the actual decline in its value in order to obtain tax concessions. It need not occur throughout the life of an asset; a substantial proportion of its total value is often written off in the first year, and reduced allowances for depreciation are made thereafter.

acceptance Broadly, the act of agreeing to do something. In business and finance, it can be taken in various ways. 1. Acceptance is one of the two stages of negotiating a *contract*: offer and acceptance. 2. It is the act of writing a bill of exchange, by which the acceptor accepts the bill and agrees to pay the drawer. 3. It is used to denote a bill that has been endorsed in the above way and has thereby been accepted.

acceptance credit A way of financing a sale to a foreign buyer in which a commercial bank or merchant bank provides a credit to the foreign creditworthy importer, who can draw a bill of exchange against the credit. The bank charges a commission to the seller (exporter).

acceptance for honour Also called acceptance supra protest, the acceptance/payment of a dishonoured bill of exchange, to preserve the honour of the person who drew or endorsed the bill.

acceptance house The US term for an *accepting house*.

acceptance supra protest See *acceptance for honour*.

accepting bank An alternative term for an **accepting house**.

accepting house (US acceptance house) A financial institution whose business is concerned mainly with the negotiation of bills of exchange, by either guaranteeing or accepting them. Also called an accepting bank, it usually operates in the same way as a **merchant bank**.

acceptor The person who accepts liability for a bill of exchange (by signing it on the face).

accommodation bill A bill of exchange signed by one person in order to help another to raise a loan. The signatory (accommodation party) is acting as guarantor, and normally does not expect to pay the bill when it falls due. Accommodation bill a are known variously as kites, windbills or windmills.

account (a/c, acc or acct.) In general terms, any note kept of a financial transaction, often also referred to as *accounts*. There are two more specific meanings. 1. In banking, it designates an arrangement made to deposit money with a bank, building society or other financial institution. There are various types of such accounts, with different conditions of withdrawal, rates of interest, minimum deposits, and so on. 2. On the London Stock Exchange, it is a period of two weeks (usually extended to three weeks when bank holidays occur) in which trading is carried out. Broadly, transactions are made in the two weeks of the account and the relevant paperwork is carried out during the following week, followed by payments (settlements) made on the sixth business day after the end of the account. This method of working allows transactions to be made with deferred payment, enabling *speculation* to take place.

account analysis The analysis of the annual results of a company, including the balance sheet, cashflow statement, and profit-and-loss account, with a view to deciding whether or not its shares would be a good investment. See also **accounting ratio**.

account day On th London Stock Exchange, the sixth business day after the end of an *account*, on which deals are settled.

account executive In the UK, most commonly a person in advertising who is responsible for the service to one client. In the USA, it is an alternative term for **stockbroker** (having the power of an agent).

accounting rate of return (ARR) The anticipated net profit from an investment, calculated as a percentage of investment.

accounting ratio Also called financial ratio, a ratio, calculated from figures in a company's accounts, that is used to assess its performance or financial viability by market analysts and potential investors. There are many such ratios, and all of the following have separate entries in this Dictionary: earning per share, fixed asset turnover, gross margin, interest cover, liquidity ratio, net profit percentage, proprietorship ratio, rate of collection of debtors, rate of payment of creditors, rate of return of gross assets, rate of return on shareholders' equity, rate of stock turnover, total asset turnover and working capital ratio.

Accounting Standards Board (ASB) An organization established in the UK in 1990 to set up and improve standards in the world of accountancy.

accounts payable The accounts on which a company owes money (for which it has been invoiced), also termed trade creditors.

accounts receivable The accounts on which money is owed to a company (for which it has issued invoices), also called trade debtors.

accounts receivable financing A type of short-term financing that uses accounts receivable as collateral.

accredited Describing somebody who is authorized to act on behalf of a company or individual.

accrual The gradual increase in something by addition over a period of time (and not resulting from a specific transaction). *See also* ***accrued charge***.

accrual rate The number of years of an employee's service that define his or her pension rights. It is usually expressed as a fraction of 60 and applied to the final salary to give the pension entitlement. The use of a figure of less than 60 is termed accelerated accrual.

accruals concept A principle used in accounting by which income and expenditure are taken into the profit-and-loss account for the period in which they occur. This method of accounting is useful in that it pulls together receipts and the costs incurred in generating them, avoiding a time lag between the time income is received and the time liability becomes due.

accrued benefits Under a company pension scheme, the pension benefits to which a person is entitled up to a certain point in time, regardless of whether or not he or she stays in the job.

accrued charge Also called accrued liability, a charge that has not been accounted for or paid. For example, demand for rent made in arrears must appear on the accounts as an accrued charge, because the service had already been used but not paid for. See *accrual*.

accrued dividend A dividend payment that is due to shareholders but not paid, the capital being retained by the company to finance expansion.

accrued income scheme A tax rule in the UK which regards the interest that accrues after the last interest payment on a sold interest-bearing security (worth not more than £5000) and the date of sale as belonging to the buyer. The seller can therefore deduct this amount from his or her taxable income.

accrued interest An interest payment that is due, but not yet received.

accumulation units The units a person holds in a *unit trust* that are bought by reinvesting previous income from the trust.

acid-test ratio Also called acid ratio, both are alternative terms for *liquidity ratio*.

acquisition The take-over of control of one company (the target company) by another or by an individual. The purchase of an equity stake in the target is the usual method of acquisition.

across-the-board Describing a movement in market prices that affects the majority of stocks in the same direction, up or down.

ACT Abbreviation of *advance corporation tax*.

acting in concert Describing the actions of investors who work togther for a common purpose. See *concert party*.

active bond crowd The members of the New York Stock Exchange who do most of the trading.

active market The situation affecting a bond, commodity, share or whole market for which there is a heavy volume of trading.

active partner A member of a partnership who has contributed to the capital and takes part in its management. See also *sleeping partner*.

actual On a commodity market, a commodity that is available for immediate delivery (or sale). It is also called a physical.

actual price On a commodity market, the price of a commodity that is available for immediate delivery (or sale). It is also called the a physical price or spot price.

actuary A statistician employed by an insurance company to calculate the likelihood of risk (particularly life expectancy) and advise insurers on the amount of premium to be charged for each type of risk and how much to set aside to cover it.

additional voluntary contribution (AVC) An extra sum paid into an occupational pension scheme by an employee to increase the size of the pension.

adjustable-rate mortgage (ARM) A mortgage whose rate of interest rises and falls along with interest rates in general. There may be a cap or ceiling defining the maximum possible rate. *See also* **teaser**.

adjustable rate-preferred (ARP) stock A US term for a type of preference share whose dividend is tied to the rate of interest on Treasury bills. The shares are convertible (to ordinary shares, US common stocks) at a fixed price and date.

adjustment speed The speed of adjustment that changes in the economic situation bring about. Commodity markets, foreign exchange markets and money markets tend to adjust rapidly in response to even small changes in supply and demand, for example.

administration Broadly, the sum of the actions involved in the organization or management of a company. In law, it is either the winding-up of the estate of a deceased person in the absence of an executor or in the event of intestacy, or it is the winding up of a company. Both cases involve the court appointment of somebody to act as administrator.

administration order A UK County Court order requiring the *administration* of the estate of a debtor, who usually has to pay the debts by instalments in order to avoid bankruptcy.

administrative receiver A person appointed by the court to manage a company's assets on behalf of **debenture** holders or other secured creditors.

administrator 1. A person appointed (usually by the court) to manage somebody else's property. 2. A person appointed by the court to manage the affairs of somebody who has died without making a will (intestate). Proof of his or her authority is a letter of administration issued by the court.

ADP (ISO) code Andorra. It has no currency of its own – there are mainly Spanish pesetas in circulation. It will adopt the euro/cent from 2002.

ADR Abbreviation of *American depositary receipt*.

ad referendum When referring to a contract, a term which indicates that while the contract has been signed and agreed, there are still some matters to be discussed.

ADST Abbreviation of *approved deferred share trust*.

ad valorem Latin for according to value. In taxation it indicates that tax is calculated as a percentage of the value of the transaction, rather than at a fixed rate; e.g. value added tax (VAT) is paid as a percentage of the cost of the goods or services and is therefore ad valorem, whereas car road tax in the UK is mostly paid at a fixed rate.

advance 1. A general term for a *loan*. 2. A part-payment for work contracted made ahead of the total payment, i.e. before all the goods or services contracted for have been rendered. Sometimes, if payment depends on sales, the advance is set against those sales.

advance corporation tax (ACT) Corporation tax is often levied in two parts. The first part is levied on the distribution of profits (of a company) and is termed advance corporation tax. The second part of the tax is estimated on the company's earnings. *See corporation tax*.

adventure A speculative venture, especially one that involves foreign dealings.

adverse selection The concept of disproportionate risk: those who are more prone to suffer loss or to make claims than the average risk.

advise fate A request from a collecting banker to a paying banker to confirm that the cheque or bill to which it refers has been honoured. This confirmation cannot be given until the paying banker receives the cheque, because the account to which it refers may have had other debits made to it, or the payer may stop the cheque. It is a speedy method of confirmation, and its circumvents the use of a banker's clearing house.

advisory funds Funds for investment deposited with a bank that can be invested only after consultation with the depositor.

AED (ISO) code United Arab Emirates – currency dirham.

AEX Abbreviation of *Amsterdam Exchanges*.

AFA (ISO) code Afghanistan – currency afghani.

AFBD Abbreviation of *Association of Future Brokers and Dealers*.

aggregation risk

affidavit A statement or declaration made in writing and witnessed by a commissioner for oaths (such as a solicitor), often used for legal proceedings.

Afghanistan currency afghani (AFA), divided into 100 pule.

after date Words written on a bill of exchange which indicate that it will become due a certain (specified) period after the date on the bill.

after-hours dealing Trading on official exchanges outside normal trading hours. As a result, prices might change considerably between the previous day's closing and the next day's opening.

aftermarket 1. Trading in stocks and shares after they have made their initial debut on the stock market. 2. The market in components and services arising after a product has been sold. It is also known as the add-on market.

after sight Words written on a bill of exchange which indicate that the period for which the bill is drawn is to be calculated from the date on which the acceptor (drawee) first saw (or accepted) it.

after-tax income The income that remains after the payment of direct taxes (although some indirect taxes may still be due).

age admitted A term in a life assurance policy that evidence of age has been provided by the assured. No further proof is needed in the event of a claim.

age allowance A UK tax allowance made to a person over the age of 65 or a married couple where one partner is over that age. It increases for those over 75.

agency 1. A person or company that represents another in a particular field. 2. A contractual agreement by which one party agrees to represent another, the agent's word becoming as binding in the affairs of the other as if the latter had acted on his or her own behalf.

agency bill A bill of exchange that is accepted by the local branch of a foreign bank.

agent A person or company that has entered into a contract of *agency* with another party, called the *principal*, and acts as its representative, usually in buying and selling goods or services. Normally an agent does not own the principal's property, but must follow the principal's instructions.

aggregation risk The multiplying up of risk when trading securities in more than one problematic market.

agio A commission or charge (the "turn") made by a bank or bureau de change in return for converting cash from one currency into another.

agorot A subdivision (1/100) of the Israeli shekel.

AIBD Abbreviation of *Association of International Bond Dealers*.

AIM Abbreviation of *alternative investment market*.

air-pocket stock Stock whose price suddenly falls, usually after rumours of the company's poor performance.

Albania currency Albanian lek (ALL), divided into 100 qindarka.

Algeria currency Algerian dinar (DZD), divided into 100 centimes.

alienation of assets The selling by a borrower of assets that have been used as security for a loan, usually disallowed by a clause in the loan agreement.

alligator spread Profit made on an option that is instantly snapped up by the broker as commission, leaving nothing for the investor.

all-in Including everything, most often used to describe a price or service.

allonge A slip attached to a bill of exchange that provides extra space for endorsements, now rarely needed with the decline in the use of such bills.

All Ordinaries Share Price Index Often shortened to All Ordinaries, a weighted index of 250 companies that trade on the Australian Stock Exchange.

all-or-none order An instruction to buy or sell a security directing a futures broker not to carry out the order unless it can be fulfilled in its entirety.

allotment letter See *letter of allotment*.

allotment note A document that authorizes the master of a ship to pay a crew member's wages direct to his wife, family or bank.

allotment of shares When a company issues shares by publishing a prospectus and inviting applications, allotment is the assignment of shares to each applicant. In cases where the issue is oversubscribed, shares are allotted in proportion to the quantity requested and so applicants do not always receive the number of shares they originally requested. See also *letter of allotment*.

allotment subscribed The allocation (and hence reduction) of a security,

amortizing mortgage

such as a eurobond, apportioned to the individual subscriber in an oversubscribed issue.

allowance 1. Money that is allotted (allowed) to individuals for a specific reason, or a provision made for unusual or uncertain events. 2. The amount deducted for one of various reasons before income is calculated for tax purposes. Examples in the UK include personal allowance and married couple's allowance.

alpha A Stock Exchange categorization of the top 100 most actively traded shares with a large capitalization value. *See also* **beta; delta; gamma.**

Alternative Investment Market (AIM) A London market, established in 1995, that helps smaller companies to raise capital. It replaced the Unlisted Securities Market at the end of 1996.

ambulance stock Securities recommended to a client whose investment portfolio has done badly. The practice is especially common in Japan.

American depositary receipt (ADR) A receipt that is issued by an American bank declaring that a certain number of a company's shares have been deposited with it. ADRs are denominated in dollars and although they usually refer to non-American companies, they are traded on the American markets as US securities.

American Express (AMEX) An international credit company based in the USA.

American option An option whose buyer can exercise the right to take it up at any time before the expiry date.

American Stock Exchange (AMEX) The New York stock exchange that deals in stocks and bonds of smaller companies. It is also known as the Little Board or the Curb Exchange. Larger companies are listed on the *New York Stock Exchange*.

AMEX Abbreviation of *American Express* and *American Stock Exchange.*

amortize To pay off debts by means of payments over a period of time. More specifically, in accounting, the cost of a fixed asset is written into the profit-and-loss account over a period of years, rather than being taken into account when it is first bought. The cost of the asset is said to have been amortized when the period is over.

amortizing mortgage A mortgage in which all the principal and interest has been repaid, usually by equal payments, by the end of the mortgage term. Although the payments are equal, early payments are made up mostly of interest, whereas later payments are mostly repayments of the principal.

Amsterdam Exchanges (AEX) A market in derivatives and equities established in 1997 by the merger of the Amsterdam Stock Exchange and the European Options Exchange. It is a private limited company owned by its shareholders.

Amsterdam Stock Exchange Claimed to be the world's oldest stock exchange, founded in 1602, it adopted a screen-based trading system in 1990. In 1997 it merged with the European Options Exchange to form the Amsterdam Exchanges (AEX).

analysis The determination of the composition or significance of something. In business and finance, an analysis can be a detailed study or investigation of a particular subject, often culminating in an analyst's report, upon which people may base decisions.

analyst A person who undertakes an *analysis*.

Andorra It has no currency of its own – there are mainly Spanish pesetas in circulation (ADP) as well French francs. It will adopt the euro/cent from 2002.

ANG (ISO) code Netherlands Antilles – currency Netherlands Antilles guilder.

angel 1. A bond with a very high investment rating. 2. A person who invests in a theatrical production.

Angola currency kwanza (AOK), divided into 100 lwei.

annual bonus 1. The amount added each year to a with-profits life assurance policy, also called a *reversionary bonus*. 2. A sum awarded to employees each year in addition to their salary (perhaps based on performance).

annual increment The amount by which prices or money (often a salary) increase in the course of one year.

annualize To convert interest on a short-term to an annual basis, *e.g.* a security or commission etc. earning ½% a month would be seen to be earning the equivalent 6% p.a. by multiplying the monthly rate by 12. It can be a useful method of producing MAT (moving annual total) figures.

annualized percentage rate (APR) Also known as annual percentage rate, the rate of interest charged on a monthly basis (e.g. on a *hire*

approved deferred share trust (ADST)

purchase transaction) shown as a yearly *compound interest* rate.

annual percentage rate *See annualized percentage rate.*

annual report A document required by law to be released by public companies, describing the company's activities during the previous year. It usually includes the company's balance sheet for the year.

annual return A document that in the UK must be submitted to Companies House each year by every company with share capital, detailing such items as the address of the registered office, a list of current members, charges on the company, and so on.

annuitant A person receiving an *annuity*.

annuity A contract whereby a person pays a certain amount of money to an insurance company, either as a lump sum or as instalments, and receives periodic payments in return for life or for a specified period. Annuities are generally linked to life assurances or pension schemes.

annuity certain An annuity that is payable over an agreed period, such as 10 or 15 years, irrespective of the life or death of the annuitant.

Antigua currency East Caribbean dollar (AGD), divided into 100 cents.

anti-trust laws US legislation that was enacted to prevent the formation of monopolies. It is similar to the Monopolies and Mergers Act in the UK.

AOK (ISO) code Angola – currency kwanza.

APCIMS Abbreviation of *Association of Private Client Investment Managers and Stockbrokers*.

application and allotment A system whereby a company may issue shares. It is done by publishing a prospectus, inviting applications from institutions and individuals to buy shares, and then allotting shares to those who take up the offer. *See also* **allotment**.

apportion 1. To share out. The term is normally applied to costs. 2. The allocation (and hence reduction) of a security, such as a eurobond, apportioned to the individual subscriber in an oversubscribed issue.

appreciation An increase in value (e.g. of an investment); the opposite of depreciation. In accounting, it is the increase in value of (fixed) assets. In finance, within a floating exchange rate system, it is the increase in the value of one currency against another.

approved deferred share trust (ADST) A trust fund in which a company buys shares in itself for the benefit of its employees. A reduced rate of tax is paid on the shares, and then only after they are sold.

APR Abbreviation of *annualized percentage rate* or annual percentage rate.

APT Abbreviation of *Automated Pit Trading*.

arb Shortened form of *arbitrage*.

ARB US abbreviation of arbitrageur. *See arbitrager*.

arbitrage (general) Practice of dealing on two markets almost simultaneously in order to profit from differing exchange rates. Arbitrage may take place when dealing in commodities, bills of exchange or currencies. It also occurs in situations where prices and returns are fixed and in this sense arbitrage may be contrasted with speculation in that there is little risk involved. In the USA, the term is often shortened to arb. *See also reverse arbitrage; soft arbitrage*.

arbitrage (currency arbitrage). 1. Dealing between two (international) financial centres to make a profit (or "turn") on rates of exchange, resulting from a temporary difference in the exchange rates quoted in the two centres. 2. The act of creating funds in currency X by borrowing in another currency Y and converting it to the currency X in a swap deal.

arbitrager (US **arbitrageur**, abbreviated to ARB) A person who practises *arbitrage*.

arbitration In disputes arising out of a contract, the parties involved may either go to court or appoint somebody (an arbitrator) to settle the dispute. The agreement to go to arbitration does not preclude either of the parties taking legal proceedings if it desires.

arbitration clause A clause in a contract that details the procedure to be taken to settle disputes. *See arbitration*.

Argentina currency peso (ARP), divided into 100 centavos.

ariary Madagascar currency unit. 1 ariary = 5 Malagasy francs.

arithmetic mean *See average*.

ARM Abbreviation of *adjustable-rate mortgage*.

Armenia currency dram.

arm's length Describing a transaction negotiated and entered into by unrelated parties, each of whom acts in his or her own best interest using fair market values. It is assumed that, unless there is a related party disclosure, all transactions described in financial statements are conducted at arm's length.

ARP See *adjustable rate-preferred stock*.

ARP (ISO) code Argentina – currency peso.

ARR Abbreviation of *accounting rate of return*.

arrears Describing money that is owed but still not paid. Annuities can be paid in arrears, e.g. "yearly in arrears" means that the first annuity payment is made in one year's time.

articles of association A legally-required document that sets up the internal regulations for a UK limited company's operation and which states, among other things, the powers of directors. It is submitted, along with the *memorandum of association*, to the Registrar of Companies, where it is available for public scrutiny. Its equivalent in the USA are articles of incorporation.

artificial currency A substitute for actual currency, such as European currency units (ECUs) and special drawing rights (SDRs).

ASB Abbreviation of *Accounting Standards Board*.

ASC Abbreviation of *Australian Securities Commission*.

Asian option An option on foreign exchange or commodity prices that additionally pays the difference gained between its strike price and the average price of the underlying asset, calculated over the option's life. It is also called an average-rate option.

asked price A US term for *offer price*.

asking price The price at which foreign exchange, foreign bank notes or other securities are offered for sale.

assay The testing of a metal or ore to determine the proportion of *precious metal* it contains. Assay most often applies to metals used in coinage, and to gold and silver.

assented bond A bond whose holder has agreed to reduce interest payments or to reduce the payment of the principal amount for a rescheduling or other type or reorganization.

assented stock In a situation where a company is threatened with a take-over, assented stocks or shares are those whose owner is in agreement with the take-over. In these circumstances, there may arise separate markets in assented and non-assented stock. Assented stock may also be stock whose owner is in agreement with a proposed change in the conditions of issue.

asset Something that belongs to an individual or company and which has a value, e.g. buildings, plant, stock, but also *accounts receivable*. There are several types of assets for business purposes, and they are usually classified in terms of their availability for exchange.

asset allocation The allocation of investments, such as stocks and shares, to make up an investment portfolio.

asset allocation mutual fund A mutual fund (such as a unit trust) in which the fund manager moves investments among various securities to achieve the best return at the least risk.

asset-backed fund A fund consisting of investments that are related to *tangible assets* (such as property or shares), so that the investment participates in growth and can be regarded as a hedge against inflation.

asset-backed security A security whose collateral is the return on a financial instrument such as a mortgage.

asset-based financing Loans secured on a company's assets, especially its accounts receivable or stock.

asset cover A measure of a company's solvency equal to the ratio of net assets to debt. High asset cover implies that a company is more than marginally solvent.

asset-led marketing A type of marketing based on a company's strengths (such as its brand name), and not merely on what customers want.

asset management Broadly, the efficient control and exploitation of a company's assets, most commonly used to describe the management of any fund by a fund manager.

asset play Describing shares that an analyst regards as being undervalued (because their price does not properly reflect the company's assets).

asset stripping A practice, normally frowned upon, whereby a company is bought merely so that the buyer may sell off its assets for immediate gain.

asset value The value of the assets of a company less its liabilities. It is often divided by the number of issued ordinary shares and expressed as the asset value per share, theoretically payable to shareholders if the company were to be wound up.

assignee A person or company to whom the rights in an asset (such as a life assurance policy) are assigned.

assignment The legal transfer of a property, right or obligation from one party to another.

assignment of a life policy The transfer of the right to receive the proceeds of a life assurance policy (with the agreement of the insurer).

assignor The person who assigns something (perhaps as security or for safe keeping) to a third party, the assignee.

Association of British Insurers (ABI) The trade organization that represents UK assurance and insurance companies and issues their code of practice. It was formed in 1985 by a merger of the British Insurance Association, the Accident offices Association, the Life Office Association and the Industrial Life Office Association.

Association of Futures Brokers and Dealers (AFBD) The professional body governing the activities of the personnel working in the financial futures market within the UK. In 1991 it became part of the *Securities and Futures Authority*.

Association of International Bond Dealers (AIBD) An organization, established in Zurich in 1969, which in 1991 changed its name to the *International Securities Market Association*.

Association of Investment Trust Managers An organization, established in 1932, that looks after the interests of more than 300 investment trusts in the UK.

Association of Private Client Investment Managers and Stockbrokers (APCIMS) An organization, established in 1990, that represents private client investment managers and stockbrokers in the UK.

Association of Unit Trusts and Investment Funds (AUTIF) An organization, established in 1959 (as the Association of Unit Trust Managers), which acts as a trade organization for its members.

assumed interest rate The rate of interest an insurance company applies to annuity payments.

AST Abbreviation of *Automated Screen Trading*.

ASX Abbreviation of *Australian Stock Exchange*.

assured In a life assurance policy, the person named in it who will receive the proceeds at maturity or on the death of the person whose life is assured.

as-you-like option Also called a call-or-put option, an option whose form can be changed, if the holder so wishes, within a specified time limit.

at best Short for at the best possible price, an instruction to a broker to buy or sell shares or commodities at the best price available. See *loan*.

at call Money at call has been borrowed but must be repaid on demand. See also *loan*.

Athens Stock Exchange The only stock exchange in Greece, established in 1876, and now converted to electronic trading.

at limit An instruction to a broker to buy or sell shares or commodities with a limit on the upper and lower prices.

at par Equal, usually indicating a share price that is equal to the paid-up or nominal value.

ATS Abbreviation of *Automated Trade System*.

at sight Words written on a bill of exchange which indicate that payment is due on presentation of the bill.

at the highest possible price An instruction to a broker in which the seller does not authorize any maximum or minimum price for the fulfilment of the order. In a limited market, such as a more exotic foreign currency, it will be carried as soon as possible.

at the lowest possible price An instruction to a broker in which the buyer does not authorize any maximum or minimum price for the fulfilment of the order. In a limited market, such as a more exotic foreign currency, it will be carried as soon as possible.

at-the-money option An option where the strike price equals the market price of the asset (e.g. in a currency market it will equal spot).

at the opening order On futures and options exchanges, a market when there is a range of prices at the opening of business.

AUD (ISO) code Australia – currency Australian dollar.

auction Method of selling goods, property or land in public. The auctioneer acts as an agent for the seller, offers the goods and normally sells to the highest bidder (for which service the auctioneer charges a commission). After the item is knocked down, the auctioneer is also an agent of the buyer. An advertisement for an auction is not legally an offer for sale but an invitation to attend.

auctioneer See *auction*.

authorized capital 21

auction system An order-driven stock exchange system in which brokers and dealers bid for stock using open outcry (or an auction), as on the New York Stock Exchange.

audit An examination of a company's accounts. It is a legal requirement in the UK that the accounts of limited companies over a certain size (and certain other organizations) be scrutinized annually by an independent auditor. This is termed a statutory audit, from which small companies (with a turnover of not more than £90,000 and not more than £1.4 million on the balance sheet) are exempt.

auditor A person appointed by a company or other organization to carry out an audit. In the UK, in order to act as an external auditor he or she must be registered or a member of a recognized supervisory body.

auditors' report A report produced by external auditors appointed to audit a company's accounts, giving an opinion of the financial statements. Under the Companies Act 1985, it has to be filed with the accounts at the Registrar of Companies. In the USA, an auditor's report is sometimes called the accountant's report.

audit trail A system by means of which each stage of a transaction is formally documented and recorded, so that they can be examined during an audit.

Aunt Millie A colloquial US term for an investor who lacks experience and sophistication.

aurar A subdivision (1/100) of an Icelandic krona.

Australia currency Australian dollar (AUD), divided into 100 cents.

Australian Securities Commission (ASC) An organization that supervises the trading in securities in Australia.

Australian Stock Exchange (ASX) An organization established in 1987 by the amalgamation of the previous six state stock exchanges in Australia, which in 1990 converted to total electronic trading (using SEATS: Stock Exchange Automated Screen Trading System).

Austria currency Schilling (ATS) divided into 100 Groschen. The 1999 legacy conversion rate was 13.7603 to the euro. It will fully change to the euro/cent from 2002.

authenticate To state that something is true, e.g. an auditor signs a company's accounts, thereby authenticating them.

authorized capital The amount of capital that a company is authorized to raise through the issue of shares, as set down in its *articles of association*.

AUTIF Abbreviation of *Association of Unit Trust and Investment Funds*.

Automated Pit Trading (APT) A computerized trading system that initially supplemented the open outcry market at the London International Financial Futures Exchange (LIFFE). Its main use was after 1620 hours (when the floor market closed) until 1800 hours (when the exchange closed).

Automated Screen Trading (AST) A computerized trading system that can operate 24 hours a day worldwide, now introduced in most of the world's major stock exchanges.

Automated Trade System (ATS) The first automated screen trading system, introduced in 1989 for the New Zealand Futures and Options Exchange.

aval A guarantee given by a bank at a customer's request that a bill of exchange will be paid on presentation.

AVC Abbreviation of *additional voluntary contribution*.

average Also called the arithmetic mean, or just mean, a single number or value that indicates the general tendency of a collection of numbers or values. The average of n values is the sum of the values divided by n.

average rate option Also known as an Asian option, an option that is settled at the difference between the strike price and the average market price of the underlying security.

AWD (ISO) code Abu Dhabi United Arab Emirates – currency dirham.

AXD (ISO) code Dubai United Arab Emirates – currency dirham.

AYD (ISO) code United Arab Emirates (others) – currency dirham.

Azerbaijan currency manat.

B

baby bond A type of bond offered by registered UK friendly societies to minors; the funds are tax-exempt. In the USA, it is a low-value bond (usually worth between $25 and $500) aimed at small investors.

backdate To date a document with a date that is earlier than that on which it is actually signed. Back dating indicates that the provisions of the document become effective on the back date rather than on the date of signature.

back-end loading The practice of charging investors for withdrawing funds (and thus discouraging them from doing so).

backing away The failure of a securities dealer to carry through a deal at the price he or she quoted. It is usually frowned upon in all markets.

back month On financial futures markets, those contracts that are being traded for the month that is farthest in the future.

back office The department of a financial services institution that does the "paper work", i.e., the documentation of transactions carried out by the front office.

backroom An informal term for *back office*.

back tax Also known as back duty, payment of tax on income that was not paid at the time it was earned or first claimed.

back-to-back credit Also known as countervailing credit, a form of credit by which a finance house acts as an intermediary between a foreign seller and a buyer, concealing the identity of the seller. The seller passes to the finance house the documents relevant to the sale and the house reissues them to the buyer in its own name.

back-to-back loan A type of loan between companies in different countries (and perhaps in different currencies) employing a bank or finance house which uses funding from a third party to provide the loan.

back-up credit Guaranteed credit from a bank or banks that backs a note issuer or Euronotes, used when any of the notes do not get purchased.

backwardation 1. In a commodity or financial market, the situation where the forward or futures price is less than the spot price. It can arise because of excessive present demand, which is expected to fall later. *See also* **contango**, which is the opposite effect. 2. In stock markets, the situation where the highest bid price is higher than the lowest offer price, in theory enabling a purchase from one market maker to be sold to another immediately at a profit.

bad debt A debt that has not been, and is not expected to be, paid. Such losses are practically unavoidable in business (and allowances are almost always made for such instances), although some bad debts may be sold to a factoring company, which attempts to recover the debt on its own account.

Bahamas currency Bahamian dollar (BSD), divided into 100 cents.

Bahrain currency Bahrain dinar (BHD), divided into 1000 fils.

baht The standard currency unit of Thailand, divided into 100 satang.

bailing out The practice of quickly selling an investment regardless of the price obtained (perhaps because losses are rising too quickly to be sustainable).

baiza A subdivision (1/1000) of the Omani rial.

balanced mutual fund A mutual fund that is invested in a spread of ordinary shares, preferential shares and bonds as a means of maximizing returns and minimizing risk.

balance of payments (BOP) An account of all recorded financial exchanges made between the residents of a country and those of other countries. The balance of payments is divided into the current and capital accounts. The current account takes stock of all visible and invisible trade (the *balance of trade* is part of the balance of payments current account), and the capital account includes all movements of capital in or out of the country.

balance of trade (BOT) Also known as the visible balance, the difference in value between a country's visible imports and visible exports. When the total value of visible imports is more than the value of visible exports, it is known as an adverse balance of trade. *See* ***balance of payments***.

balance sheet A statement that shows the financial position of a company in respect of its assets and liabilities at a certain time, often the last day of its accounting period, which must be included in the company's financial accounts. It must also give a true and fair view of the company's affairs. After listing the fixed and current assets, and the

bank loan 25

liabilities (part 1), the statement indicates how they were financed (part 2). The totals of parts 1 and 2 should be equal – they must balance. The balance sheet should also show the corresponding figures for the previous accounting period. In the USA, a balance sheet is sometimes known as a statement of financial condition or position.

balloon A large irregular part-payment of a loan, made when funds are available. Such an arrangement is termed a balloon loan.

balloon interest A higher rate of interest on securities that have later maturities.

balloon mortgage See *non-amortizing mortgage*.

ballot In general terms, a method of voting by marking a paper. More specifically it is a method of allotting shares to applicants in the event that the share issue is oversubscribed. All applicants are entered for the ballot and those drawn at random receive some or all of the shares applied for.

Baltic Exchange Shortened form of *Baltic International Freight Futures Exchange*.

Baltic International Freight Futures Exchange (BIFFEX) Usually known by its shortened name Baltic Exchange, a facility for the purchase and sale of freight futures, transferred to *London Futures and Options Exchange* in 1991.

bancassurance The combining of the businesses of banking and life assurance (and pensions), usually within an existing bank or building society.

Bangladesh currency taka (BDT), divided into 100 poisha.

bani A subdivision (1/100) of the Romanian leu.

bank An organization that carries on the business of banking and is so authorized by the central bank (the Bank of England in the UK). See also *central bank; licensed deposit taker; merchant bank*.

Bank Insurance Fund (BIF) An organization that offers insurance to US banks to cover all deposits up to $100,000. It was established in 1933 as the Federal Deposit Insurance Corporation.

bank loan A loan from a bank. A modest personal loan does not normally require security. Larger loans and loans to companies generally have to be secured.

banknote Paper currency, a note issued by a bank (the Bank of England in the UK) that promises to pay its bearer on demand the face (par) value of the note. *See also* **legal tender**.

Bank of Documentary Credit Insurance (BDCI) An organization that provides guarantees against losses to Canadian banks that finance export business. It is part of the Canadian Export Development Corporation.

Bank of England The central bank of the UK. Founded in 1694, it now has various functions including the supervision of other banks, managing monetary policy, and acting as a banker's bank and lender of the last resort. It also issues banknotes in the UK.

Bank of France The central bank of France. Founded in 1800, it changed composition in 1994 (following the Maastricht Treaty) to give it a higher degree of autonomy in formulating monetary policy.

Bank of Japan The central bank of Japan. It manages monetary policy and acts as lender of last resort; it also issues banknotes. The supervision of other banks, however, is undertaken by the Banking Bureau.

Bank of Scotland A commercial bank in Scotland which, while not a central bank, issues its own banknotes.

bank rate The official rate of interest charged by the central banks as lender of the last resort, for instance by the Bank of England when lending to discount houses. The term has fallen out of use in the UK, to be replaced by *minimum lending rate*.

bankruptcy The state of an individual or unincorporated body that is unable to pay its debts, as determined by the court. A similar situation involving a limited company is termed *insolvency*.

bank statement A record of deposits and withdrawals from an account with a bank or building society.

Barbados currency dollar (BBD), divided into 100 cents.

barbell portfolio A US term that describes an investment portfolio consisting mainly of short-term bonds and long-term bonds, with few of intermediate date.

bargain In London Stock Exchange jargon, any deal struck that involves the buying and selling of shares.

bargaining The act of negotiating a price or other terms.

barometer stock A *blue-chip* security whose price is regarded as indicative of the state of the market. A similar US term is bellweather security.

barter Also called countertrading, the trading of goods or services without using money (as opposed to a sale, when some form of money is involved).

base currency Every exchange rate consists of a quoted currency against a base, or reference currency. For example, if the euro is quoted at 1.1052 - 1.1096 to the US dollar, the US dollar is the base currency.

base metals On commodity markets, copper, lead, tin and zinc (i.e. not *precious metals*).

base period The time period selected for the base for an *index number* series. The index for a base period is usually 100, and any changes in prior or subsequent periods are expressed relative to it.

base rate The rate of interest charged by UK banks on loans to their prime corporate customers. It represents the minimum amount of interest a bank charges on a loan and higher quotations reflect any increased current market pressures and/or the risk involved in the loan.

base year The starting year for s system of *index-linking*, generally allocated an index number of 100.

basic rate Formerly the standard rate, the normal rate of UK income tax, equal to 23% in 2000/2001. All taxable income above a certain amount attracts tax at the basic rate (although there is a lower rate for income below that amount), as long as it does not exceed an upper limit, beyond which a higher rate of tax (currently 40%) is payable.

basis 1. The difference between the spot price and a futures contract price. 2. The value of an asset for tax purposes.

basis point A unit used to measure the rate of change of investment payments for bonds or notes. Each basis point is equal to 0.01% (one-hundredth of a percentage point), e.g. 25 basis points is 0.25%. See also *minimum fluctuation*.

basis price An alternative term for *strike price*.

basket trade The trading of securities that include all the *Financial Times Stock Exchange 100 Index* (FTSE 100) shares.

BBD (ISO) code Barbados – currency dollar.

BCF (ISO) code Benin – currency CFA franc.

BDCI Abbreviation of *Bank of Documentary Credit Insurance*.

BDT (ISO) code Bangladesh – currency taka.

bear A stock exchange dealer or analyst who believes that prices or investment values will go down.

bear closing A situation that occurs when a dealer has sold shares or commodities that he does not yet own and then buys them back, at a lower price, this making a profit.

bearer Somebody who holds a bill of exchange, cheque or certificate. If the document is marker "pay bearer", he or she may present and cash it.

bearer bond A bond payable to the bearer rather than to a specific, named individual. It usually has detachable coupons that are sent to the issuer for regular interest payments.

bearer scrip A temporary document that acknowledges acceptance of an offer form and a cheque for a new issue, exchanged for a bearer bond when the bond is available (or when all instalments have been paid).

bearer stocks Like bearer bonds, securities that are payable to the bearer, not to a named holder.

bear hug In corporate finance, an informal term for notice given to the board of a target company that a take-over bid is imminent.

bearish Describing somebody or something (e.g. a market) with the qualities of a *bear*.

bear market A situation in which share prices are falling (bears are speculators who sell shares in anticipation of falling prices).

bear position The position of an investor whose sales exceed his or her purchases and who therefore stands to gain in a falling, or bear, market.

bear raid Vigorous selling in concert in order to force down the price of a particular commodity or share. *See* **concert party**.

bear squeeze A situation in which bears who have been *short selling* are faced with a price rise rather than a fall.

bed-and-breakfast deal A transaction that is used to minimize the impact of capital gains tax. A shareholder sells his or her holding after trading closes for the day, for tax purposes. Next morning, the same shareholder buys the holding back. In the USA, it is called a swap.

BEF (ISO) code Belgium – currency Belgian franc. The 1999 legacy conversion rate was 40.3399 to the euro. It will fully change to the euro/cent from 2002.

Belarus (also known as Belorussia, Byelorussia) currency rouble, divided into 100 kopecks.

Belfox Abbreviation of *Belgian Futures and Options Exchange*.

Belgian Futures and Options Exchange (Belfox) An exchange in Brussels, established in 1991, that trades in government bonds and stock options.

Belgium currency Belgian franc (BEF), divided into 100 centimes.

Belize currency dollar (BZD), divided into 100 cents.

below par Describing a share price that has fallen below the nominal value at which it was issued.

bellweather security *See barometer stock.*

beneficial owner 1. When a shareholding is held by a nominee such as a stockbroker, the nominee's name appears on the register of shareholders. The real owner is known as the beneficial owner. 2. The owner of the beneficial interest in a property. It may not be the legal owner, but he or she has the rights in the benefits.

beneficiary A person who gains money or property from something; e.g. from a financial transaction such as a life assurance policy, a will or a trust.

Benin currency CFA franc (BCF); there is no subdivision.

bequest A gift of money or property made to a beneficiary under the terms of a will. It may also be called a legacy.

Bermuda currency Bermudan dollar (BMD), divided into 100 cents.

BES Abbreviation of *Business Expansion Scheme*.

best advice A term reflecting the fact that legally a financial adviser must recommend a suitable product to meet a client's needs. An independent financial adviser must offer best advice from all the financial products available in the marketplace. A tied agent must offer best advice from the range of products on offer by his or her company.

best execution rule The requirement that a stockbroker must obtain the best available price when buying or selling securities on behalf of a client.

best price An order to buy or sell something at the best price available at the time.

beta A measure of the relative volatility of a security's price. A balanced portfolio is likely to have a factor or coefficient of about 1. One with only half the movement of the market as a whole will have a factor of 0.5, while conversely one with double the degree of change will have a factor of 2, and so on.

beta shares (US **beta stocks**) Second-line shares, as opposed to the less numerous highly-capitalized alpha (first-line) or more numerous gamma (third-line) shares.

betting See *bookmaker; gambling*.

BGL (ISO) code Bulgaria – currency Bulgarian lev.

BHD (ISO) code Bahrain – currency Bahrain dinar.

Bhutan currency ngultrum.

bid An offer to buy something (e.g. shares) at a certain price. A seller may make a certain offer and a prospective buyer may make a bid. The bid cancels out the offer. More especially, a bid is an offer by one company to buy the shares of another – a take-over bid.

bidder Somebody who makes a bid for something or who is willing to buy at a specified price in a two-sided deal.

bidding ring A group of dealers acting in concert in order to drive prices up or down. The practice is illegal. *See also* **concert party**.

bid-offer spread The difference between the *bid price* and the *offer price* offered by a market-maker.

bid price The price a market-maker is prepared to buy at (e.g. for a currency).

bid rate The rate of interest offered for deposits.

BIF (ISO) code Burundi – currency Burundi franc.

BIF Abbreviation of *Bank Insurance Fund*.

BIFFEX Abbreviation of *Baltic International Freight Futures Exchange*.

Big Bang A popular term for the deregulation of the London Stock

Exchange on 27 October 1986. Among the changes implemented were the admission of foreign institutions as members of the Exchange, the abandonment of rigid distinctions between stockbrokers, jobbers and bankers, and the abolition of fixed commissions.

Big Board A nickname for the New York Stock Exchange.

big ugly A colloquial US stock exchange term for a share that fails to attract buyers.

BIIBA Abbreviation of *British Insurance and Investment Brokers Association*.

bill 1. A list of charges to be paid on goods or services. In this sense the usual US term is check. 2. A document that promises to pay somebody a certain amount of money. In this sense the US meaning of the term is banknote. 3. A document that describes goods, most often used in dealings with customs. 4. Short for *bill of exchange* (US draft).

bill broker A person or company that buys or sells bills of exchange and Treasury bills, either on their own account or as an intermediary.

bill-discounting interest rate The rate of interest charged by a central bank when lending money to a discount house. *See also* **bank rate**.

billion Now taken to mean one thousand million (1,000,000,000), although formerly in the UK equal to a million million.

bill of exchange (usual US term *draft*) A document indicating that one party (the drawee) agrees to pay a certain sum of money on demand or on a specified date, to the drawer (the person named on the bill). Two very familiar bills of exchange are cheques and banknotes. Another type of bill of exchange is used by the government to regulate the money supply.

bill of imprest An order whose bearer is entitled to have money paid in advance.

bill rate The rate at which a bill of exchange is discounted.

bills in a set Foreign bills of exchange were invariably made out in triplicate and sent to the drawee separately as an insurance against loss. The copies were known as bills of set. The practice has fallen into disuse with the rise of electronic methods of funds transfer.

BIP Abbreviation of the ECGD's *bond insurance policy* covering contract bonds and guarantees.

birr The standard currency unit of Eritrea and Ethiopia, divided into 100 cents.

Black Monday Monday 19 October 1987, when huge losses were sustained on the equity (shares) market.

Black Wednesday 16 September 1992, the day sterling left the Exchange Rate Mechanism (ERM). The result was a fall of 15% in sterling against the Deutschmark.

blank bill A bill of exchange on which the payee is not specified.

blank cheque A cheque that has been signed (and possibly dated) by the drawee but which does not specify the amount to be drawn.

blank endorsement 1. A blank cheque endorsed on the reverse. 2. A type of reference that can freely be used by the endorsed person, e.g. a statement given by a referee for distribution with a curriculum vitae.

blanket rate A fixed (unchanging) charge that covers a series of transactions or services.

block 1. A (large) group of something (e.g. shares). 2. An obstruction or prevention of entry or exit, as in a blocked account.

blowout An informal term that refers to unexpectedly strong sales of something, e.g. a new offering of shares or securities

blue-chip Describing an investment that is regarded as extremely safe, without being as guaranteed as a gilt-edged security (gilt). It also describes a company whose shares are regarded as an extremely safe investment.

blue-sky Describing a security that is worthless or highly speculative, or something with no particular aim.

blue-sky laws The laws in some US states that are intended to protect investors, including broker licensing and the supervision of the issue of securities.

BMD (ISO) code Bermuda – currency Bermudan dollar.

BND (ISO) code Brunei – currency Brunei dollar.

board of directors The decision-making group consisting of all the directors of a company, who are legally responsible for their actions. The board of directors is specifically charged with the management of the company, and in the case of a public limited company (plc) is elected by the shareholders at the company's annual general meeting

bond discount 33

(AGM). In the USA, the board of directors draws up company policy and appoints executives to run the company. It is sometimes known simple as "the board".

boilerplate language Colloquial US term for legal language in the fine print of many documents.

boiler room A little-known firm of brokers or dealers that sells securities over the telephone.

bolivar The standard currency unit of Venezuela, divided into 100 centimos.

Bolivia currency boliviano (BOP), divided into 100 centavos.

boliviano The standard currency unit of Bolivia, divided into 100 centavos.

bolsa Spanish for stock exchange.

Bolsa de Valores de Lisbon The *Lisbon Stock Exchange*.

Bolsa Mexicana de Valores The *Mexican Stock Exchange*.

Bombay Stock Exchange (BSE) Formally The Stock Exchange, Mumbai, is India's largest and oldest stock exchange which, along with others, is regulated by the Securities and Exchange Board of India.

bona fide Latin for in good faith. It usually appears in reference to contracts, especially contracts of insurance. The term is also used simply to mean honest or trustworthy.

bond A security issued at a fixed rate by central government, local authorities or occasionally private companies. In this case it is essentially a contract to repay money borrowed, and as such represents a debt. Normally bonds are issued in series with the same conditions of repayment and denominations. It is also known as a fixed-interest security.

bond broker A dealer in bonds on the floor of an exchange or, in the USA, one who deals with over-the-counter issues of government and municipal bonds.

bond discount The amount by which the face value of a bond exceeds its market price. Unsold fixed-coupon bonds are discounted when market interest rates rise. Discounts also result when supply exceeds demand and with a reduction in a bond's credit rating. In the opposite situation, with the market price is higher than face value, the difference is called a *bond premium*.

B

bond premium The amount by which the market price of a bond exceeds its face value. A premium may also arise when a bond is redeemed before maturity and the holder is compensated for any lost interest. *See also* **bond discount**.

bond-rating agency An organization which assesses the creditworthiness of other organizations, such as companies and national and local governments, that issue bonds.

bond swap The simultaneous selling of one bond issue and the buying of another.

bond washing The practice of buying bonds cum dividend and selling them ex dividend, to reduce the rate of tax payable on the transaction. The dividend on the bond becomes a capital gain, on which a lower rate of tax is payable than if tax were paid on the proceeds of the dividend income. Because of changes to the tax laws in the UK there is no longer scope for this kind of manoeuvring, although it still happens in the USA.

bond with warrant A fixed-rate bond which has attached to it a warrant that gives a long-term option (usually related to ordinary shares). The bond and the warrant can be split and sold separately. *See also* **convertibles**.

bonus issue An alternative term for *scrip issue*.

bookmaker Usually shortened to bookie, a person who accepts bets and pays money to winners of such bets. He or she "makes book" (calculates the odds offered) on the outcome of (usually) a sporting event, traditionally a horse race. The bookmaker, who in the UK must be licensed, may operate at the sporting venue or through licensed betting shops. A bookmaker who deals mainly in bets in horse races may use the grander title of turf accountant. *See also* **gambling**.

book value Also called written-down value, the value shown in a company's books for an asset or liability (or owner's equity), taking due account of any depreciation. Of a company as a whole, it is the amount by which total assets exceed total liabilities (*i.e.*, the net assets).

boom A popular term for a period when employment, prices and general business activity are at a high level and resources are being used to the full.

bootstrap A term used mostly in the USA, where take-over activity is more common, to describe a cash offer for a controlling interest in a company which, if accepted, is followed by another offer (usually at a lower price) for the remainder of the shares.

BOP (ISO) code Bolivia – currency boliviano.

BOP Abbreviation of *balance of payments*.

borrow On commodity markets, to simultaneously buy (at current prices) and sell forward.

borrower A company, person or organization that obtains a loan, usually after having to put up some form of security.

borrowing See *lending*.

Borsa Valori The chief *Milan Stock Exchange*.

Börse German for stock exchange.

Boston Stock Exchange (BSE) An exchange, founded in 1834, that deals only in equities of its more than 2000 listed companies using an automated trading system

BOT Abbreviation of *balance of trade*.

Botswana currency pula (BWP), divided into 100 thebe.

bottom fishing The practice of buying shares in a falling market in the expectation that the market will improve and the shares can be sold at a profit.

bottoming out An informal term for a very sudden and serious fall in market prices.

bounce A sudden rise in the value of a share that has been performing badly.

bourse French for stock exchange. *The Bourse* is the Paris Stock Exchange (see *Paris Bourse*).

boutique A type of financial services company, which operates in much the same way as a High Street shop, into which customers may walk to seek investment advice and services. It is also known as a financial supermarket.

box spread A complicated combination of a long-call option held against a short-put option, both at the same exercise price, and a short-call option held against a long-put option, again at the same exercise price.

bracket creep A situation that occurs when inflation forces groups of people into the next tax or income bracket. Normally brackets are fixed annually to account for inflation, but bracket creep can occur if inflation runs at a higher level than anticipated.

36 Brady bonds

Brady bonds Dollar-denominated, interest-bearing securities issued, in order to reschedule international debt, by Argentina, Venezuela and other South American countries in the 1990s. Collateral security was provided by interest-free US government securities. They were named after US Treasury Secretary Nicholas Brady, who devised them.

Brazil currency real (BRC), divided into 100 centavos.

break A sudden or substantial drop in prices following a period in which prices have been rising steadily.

break even (verb) To cover one's costs, making neither a profit nor a loss.

breakeven (noun) A situation in which the revenue from an activity/investment exactly covers the cost of that activity/investment.

break-forward On the money market, a combination of a currency option contract and a forward-exchange contract, which can be broken at a pre-set fixed rate of exchange if the exchange rates move in favour of the investor.

breaking an account The act of closing an account and transferring the balance to another one.

breakout What happens when a share or commodity price breaks a previously fixed, or at least stable, pattern.

Bretton Woods Agreement An international agreement between the USA, Canada and the UK formulated at a conference held at Bretton Woods, New Hampshire, in 1944. It defined a new system of international monetary control that resulted in the setting up of the International Monetary Fund (IMF) and the International Bank for Reconstruction and Development (World Bank).

BRC (ISO) code Brazil – currency real.

bridge financing Any form of short-term funding in anticipated arrival of funds, whether from a venture company on the verge of raising new capital or a bridging loan for a home buyer who needs to pay for a property before receiving the proceeds on the sale of the previous one.

bridging loan See *bridge financing*.

Britannia coins Gold coins minted in the UK in 1987 for investors in competition with the Krugerrand. They were available in denominations of £10, £25, £50 and £100.

British Insurance and Investment Brokers Association (BIIBA) An organization established in 1977 to represent registered insurance brokers and investment intermediaries, promote training and offer advice.

British Venture Capital Association (BVCA) The trade association of some 100 companies that deal in *venture capital*.

broker Broadly, an intermediary between a buyer and a seller, a mercantile agent. There are several forms of broker, the job title referring to what it is that a particular broker deals in; e.g. a stockbroker deals in stocks and shares. Most brokers' earnings take the form of commission. In the USA, a broker is more often known as a brokerage house.

brokerage A payment made to a broker for services rendered, also known as a broker's *commission*.

brokerage account A US term for a stockbroker's record of an individual client's sales and purchases of securities.

broker-dealer A firm that acts in the dual capacity of commodity dealer for its clients and as dealer for its own account.

broker-trader On the London International Financial Futures Exchange a firm that acts as both broker and trader for its own account. It is similar to a *broker-dealer*.

Brunei currency Brunei dollar (BND), divided into 100 cents.

Brussels Stock Exchange An exchange established in 1801 and now the centre of trading in local shares in Belgium (since the closure of the Antwerp Stock Exchange in 1997). It operates as a limited liability cooperative.

BSD (ISO) code Bahamas – currency Bahamian dollar.

BSE Abbreviation of *Bombay Stock Exchange* and *Boston Stock Exchange*.

bubble An industry or trend with no substance to it, such as a high-priced asset that people buy because they think that its price will continue to rise and they will be able to sell at a profit. A bubble usually bursts with more-or-less disastrous consequences for those involved. Probably the most famous bubble was the South Sea Bubble, which burst in 1720.

bucket shop A popular term for brokers of stocks, shares and commodities who are not recognized members of any exchange.

budget A plan that details expected future income and outgoings from an activity, normally over the span of a year. It is often referred to in controlling the activity. A budget is also the sum of money set aside for a given activity or project.

budget account An account with a bank or building society that provides an agreed revolving overdraft facility (usually for coping with temporary illiquidity).

buffer stock On the commodities markets, stocks that are held by a designated agency for release at certain strategic times in order to stabilize prices and markets.

BUK (ISO) code Myanmar (formerly Burma) – currency kyat.

building and loan association A US organization roughly equivalent to a building society in the UK. It is also known as a savings and loan association.

Building Societies Commission A regulatory organization for building societies set up under the Building Societies Act 1986, due to be absorbed into the Financial Services Authority (FSA).

building society A financial institution in the UK that accepts deposits, on which it pays interest, and lends money, originally only in the form a mortgage to enable people to purchase residential property. Many building societies now issue cheque books and plastic cards, and so operate in much the same way as a bank.

Bulgaria currency Bulgarian lev (BGL), divided into 100 stotinki.

bulge A sudden short-term rise in the price of a commodity, a share or a whole market.

bull A stock exchange dealer or analyst who believes that prices or investment values will increase. On this conviction, the dealer buys now and profits later by selling at a higher price.

bulldog bond A sterling-denominated security issued by a foreign government for sale on the UK market.

bullet 1. The final payment of a loan usually consisting of the whole principal (previous payments being of interest only). 2. A security that pays a guaranteed (fixed) interest at a specific date.

bullion Bars or ingots of a precious metal (such as gold or silver), as opposed to coins made from these metals. 24-carat gold bars are

busted convertible

available in weights of 5, 10, 20 and 50 grams. Gold bullion consists of 11.3-kilogram (400-ounce) bars.

bullion market A market at which precious metals and gold and silver coins are traded. *See also* **London Bullion Market Association**.

bull market A situation in which share prices are rising.

bull position The position of an investor whose purchases exceed his or her sales, and therefore stands to gain in a rising, or bull, market.

Bundesbank Full name Deutsche Bundesbank, the central bank of Germany, established in 1957 with headquarters in Frankfurt.

Bundesliquiditätsschatzwechsel A German one-year Treasury bill, introduced in 1993 to mop up excess non-banking liquidity but included here mainly because it is the longest one-word entry in the Dictionary! Understandably it is usually shortened to *Bulis*.

Burkino Faso (formerly Upper Volta) currency CFA franc (HVF); there is no subdivision.

burn rate When a company starts trading using venture capital, the rate at which the company consumes capital in financing fixed overheads. *See* **venture capital**.

Burundi currency Burundi franc (BIF), divided into 100 centimes.

business cycle The fairly regular swings in economic activity (demand and output) that tend to repeat every few years.

Business Expansion Scheme (BES) A scheme to encourage new businesses whereby the UK government gave tax relief on investment in certain share issues. It was replaced by the ***Enterprise Investment Scheme*** in 1994.

business rates A tax levied by local councils on business premises in the UK. There is a uniform rate, applied to the value of the premises as decided by the District Valuer.

bust An informal term for bankrupt.

busted bond A bond whose issuer has defaulted on the loan raised to fiance the issue. Valueless except as collectors' items, busted bonds are also called old bonds.

busted convertible A convertible whose conversion facility has no value because of the very low price of the ordinary shares it converts to. It is therefore traded just like a fixed-income investment.

butterfly A complex type of option dealing in which two identical options are bought and sold at the same time as two others, one with a lower exercise price and one with a higher exercise price (all with the same expiry date).

buy-back A company that is originally financed by venture capital may pay back the capital invested either by seeking a quotation or by being taken over. In either case, it will be buying itself back from the venture capitalist.

buyer's market A market in which there are too many sellers and not enough buyers, so that buyers are in a position to influence prices or conditions of purchase.

buyers over On the stock exchange, a situation in which there are more buyers than sellers. The opposite is sellers over.

buy forward To buy shares, commodities, and so on for delivery at a later date. In essence, buying forward is speculation on the current price, i.e. that it will rise in the future and the buyer will then be able to sell at a profit.

buy in 1. On the options market it is a hedge whereby the writer of the option buys a matching option (the only difference being in the premiums). The second thereby offsets the first, and the profit or loss is restricted to the difference between the premiums. 2. On the Stock Exchange any transaction in which a trader is unable to deliver the shares on time and so has to seek them from another source.

buying price The price at which a market-maker is prepared to buy (e.g. a currency).

buy on close Practice of buying contracts on a financial futures market at a price within the closing range. *See also* **buy on opening.**

buy on opening Practice of buying contracts on a financial futures market at a price within the opening range. *See also* **buy on close.**

buy on the bad news Policy of buying a currency or security after hearing any bad news about it in the expectation that its price will fall as a result. Such a technique can indeed be quite profitable if the bad news proves to be only temporary.

buy order An order to buy a specified security at market or another stipulated price.

buy-out The purchase of a controlling interest in a company's shares, as in a *management buy-out*.

buy-to-let mortgage An alternative term for *investment home loan*.

BVCA Abbreviation of *British Venture Capital Association*.

BWP (ISO) code Botswana – currency pula.

BZD (ISO) code Belize – currency dollar.

C

cabinet crowd The members of the New York Stock Exchange who deal in rarely-traded bonds.

CAC index An index of ordinary shares of 40 of the 100 largest companies quoted on the Paris Stock Exchange (Bourse).

CAD (ISO) code Canada – currency Canadian dollar.

calendar spread The simultaneous sale and purchase (or vice versa) of an option at the same striking price but for different dates.

call The act of demanding payment for stocks or shares, or repayment of a debt. A lender may advance money on condition that it is repayable at call (i.e. without notice).

callable bond A bond that may be called for payment before its maturity date.

call date The date on which a bond may be redeemed before it reaches maturity. In the USA a bond so redeemed is said to be called away.

called-up share capital The face value of a company's shares that the shareholders have actually paid for.

call money A type of loan made by a bank, which must be repaid on demand. It is also known as money at call.

call option An option to buy shares, commodities or financial futures at an agreed price on or before a future agreed date.

call-or-put option An alternative term for *as-you-like option*.

callover A method of trading on a stock exchange whereby the securities listed are called out in order, and dealers make bids or offers for each security according to their instructions.

callover price The price for a security verbally agreed at *callover*.

call price An alternative term for *redemption price*.

call provision A condition attached to a bond by which the issuer is entitled to redeem the bond at a fixed price after a specified period of time.

call risk The risk to the holder of a bond that it may be redeemed before its maturity date

calls in arrears When a company issues shares under phased terms of payment, the difference that can arise between called-up capital and paid-up capital if shareholders do not pay instalments.

call warrant A warrant that entitles its holder to purchase the underlying asset at a specified date and price, often used in gold trading.

Cambodia currency riel.

Cameroon currency CFA franc (CMF); there is no subdivision.

Canada currency Canadian dollar (CAD), divided into 100 cents.

cancellation price The lowest price a unit trust manager can offer for the redemption of units (on a particular day).

cap 1. An upper limit on a charge, such as an interest rate (which could then not rise above the limit despite financial trends that are adverse to the lender) 2. An abbreviation of capitalization, as in cap issue.

cap-and-collar mortgage A variable-rate mortgage with fixed upper and lower limits on the interest rate.

Cape Verde Islands currency Cape Verde escudo (CVE), divided into 100 centavos.

capital An imprecise term that, unqualified, generally refers to the resources of an organization or person (such as cash, equipment or skills), as contributed by the owners (i.e. the owners' equity). More precisely it is the total value of assets less liabilities.

capital adequacy A legal requirement that a financial institution should have enough capital to meet all its obligations and fund the services it offers.

capital allowance An amount deducted from a company's profits before tax is calculated, to take into account depreciation of capital assets (such as vehicles, plant and machinery, and industrial buildings).

capital asset pricing model (CAPM) A method of weighing risk and return to achieve the best equity value of a company in planning its financial policy.

capital assets Another term for *fixed assets*.

capital budget A budget that details proposed outgoings to obtain long-term assets, i.e. a company's capital expenditure. It involves longer timescales than a cash budget. It is also known as a capital expenditure budget or capital investment budget.

capital costs The expenditure on capital goods, for example *fixed assets* such as plant, or on *trade investments* and *current assets*. Capital costs are classed as below the line for accounting purposes. They are also known as capital expenditure, capital investment, investment costs or investment expenditure.

capital employed The capital that a company uses to finance its assets. It is taken to be the sum of the shareholders' funds, loans and deferred taxation.

capital expenditure An alternative term for *capital costs*.

capital flight Also called flight capital, capital removed from a country that seems to be politically (or economically) unstable, and taken to a more stable environment.

capital gain A gain made from a capital transaction, such as the buying and selling of assets. It is the amount by which the proceeds exceed the cost.

capital gearing Also called leverage, especially in the USA, the relationship between a company's funds derived from ordinary shares and long-term, fixed-interest rate funds such as preference shares and debentures. It is the ratio of the company's debts to total capital or shareholders' funds. High gearing, i.e. a high proportion of debt, generally represents a speculative investment.

capital growth An increase in the value of an investment over a period of time.

capital-intensive Describing a business in which capital is the most important and costly factor of production. Thus, an industry in which the major cost is the purchase and maintenance of machinery (fixed assets) is capital-intensive.

capitalization 1. The conversion of a company's reserves into share capital by issuing more shares (a scrip issue). 2. The total amount of capital available to a company in the long term. 3. The process of providing such capital.

capitalization issue An alternative term for *scrip issue*, also called a bonus issue.

capital loss A negative *capital gain*, resulting from selling an asset at a lower price than it originally cost. It is also called allowable capital loss.

capital market A market made up of the various sources of capital for medium- or long-term investment in new and already existing companies (as opposed to the money market, which generally deals in short-term funds). In the UK it is centred on the London Stock Exchange and the Alternative Investment Market (AIM). *See also* *financial market*.

capital outlay Expenditure on fixed assets such as machinery (i.e. involving capital costs).

capital shares Shares in a split-level investment trust whose holders receive the capital values of the trust's assets when it is liquidated. *See also* *income shares*.

capital stock 1. The value of all the capital goods owned by a company, industry or nation after depreciation has been taken into account. 2. The US term for a company's equity shares.

capital structure The make-up of a company's borrowings in terms of the proportions of owners' equity, short-term debt and long-term debt. The complete financial structure includes also its assets and any other liabilities.

capital transfer A gift or bequest from one person to another (not part of earnings). *See* the next entry.

capital transfer tax (CTT) From 1974 to 1986, a UK tax that replaced estate duty, payable on the estate of somebody who had died; it also applied to large gifts of money or other wealth. It was superseded by *inheritance tax*.

capped floating-rate note A *floating-rate note* (FRN) with a pre-arranged maximum (cap) on its coupon.

capped mortgage A variable-rate mortgage with a fixed upper limit on the interest rate.

captive Describing an investment services business that is owned by a financial institution that provides related services (such as a car sales outlet that offers credit facilities being owned by a finance house).

CAR Abbreviation of *compound annual return*.

carat 1. A measure of the fineness (purity) of gold. Pure gold is 24 carat; 9-carat gold, foe example, is 9/14 gold and 15/14 another metal (usually copper). 2. A unit of weight for gemstones equal to 200 milligrams.

Caribbean Common Market (CARICOM) An organization established in

Caribbean Free Trade Association (CARIFTA)

1973, with headquarters in Georgetown, Guyana, by 13 English-speaking Caribbean countries for purposes of mutual trade.

Caribbean Free Trade Association (CARIFTA) An organization that set up a free trade area in the Caribbean, superseded in 1973 by the *Caribbean Common Market (CARICOM)*.

CARICOM Abbreviation of *Caribbean Common Market*.

CARIFTA Abbreviation of *Caribbean Free Trade Association*.

carry Money borrowed or lent in order to finance trading in *futures*. The process of borrowing and lending in this way is known as carrying.

carrying market A market for commodities where a durable commodity accepted for delivery in one month is stored and delivered in a later month.

carry over 1. To postpone payment on a bargain traded on a stock exchange from one settlement day to the next. 2. The amount of a commodity that is left over from the previous year or season.

cartel A group of companies that come together to monopolize a market, agreeing between them which company presides over which area of operation. Cartels are illegal in the UK and USA.

case of need Words written on a bill of exchange that name a person the holder can apply to if it is not honoured at maturity.

cash Ready money (legal tender such as coins and notes), or to convert something (such as a cheque) into ready money.

cash and carry The buying of commodities spot (at the current price) with the intention of selling later at a profit.

cash and new On a stock exchange, a method of postponing payment on a bargain until the next settlement day. The investor begins with a bargain for which he or she would like to postpone payment. Towards the end of the account (period), a deal is made that is opposite to the first (i.e. the investor either buys or sells a similar instrument). The original position is then restored by yet another purchase or sale, to be settled on the next settlement day. In effect, the investor negates the original position and then returns to it in the next account.

cash book In book-keeping, a book in which all receipts and payments are recorded in the first instance.

cash budget A forward plan of day-to-day income and expenditure.

cash card A plastic card that allows the holder, by using a personal identification number (PIN), to withdraw cash from branches of his or her bank or building society through a cash dispenser (automated teller machine, or ATM). It often also allows access to such facilities as a display of the account balance and ordering bank statements and cheque books.

cash cow A product or aspect of business that continues to provide a healthy revenue after its initial launch, with relatively little extra investment.

cash deal An arrangement or transaction concluded with a cash payment. On the stock exchange, it is a deal to be completed on the next trading day.

cash dealing Describing stock exchange deals that must be settled on the following settlement day. Such bargains are said to be for cash settlement rather than account settlement.

cash discount A reduction in the price of goods or services in return for (prompt) payment in cash. Discounts allowed in this way are classified as expenditure. To the receiver of the discounts, they are regarded as revenue.

cash dividend A dividend paid in cash (rather than in shares).

cashflow The movement of money through a company from when it is received as income (or borrowing), to the time it leaves the company as payments (for example, for raw material, wages, and so on). A negative cashflow occurs when there is too little money coming in to pay for all the outgoings. Conversely, a positive cashflow occurs when a company receives income before it is due to pay outgoings.

cash in advance (CIA) A method of payment in which the purchaser pays for goods or services before delivery.

cash market A deal in the cash or spot commodity market that is completed, with payment made on delivery (unlike the *futures* market).

cash on delivery (COD) A distribution system whereby the person in receipt of goods makes payment for them on the spot to the deliverer. Such a system is operated by the UK Post Office, where it is the postman or woman who takes receipt of payment.

cash settlement On a derivatives market, to pay cash at the current market price for a security rather than take delivery of the underlying instrument.

48 cash surrender value

cash surrender value The amount an assurance company will return to the policyholder on cancellation of a life assurance policy.

cash with order (CWO) The terms of an agreement by which goods are supplied only if payment is made in cash at the time the order is placed.

CAT Abbreviation of *computer-assisted trading*.

Catmark A UK government scheme for checking Charges, Access and Terms of *Individual Savings Accounts* (ISAs).

CATS Abbreviation of *certificate of accrual on treasury securities*.

caveat emptor Latin for "buyer beware". In legal terms this maxim means that a buyer of goods should use his or her own common sense, and that the law is not prepared to aid someone who buys goods foolishly.

caveat subscriptor Latin for "signer beware", meaning that anyone who signs a document is bound by its contents, regardless of whether or not he or she has read it, or understands its legal implications.

CBOE Abbreviation of *Chicago Board Options Exchange*.

CBOT Abbreviation of *Chicago Board of Trade*.

CD Abbreviation of *certificate of deposit*.

CEDEL Abbreviation of *Centrale de Livraison de Valeurs Mobilières*.

ceiling The highest price or interest rate allowable on a deal.

Central African Republic currency CFA franc (CFA); there is no subdivision.

central bank A bank that carries out government economic policy, influences interest and exchange rates, monitors the activities of commercial and merchant banks, and usually issues currency. In this way it acts as the government's banker and is the lender of last resort to the banking system. In the UK it is the Bank of England and in the USA the Federal Reserve Banks.

Centrale de Livraison de Valeurs Mobilières (CEDEL) An organization of international banks, established in Luxembourg in 1970 as a settlement system for trading in Eurobonds. It acts as an agency for the collection of dividends and as a clearing house.

Central Gilts Office (CGO) A computerized book-entry transfer system for gilt-edged stock (gilts) established in 1986 by the Bank of England and the Stock Exchange. It ensures automatic "same-day" payment for the electronic transfer of stock.

charge 49

certificate of accrual on treasury securities (CATS) In the USA, zero-coupon bonds issued by the Treasury Department.

certificate of bonds A document issued to a registered bond holder confirming that the bonds are registered in his or her name.

certificate of deposit (CD) Essentially, a document (originally issued by merchant banks) declaring that a certain sum had been deposited with a bank. Sterling certificates of deposit refer to long-term fixed deposits of sums over £10,000 and therefore offer high interest rates.

certified cheque A banker's draft or customer cheque guaranteed by the bank on which it is drawn (also sometimes called a marked cheque).

CFA (ISO) code Central African Republic – currency CFA franc.

CFA Abbreviation of Communaute Financière Africaine – belongs to the French franc zone.

CFP Abbreviation of Colonies Françaises du Pacifique – belongs to the French franc zone.

CFTC Abbreviation of *Commodity Futures Trading Commission*.

CGF (ISO) code Congo – currency CFA franc.

CGO Abbreviation of *Central Gilts Office* and *collateralized bond obligation*.

Chad currency CFA franc (TDF); there is no subdivision.

chairman 1. A person who chairs a meeting, also called a chairperson or simply "chair". 2. The most senior director of a company, full title Chairman of the Board of Directors.

CHAPS Abbreviation of *Clearing House Automated Payments System*.

Chapter 7 A clause in US company law that provides for the winding up (liquidation) of a company that is unlikely to recover a viable financial position. It is part of the Federal Bankruptcy Act 1978.

Chapter 11 A clause in US company law that enables a company to continue to operate after it has been declared bankrupt (under the direction of the court), so that it may find a way to pay its creditors. It is part of the Federal Bankruptcy Act 1978 and roughly equivalent to the UK's administration.

charge 1. An obligation to meet a debt, a debit to an account, or the process of debiting. 2. A legal interest in land agreed by a borrower to secure a loan (mortgage) that gives the lender (often a bank or building society) a priority right to repayment when the land is sold. 3. A creditor's interest in company property, which must be registered with the Registrar of Companies

chartered company A UK company that is incorporated by Royal Charter. The main difference between a chartered company and an ordinary company is that the former is treated as an individual person in law.

chartism The activities of a *chartist*.

chartist A stock market or economic analyst who believes that trends (e.g. in price movements and so on) follow recognizable patterns and so predicts future trends with the aid of charts.

chasing the market The act of buying a security at a higher price than intended (because prices have risen) or selling at a lower price than intended (because prices have fallen).

cheap money Also called easy money, money borrowed at a low rate of interest, usually consisting of funds made available by authorities wishing to encourage investment or economic activity.

cheque The most familiar form of bill of exchange, used to transfer funds from a bank account to somebody else. It is also a common way of drawing cash from a current account.

cheque card A plastic card with a magnetic strip and bearing the holder's name, signature and account details which guarantees payment of cheques up to a certain value (between £50 and £250). Some cheque cards have additional functions, such as acting as a *cash card*, *credit card* or *debit card*.

CHF (ISO) code Switzerland – currency Swiss franc.

Chicago Board of Trade (CBOT) The world's largest futures and options exchange, established in 1848, which today deals mainly in financial futures.

Chicago Board of Trade Clearing Corporation An organization that is independent of the Chicago Board of Trade but maintains CBOT's top credit rating by guaranteeing all of its deals.

Chicago Board Options Exchange (CBOE) A major world market in options, established in 1973.

Chicago Mercantile Exchange (CME) A major world market established in 1919 to deal in commodities, which today deals particularly in cash and financial futures. Its US nickname is Merc.

Chicago Stock Exchange (CHX) The former Midwest Stock Exchange, formed in 1949 from exchanges in Chicago (itself dating from 1882), Cleveland, Minneapolis-St. Paul and St. Louis. It adopted its present name in 1993. It deals only in shares, mostly through an automated dealing system.

chief executive Also known as the chief executive officer (CEO), the person responsible for the day-to-day running of a company, usually the managing director.

chief executive officer (CEO) See *chief executive*.

Chile currency Chilean peso (CLP), divided into 100 centesimos.

China currency yuan (CNY).

Chinese wall An artificial barrier erected in any business where confidentiality between departments is a legal requirement. The Chinese wall has become necessary since the Big Bang changed the London Stock Exchange to a dual capacity system in 1986. The purpose of the wall is to prevent insider dealing.

CHIPS Abbreviation of *Clearing House Interbank Payments System*.

choice price When comparing different market-makers' bid-offer spreads on a futures market, an identical bid and offer price.

chon A subdivision (1/100) of the South Korean won.

churning An informal term for a broker's practice of buying and selling of stocks and shares solely in order to generate higher commission income. The practice is illegal in the USA if the activity is not in the client's best interest.

CHX Abbreviation of *Chicago Stock Exchange*.

CIA Abbreviation of *cash in advance*.

CIF (ISO) code Ivory coast (Côte d'Ivoire) – currency CFA franc.

circuit breaker A method of limiting the overall movement (up or down) of share prices, used on the Tokyo Stock Exchange in an attempt to maintain stability.

City, The The financial district of London, situated in the City of London. It covers an area of roughly one square mile and for this reason is also sometimes known as the Square Mile.

52 City code

City code A voluntary system of regulation applied to take-overs and mergers on the UK Stock Exchange.

clean 1. Free from debt (*e.g.* a clean balance sheet). 2. Without documents (e.g. a clean bill of exchange).

clean bill A bill of exchange that has no documents or special conditions attached to it.

clean price The price of a gilt-edged security (gilt) excluding any interest that has accumulated since the last payment of a dividend.

clear 1. To have something authorized. 2. To sell goods in order to make room for new stock. 3. A period of so many days, or a sum of money on which there is nothing additional to be paid.

clearance 1. The receipt of money from a bill or cheque. 2. The completion of necessary formalities before goods can enter or leave the country (such as customs duty). 3. The completion of the necessary formalities before an aircraft or ship can depart.

clearing The practice of organizing the payment of financial instruments (such as cheques). In the UK, commercial banks are usually members of the Banker's Clearing House, which settles their daily balance.

clearing cycle The process by which payments by cheque are transferred from the payer's account to the payee's account. It usually takes two or three days.

clearing house A financial institution that specializes in clearing debts between its members. The best-known type is a banker's clearing house, which clears cheques between the major banks.

Clearing House Automated Payments System (CHAPS) An organization established in 1985 as part of the Association for Payment Clearing Services (APACS), that provides a guaranteed same-day electronic transfer of sterling funds within the UK.

Clearing House Interbank Payments System (CHIPS) A US organization established in 1970 that provides on-line electronic transfer of funds in US dollars, mainly for international transactions.

close 1. On a financial futures market, the 30 seconds before trading closes for the day. 2. To cover an open position on a futures or options market by making a further transaction. 3. Another term for closing price.

close company A company whose shares are held privately, by a few people (usually not more than five), and not traded on a stock exchange. The US term is closely-held company.

closed-end fund A fund with fixed capital, as opposed to an open-ended fund. Sums held by investment companies are closed-end funds (investment trusts).

closed fund A unit trust that has gown too large and no longer issues shares.

closely-held company A US term for a *close company*.

close market A market in which there is very little difference between bid and offer prices.

close out Counterbalancing transactions in two or more financial instruments that leaves the investor neither in credit nor in debt (a net zero position).

closing bid The last bid at an auction or, more generally, the bid that is successful.

closing price The price of shares at the close of trading each day on a stock exchange.

closing purchase The purchase of an option that closes an open position.

closing range On a financial futures market, the highest and lowest prices recorded during the close.

closing sale On an options market, a transaction in which an option is sold in order to close a position. *See also* ***last sale***.

CLP (ISO) code Chile – currency Chilean peso.

CME Abbreviation of Chicago Mercantile Exchange.

CMF (ISO) code Cameroon – currency CFA franc.

CMO Abbreviation of *collateralized mortgage obligation*.

CNAR Abbreviation of *compound net annual rate*.

CNY (ISO) code China – currency yuan.

COB Abbreviation of *Commission des Opérations de Bourse*.

COD Abbreviation of *cash on delivery*.

codicil A legal addition to a will (amending its terms).

coinsurance A method of sharing insurance risk betweens several insurers. The policyholder deals with the lead insurer, who issues documents and collects premiums. The policy details the shares held by each company.

cold call A sales practice (by, *e.g.*, brokers) of approaching a potential customer, by telephone, e-mail or in person, without any prior introduction. It is also termed an unsolicited all.

collar In return for a premium, an option that guarantees a borrower a fixed maximum interest (cap) and fixed minimum interest (floor) for a loan.

collateral Strictly, *security* that is put up for a loan by a third party, as opposed to the borrower's own personal security.

collateral agreement A contract or agreement that runs in parallel with an existing one.

collateralize US term for the act of putting up assets as security to obtain a loan.

collateralized bond obligation (CGO) A US bond of investment grade secured against a portfolio of high-yield bonds (junk bonds).

collateralized mortgage obligation (CMO) A US bond secured against a portfolio of mortgages issued by the Federal Home Loan Mortgage Corporation.

collateral security A second *security* for a loan put up by a third party, often in addition to the borrower's personal security.

collectibles A blanket term for any items – from antiques to postage stamps – collected by investors because their value is expected to rise

Colombia currency Colombian peso (COP), divided into 100 centavos.

colon The standard currency unit of Costa Rica, divided into 100 centimos.

COLTS Abbreviation of *Continuously Offered Longer-term Securities*.

COMEX Abbreviation of *Commodity Exchange of New York*.

comfort letter An independent auditor's letter that guarantees that information in a new company's prospectus has remained unchanged between the preparation of the prospectus and its distribution. It is a legal requirement in the USA.

Comisión Nacional del Mercado de Valores The *Madrid Stock Exchange*.

commercial bill A bill of exchange that is not a Treasury bill.

commercial credit company An alternative name for a *finance house*.

commercial loan A short-term loan intended to provide a company with seasonal working capital.

commercial paper (CP) A corporate debt in a tradable form. In the USA, the commercial paper is a short-term, non-bank market in which firms lend money to each other without the intervention of a financial intermediary.

commission Money paid to an agent or other intermediary, usually as a percentage of the sum involved in the transaction.

commission agent An agent who is paid a *commission*, usually calculated as a percentage of the value of purchases or sales made overseas.

commission broker A dealer on the US stock exchange who buys or sells securities (for the public) in return for a commission.

Commission des Opérations de Bourse (COB) The official supervisory organization, established in 1967, of French stock exchanges. Belgium has a similar organization of the same name.

commitment fee A charge levied by a lender for keeping (a specified amount of) credit available

commodity 1. Raw materials and foods, especially such goods as cocoa, coffee, jute, potatoes, tea, etc., which may also be traded. 2. In economics, any tangible goods that are traded.

commodity-backed bond A bond linked to the price of some underlying commodity, favoured as a hedge against inflation.

commodity broker A broker who deals in commodities, usually in a commodity market.

commodity exchange A commodity market on which *actuals* and *futures* are traded.

Commodity Exchange of New York (COMEX) A commodity market established in 1870 that deals mainly in futures contracts for metals.

Commodity Futures Trading Commission (CFTC) A US organization established in 1974 that regulates the country's commodity futures exchanges, particularly in agricultural products and derivatives.

commodity market A market on which commodities are traded (*see commodity*).

common market Any market organization among countries that have a common external tariff (unlike a free-trade area). The EU is a modern example.

common shares A US term for equity shares, with a stated face value that does not relate to the true value.

common stocks A US term for *ordinary shares*, representing a company's equity capital.

company An enterprise that has been legally incorporated to produce certain goods or provide certain services, or to transact any other type of business. There are strict legal requirements of a UK company, as set out in the Companies Acts.

company doctor A person who is brought into a company, usually at board level, that is on the brink of liquidation. A company doctor often has powers to administer very strong medicine in order to put the company back on its feet.

company limited by guarantee A company whose shareholders' liability is limited to the amount that they guarantee to pay if liquidation occurs (rather than by the amount of equity they hold).

company pension A pension scheme that is funded by contributions from the employer, with or without contributions also from the employees. It is more commonly known as an *occupational pension*.

company secretary A person who is responsible for ensuring that his or her company complies with company law.

compliance In a financial institution, the activity that makes sure that the organization's operations comply with regulatory and statutory requirements, i.e. are within the law as it applies to such institutions. Many organizations have a compliance officer to check that this happens.

compensation fund A fund financed by members of the London Stock Exchange that compensates investors for losses incurred because of failure of a member.

compound annual return (CAR) The total return on a sum invested or lent over a period of a year, including the return on interest previously accrued. *See also compound net annual rate*.

compound interest A rate of interest calculated by adding interest previously paid to the capital sum plus previous interest payments. After n years a sum S invested at x per cent compound interest is worth $S[100 + n)/100]^n$. See also **simple interest**.

compound net annual rate (CNAR) The return, after deduction of tax at the basic rate, of interest from a deposit or investment that includes the return on interest previously accrued. See also **compound annual return (CAR)**.

compound option An option to purchase an option (at a specified date and price).

compound reversionary bonus For an endowment policy, a reversionary bonus that is calculated both on the basic sum assured and the annual reversionary bonuses already earned.

comptroller A mainly US term for the chief financial officer of a group of companies or the financial director of a single company. The title should not be confused with that of controller, who is the chief accounting executive, although not all companies preserve the distinction. Both titles are pronounced in the same manner.

concentration risk The risk of holding or trading in just one or two financial instruments or in just one sector of the market.

concert party A group of people who come together secretly to act "in concert", that is, to orchestrate a market in the group's favour. For example, two or more people may form a concert party to buy shares in a company in order to effect a take-over. Such action is illegal.

concession 1. The right to use somebody else's property as part of a business. 2. An allowance made to somebody who would otherwise be charged.

conditional bill of sale A bill of sale by which the owner of the goods transferred retains the right to repossess them.

conditional endorsement An endorsement on which the endorser has added a condition, which has to be fulfilled before the endorser receives the proceeds of the bill.

conglomerate A very large public company that is extremely diverse and probably international in its operations. It generally consists of a holding company and its subsidiaries.

Congo currency CFA franc (CGF); there is no subdivision.

consideration 1. In most forms of contract, the agreement is made binding by the promise or payment of a sum of money or other favour from one party to the other. Such a payment or favour is known as a consideration. 2. In buying securities, it is the amount paid before deduction of commission and tax. 3. The term is also used informally for any kind of payment.

consignee A person or company to which goods are sent.

consignment A shipment of goods sent or delivered at the same time, usually to an agent for selling on to somebody else (the consignee). *See also **on consignment**.*

consignment note A document sent with a consignment of goods, to be signed by the consignee or his agent upon receipt of the goods. It may also be known as a waybill.

consignment stock The stock held by an agent or dealer that legally belongs to somebody else. The dealer can, in law, sell it or return it unsold to the rightful owner.

consignor A person or company that dispatches goods (to a consignee).

CONSOB Abbreviation of *Commissione Nazionale per le Società e le Borsa*. See **Milan Stock Exchange**.

Consol An abbreviation of Consolidated Stock or Consolidated Loan, a form of fixed-interest government security that has no redemption date.

consolidated loan A loan arranged so as to combine and refinance several other existing debts and calculated to result in an overall reduction in (monthly) repayments.

consolidation 1. In accounting, the practice of putting together the accounts of subsidiary companies of a group, to calculate the overall results for the group as a whole. 2. In share dealings, the practice of combining a number of low-priced shares, to produce a realistically marketable lot.

consortium A group of companies that come together to bid for a certain project. It is usually dissolved after that one project is completed. It is similar to a syndicate, but more short-term.

consumer credit Short-term personal credit for a specific purchase, such as a bank loan, credit card or incorporated into a hire-purchase agreement.

Consumer Credit Act 1974 The legislation in the UK that safeguards people who take out personal credit worth up to £15,000. It covers bank loans, credit cards, credit sale agreements, hire-purchase agreements and mortgages (bank overdrafts are excluded).

consumer interest The interest charged for *consumer credit*.

consumer price index (CPI) The US term for *retail price index*.

contango A stock exchange term for a delayed settlement of a bargain from one account to the next. A premium then becomes payable. The term is also used more frequently in futures trading to mean the opposite of *backwardation*.

contingent annuity An annuity that does not begin payment until a specified event has occurred (such as the death of one spouse in a husband-and-wife joint annuity). It is also known as a reversionary annuity.

continuation An alternative term for *contango*.

Continuously Offered Longer-term Securities (COLTS) Variable-rate zero-coupon bonds with a fixed 3- to 30-year term offered on a continuous basis by the World Bank (International Bank for Reconstruction and Development).

contract A legally binding agreement between two parties, or the act of forming such an agreement. It may be a *verbal contract* or a *contract in writing*. See also *consideration*.

contract bond An alternative term for a *performance bond*.

contract by deed A type of contract that is binding only if made by deed (such as conditional bills of sale and mortgages of land).

contracting out The withdrawal from the State Earnings-Related Pension Scheme (SERPS) by an occupational pension scheme.

contract in writing A written contract, required for various purposes such as bills of exchange, transfers of shares and credit sale or hire-purchase agreements.

contract note A document issued by a broker setting out details of a recent transaction, such as buying or selling price, inclusion or exclusion of benefits (dividends), tax, fee and commission.

contra proferenten rule A nickname for the following Latin maxim: *verba chartarum fortuis accipiumtur contra proferentem* – the words of the contract are construed more strictly against the person proclaiming them. In effect, the rule means that if a contract is ambiguous, it will be construed in a way that is the least advantageous to the party that drew up the contract.

contrarian An informal term for a speculator in stocks and shares who goes against short-term trends; e.g., a contrarian may decide on a buying policy in a bear market.

contributory pension A pension for which an employee makes contributions during his or her working life. The contribution is usually a percentage of the employee's gross salary, deducted at source and added to the employer's contribution.

controlling interest The holding of more than 50% in the voting shares of a company, necessary for a successful take-over. A director with more than 20% of the voting shares is also said to have a controlling interest.

conventional mortgage A fixed-rate, fixed-term loan from a bank or building society for the purchase of residential property.

convergence The gradual movement of a future contract's price towards that of the underlying commodity as contract approaches maturity.

conversion price The price at which convertible bonds, debentures or preferred shares can be converted into ordinary shares.

convertible capital bond A financial instrument that is similar to *convertible loan stock* except that it its conversion takes place in two stages: first to preference shares and then to ordinary shares.

convertible currency A currency that can be changed into any other currency.

convertible loan stock A type of loan stock (such as a debenture) with the right of conversion into preference shares or ordinary shares at some time in the future. Government stock that can be converted into new stock (instead of repayment) is also known as convertible loan stock.

convertibles Loan stock, bonds, preference shares and debentures that can easily be converted into ordinary shares at predetermined dates. They usually have a stated maturity date and pay a fixed rate of interest. In the USA they are known as converts.

convertible term assurance A type of life assurance that allows the

corporation tax (CT)   61

policyholder to convert to an endowment assurance policy or a whole life policy without any further medical examination.

conveyance A legal document that transfers ownership of land and/or buildings from one owner to another.

cooling-off period A period of ten days (in the UK) during which a person who has agreed to a certain form of contract (such as a credit sale or hire-purchase agreement) may withdraw from the agreement and have his or her money repaid. Such a period exists in order to minimize the effects of hard selling that some companies or their agents undertake.

cooperative An organization run by a group of people who each have a say in its management and a financial interest in its profitability. It may be a group of producers (such as farmers), consumers (in retail cooperatives) or the workers themselves (as in some Communist countries).

COP (ISO) code Colombia – currency Colombian peso.

Copenhagen Stock Exchange A non-monopoly public limited company (since 1995) that runs the stock exchange in Copenhagen, using an electronic order-driven system.

cornering the market The act of building a virtual monopoly in particular goods or services, so that the monopolist is able to dictate price.

Corn Exchange A London commodity exchange that deals in such commodities as cereals and animal foodstuffs.

corporate bond A bond issued by a company or corporation, which most frequently occurs in the USA.

corporate equity The net assets of a company that remain after paying creditors and holders of debentures and preference shares, available for distribution as dividends to the holders of ordinary shares.

corporation A large company, usually with several subsidiary companies. In the USA, it is a company that has been incorporated under US law. The term is therefore a virtual synonym for the British term company. Its is often abbreviated to corp.

corporation tax (CT) tax levied on a UK company's profits. The rate depends on the amount of profit, starting at 10% for companies whose profits are less than £10,000, rising to 20% for companies with profits of between £10,000 and £300,000, rising to 30% for companies making more than $1.5 million. *See also* **advance corporation tax**.

corset Normally the Supplementary Special Deposits Scheme, a former Special Reserve account used by the Bank of England between 1973 and 1980 to add to the constraints of Special Deposits required of commercial banks (to limit their ability to grant loans and thus control the money supply).

Costa Rica currency colon (CRC), divided into 100 centimos.

cost-based pricing The pricing of goods or services in terms of their production costs, as opposed to taking account of market conditions.

cost accountant An accountant who specializes in reckoning the cost of manufacturing a unit of product, taking into account such variables as cost of raw materials and labour, and thereby making a projection of probable cost at the planning stage of a project. This in turn enables the manufacturer to tender a price to a prospective buyer.

cost accounting The work undertaken by a *cost accountant*.

costing The practice of working out how much a product will cost to produce, taking into account costs such as raw materials, labour, overheads, and so on. A frequent alternative term is costing-out.

cost of capital The average of the costs to a company of its various kinds of capital (bonds, debentures, loans, shares, retained profit, and so on).

cost of living index An alternative term for *retail price index*.

cost-plus A system of charges whereby the buyer pays the cost of the item plus a profit to the producer or a commission to the seller.

cost-push inflation A theory that inflation is caused by increases in the cost of manufacturing prices, thus pushing up overall prices to the consumer. *See also* **demand-pull inflation**.

Côte d'Ivoire (formerly Ivory Coast) currency CFA franc (CIF); there is no subdivision.

Council Tax A tax levied by local councils on the occupants of homes in the UK, which are allocated to one of seven bands (each attracting a different level of tax as set by the local council) by the District Valuer. Certain people, such as sole occupants, pay lower rates of tax.

countercyclical shares Share whose value tends to rise when the economy or prices in the market as a whole are falling (such as shares in companies that produce medicine or food).

counterparty Either of the parties to a contract.

counterparty risk The risk that either of the parties to a contract (such as the purchase or sale of a security) will for whatever reason fail to honour his or her side of the agreement.

countertrading An alternative term for *barter*.

countervailing credit An alternative term for *back-to-back credit*.

coupon 1. A document attached to a bond, which must be detached and sent to the paying party in order for the bond holder to receive interest payments. Each payment is detailed on the coupon for each payment period. 2. An alternative term for interest that is payable on a fixed-interest security.

coupon bond An alternative term for *bearer bond*.

coupon interest rate The rate of interest payable on a bond's face value.

covenant Broadly, any form of agreement; or more specifically, an agreement taken out between two parties, stating that one party agrees to pay the other a series of fixed sums over a certain period of time.

cover 1. Any form of security (i.e. collateral). 2. In financial futures, the buying of contracts to offset a short position. 3. The number of times a company could theoretically pay dividends to shareholders from its earnings. 4. To make enough money in selling products or services to pay for their production.

covered bear A dealer who sells shares or commodities he owns, hoping to buy them back later at a lower price (i.e. he or she is not taking the risk of *short selling*). He or she is also known as a protected bear.

cover note A document issued by an insurance company giving cover for a short time, often one month, while a complete policy (and, possibly, an insurance certificate) is drawn up and issued.

CP Abbreviation of *commercial paper*.

crash An informal term for a very severe drop in prices on securities, financial and commodities markets.

crawling peg A method of fixing exchange rates which are fixed (pegged) but then changed slightly – weekly or monthly – to another fixed rate.

CRC (ISO) code Costa Rica – currency colon.

credit A loan of money (made by a trader before requiring payment for goods or services); or a book-keeping balance that shows a profit (*i.e.*, on the right-hand side of the account); or a person's or company's financial standing; or to add a sum to an account.

credit agency (US **credit bureau**) A company that gathers information on the creditworthiness of individuals and companies, and distributes this information (for a fee) to those providing credit facilities.

credit bureau The US term for a *credit agency*.

credit card A plastic card issued by a bank or building society that allows the user to buy goods on credit, paying all or part of outstanding sums on his or her account in monthly instalments. *See also* **debit card**.

credit crunch A situation in which *short credit* becomes scarce and thus more expensive than *long credit*.

credit freeze The action by banks to restrict the extension of credit to customers. It is also known as a credit squeeze.

credit insurance An insurance against the risk of non-payment of a commercial debt (possibly because of insolvency).

credit limit The maximum sum that a person or organization is prepared to lend to another.

credit note 1. A document that confirms the availability of funds for a future purchase (perhaps because an account has been overpaid or goods have been returned). 2. A document that confirms the transfer of credit from one account to another.

creditor A person or company that lends or is owed money (by a debtor). In company accounting, creditors who are due to be paid within a year are classified as current creditors; creditors who are not due to be paid until after a year are classified as long-term liabilities.

creditors' meeting A meeting that confirms the appointment of a receiver to a company in liquidation.

credit rating A rating assigned to a person or company that assesses creditworthiness.

credit risk When a loan is made, the risk that the borrower will be unable (or unwilling) to repay the principal and any interest owing.

credit sale A method of purchasing goods that allows the buyer to pay for them by means of instalments over a period of time. Unlike *hire purchase*, a credit sale agreement confers ownership as soon as the contract is signed.

cross-firing 65

credit scoring A method of assessing a company's or person's ability to make loans.

credit squeeze An alternative name for a *credit freeze*.

credit union In the UK, a non-profit making mutual organization that offers facilities for savings, makes small loans, and may provide basic personal insurance within a local area. In the USA, a member-owned, democratically governed, non-profit making cooperative that provides financial services to members and whose earnings are returned to the members.

creditworthy Describing a person who, from his or her record, is deemed willing and able to pay back credit. Thus a creditworthy person finds it easier to borrow (and to borrow larger sums) than somebody who is deemed to be a credit risk.

creeping inflation Regular small increases in the general level of prices.

creeping take-over A gradual increase in a shareholding through open purchase on the stock exchange with the aim of accumulating enough shares to make a take-over bid.

CREST An electronic (and therefore paperless) system introduced to the London Stock Exchange in 1996 for processing shares for the securities market. It replaced **TALISMAN** and includes registration, purchase, sales and payment of dividends as they become due.

Croatia (Hrvatska) currency kuna.

crore 1 crore = 10 million Indian rupees.

cross-border listing The practice of listing securities on exchanges in more than one country. Investors in one country can purchase shares in another country by using a broker who deals through a broker in the other country.

cross default A condition attached to a security or debt specifying that, should the borrower default on any other debt, it also counts as a default on the one with the cross-default condition.

crossed A US term for backwardation, in which one market-maker's offer price is lower than another's bid price.

cross-firing A fraud that involves opening two or more bank accounts at different banks. Money withdrawn from the first bank is backed by a cheque drawn on the second bank, and so on.

crowd A group of people who wish to trade in a particular option or future, so named because to do so they must gather around the relevant pitch on the trading floor.

crown jewel tactic A strategy undertaken by a company that is threatened by take-over, in which it sells, or offers to sell, the best part of its business to somebody other than the raider (e.g. a *white knight*), in order to make the target seem less desirable.

cruzeiro real The standard currency unit of Brazil (also called simply the real), divided into 100 centavos.

CSK (ISO) code Czech Republic – currency koruna.

CT Abbreviation of *corporation tax*.

CTT Abbreviation of *capital transfer tax*.

Cuba currency Cuban peso (CUP), divided into 100 centavos.

cum coupon Describing a security that is passed from one holder to another with *coupon* (enabling the holder to claim interest payments) attached. *See also* **ex coupon**.

cum dividend Describing shares that are sold with the right of the new holder to claim the next dividend payment. It is sometimes abbreviated to cum div. *See also* **ex dividend**.

cum new Describing shares that are sold with the right to claim participation in any outstanding scrip or rights issue. *See also* **ex new**.

cumulative preference share A kind of *preference share* whose holder can claim any dividends not paid in earlier years, as long as the company has funds to pay them. Even then, eventual payment is guaranteed before payment to holders of ordinary shares.

CUP (ISO) code Cuba – currency Cuban peso.

Curb Exchange A term for the *American Stock Exchange*.

currency 1. The coins and notes that are a country's medium of exchange 2. In banking, any foreign currency.

currency bond A bond issued in a foreign country. It is repaid in the currency of that country.

currency future A futures contract for delivery in one of the world's major currencies, often used as a hedge against currency risk.

current assets An alternative name for *circulating assets*.

current assets ratio An *accounting ratio*, a test of liquidity made by dividing a company's current assets by its current liabilities. It is also called current ratio or working-capital ratio.

current expenditure The expenditure on assets for resale, such as raw materials, rather than fixed assets. It is also known as above-the-line expenditure.

current liabilities An asset that is used by a company in its day-to-day operation, e.g. raw materials, etc.

current yield A dividend calculated as a percentage of the price paid for each share.

cushion bond A bond that can be called in before maturity (i.e. retired early).

custodian Somebody who holds securities for an investor (often a minor) and deals with all matters pertaining to them.

CVE (ISO) code Cape Verde Islands – currency Cape Verde escudo.

cyclical stocks Also called cyclicals, a US term for shares in companies that are involved in basic industries, such as the provision of raw materials, metals, and so on. They are so called because their prices on the stock market tend to rise and fall with the business cycle.

CYP (ISO) code Cyprus – currency Cypriot pound.

Cyprus currency Cypriot pound (CYP), divided into 100 cents.

Czech Republic currency koruna (CSK), divided into 100 haleru.

D

DA Abbreviation of *discretionary account.*

Daily Official List *See Official List.*

daimo bond A bearer bond that the World Bank issues on the eurobond market and on the Japanese markets.

daisy chain The buying and selling of the same stocks or shares several times, usually to make it appear that there is more activity in their trading than there really is (and thereby tempt investors).

dalasi The standard currency unit of Gambia, divided into 100 bututs.

database Data organized in such a way as to allow easy access to the most up-to-date information and its collation with older data. The term is generally applied to electronic storage devices (i.e., computers), which can store, organize and search for data more rapidly than hitherto possible. A facility that stores several interlinkable databases is called a data warehouse.

data warehouse *See database.*

date The day, month and year. In the UK these are usually stated numerically in that order (i.e., 1:2:02 is 1 February 2002). However in the rest of Europe and the USA they are recorded in the order month, day, year (i.e., 1:2:02 is January 2nd 2002). The potential for confusion is vast.

dated date The date from which a new issue of a bond or other debt interest begins to accrue interest.

dated security A bill of exchange, bond or other security that carries a specified payment or redemption date.

dawn raid The practice of buying a significant number of a target company's shares at the start of the day's trading, or before the market becomes aware of what is happening, often at a price higher than normal. The purpose of a dawn raid is to give the buyer a strategic stake in the target company, from which the buyer may launch a take-over bid.

day order An order given by an investor to a stockbroker that is valid only on the day it is given. A day order also specifies a price limit on the transaction envisaged. If it is not completed on the day in question, the order is automatically cancelled.

days of grace 1. A period of three days still allowed in the UK for the payment of a bill of exchange (except for instruments payable on demand, on sight or on presentation). 2. A period of time, either 14 or 30 days, generally allowed for the payment of an insurance premium after the due date.

day-to-day loan Also called an overnight loan, money that is borrowed particularly by a financial institution that is temporarily illiquid. It is lent to companies wishing to be paid interest on money earned in the previous day's trading. Interest rates on day-to-day loans are high and variable.

day-to-day money A type of loan made usually to a financial institution that must be repaid on demand. It is also known as money at call.

day trading Also called day trade, the creation and liquidation of the same futures position or positions within one day's trading.

DCF Abbreviation of *discounted cashflow*.

dead-cat bounce A brief rise in the stock index of a falling market. The term refers to the supposed ability of a cat always to land on its feet: if a falling cat bounces, it must be dead.

dead security A security that is backed by an exhaustible industry (such as mining), which is thus a poor risk for a long-term investment or loan.

deadweight debt A debt that does not create an asset to provide the funds to service the debt.

deal Any agreement or transaction.

dealer A merchant who operates on his or her own in a market at his or her own risk and hence is a speculator. This includes anybody who is engaged in trading on a financial market.

dealing The activity of dealers.

dear money Describing a situation in which credit is difficult to obtain (and interest rates for borrowing are consequently high), possibly because of official action to restrict the money supply. It is known as tight money in the USA.

death benefit The amount payable on the death of a life assurance policyholder.

death-valley curve The period of time during which a start-up company uses venture capital at an extremely fast rate, to the point at which it is using equity capital to finance overheads – an unhealthy state of affairs.

death-valley days An informal term for "dry" periods on financial markets, days on which little trading takes place.

debenture A long-term loan to a company made at a fixed rate of interest and usually with a specified *maturity date,* generally between 10 and 40 years. Debenture holders are numbered among the company's preferential creditors, and in the event of liquidation have preferential claims on the firm. Debentures may be treated as tradeable *securities.*

debenture capital That part of a company's capital that is issued in the form of debentures.

debenture issue An issue of debentures, whether secured or unsecured, by a company wishing to raise loan capital. The debenture holders become the company's principal creditors and have the right to preferential repayment of their loans in the event that the firm encounters financial difficulties.

debenture stock Some debentures may be divided into units and traded on an exchange; these securities are known as debenture stocks.

debit A sum owed by or a charge made on a person.

debit balance In accounting, a balance that shows a debit.

debit card A plastic card issued by banks and building societies that allows the account holder to use the card at retail outlets to debit a current account immediately (unlike a *credit card*). It is also called a payment card.

debt A sum of money, or the value of goods or services, owed by one person, group or company (the debtor) to another. It arises because the seller allows the purchaser credit. Assignable debts may be transferred in whole from one person to another; such debts therefore become *negotiable instruments.* In company accounting, the term debt is also used to describe the whole of a company's borrowings.

debt bomb The financial repercussions envisaged if a major international debtor were to default.

debt burden The cost (such as interest) of servicing a debt.

debt buy-back In international trading, an arrangement whereby a debtor nation buys back its debt at a discount for cash.

debt collecting The business of a company or organization that collects debts on behalf of other companies or individuals. *See also* ***factoring***.

debt-equity swap A method by which a lender (such as a bank) disposes of a loan to a Third World country by converting it into a holding of equity in a company in that country. Venture capital may also be provided in exchange for equity in the company being financed.

debt forgiveness In international finance, writing off part of a nation's debt, or selling the debt to a third party for a large discount.

debt instrument 1. A written promise to pay a debt. 2. A medium for obtaining a (usually short-term) loan.

debtor (Dr) A person or company that owes money, goods or services to another (the creditor).

debt rescheduling The act of lengthening the repayment period of a loan (and thereby reducing the individual payments) to assist somebody who is having difficulty in keeping to the original payment schedule.

debt retirement The repayment of a debt.

debt service ratio In international finance, a nation's annual repayments on its foreign debt divided by the value of its exports (in hard currency).

debt servicing The payment of interest on a debt.

debt swap *See debt-equity swap.*

debt-to-equity ratio A company may finance itself through borrowing or through shareholder investment, depending on current interest rates. The proportion of each source of finance is known as the debt-to-equity ratio, or gearing.

declaration The act of exercising the rights in an ***option***.

declaration of dividend An announcement by a company's directors of the amount of dividend they recommend paying to shareholders.

declaration of solvency A formal statement by a company's directors that it is seeking voluntary liquidation but that it expects to pay its creditors within at most 12 months.

decreasing-term assurance A type of *life assurance* for a specified term in which the sum assured decreases by level amounts over the duration of the policy.

deduction Money that is legally deducted from wages and salaries at source and allotted to pay taxes and (in the UK) National Insurance contributions. Payments for a *contributory pension* are also legal deductions.

deed A document that records a transaction and usually bears the seals of the parties concerned to testify to its validity.

deep discount Describing a type of loan stock that is issued at a discount exceeding 15%, or ½% per complete year between issue and redemption if less.

deep market A financial market in which many transactions can occur without affecting the price of the underlying financial instrument.

default The failure to comply with the terms set out in a contract (such as the repayment of a loan).

default notice A notice issued by a lender to a borrower who is in default on a loan (in the UK subject to the Consumer Credit Act 1974). If the notice is not complied with, the lender can seek an *enforcement order*.

default risk The risk that a borrower will not pay interest or repay the capital on a loan.

defeasance A condition built into the wording of a deed that renders it void if the condition is complied with. The term is also used for any annulment or act that renders something null and void.

defensive stock Shares in companies that are not affected by economic cycles, because they produce necessities such as food.

deferral The spreading of the benefits accruing from an asset over the whole life of the asset, rather than accounting for them in the financial year of its acquisition.

deferred annuity A type of annuity for which payments commence at a later specified date, possibly when the policyholder reaches a specific age.

deferred charges Outgoings that are not regarded as an expense in the accounting period in which they occur but which are carried forward (as an asset) and written off in a later accounting period. They are also known as a deferred costs.

deferred coupon note A bond on which interest is not paid until after a specified date. It is known in the USA as a deferred interest bond or extended bond.

deferred futures Futures contracts that are farthest away from maturity.

deferred interest bond US term for a *deferred coupon note*.

deferred ordinary shares Shares with special dividend rights, often allocated all company profits remaining after a given percentage has been paid on other kinds of shares. Such shares are usually issued to the founders of a company.

deferred pension An *occupational pension* that is paid to an employee some time after retirement from employment.

deferred start option Also termed a deferred strike option, an option whose holder can postpone setting the striking price (either to a pre-set date or indefinitely).

deficit The excess of expenditure over income, or liabilities over assets.

defined benefits scheme A type of occupational pension in which the pension provision is defined (and guaranteed; the employer has to make up the difference if the scheme fails to perform as well as expected). It is also known as a final salary pension scheme. For example, a company may provide a defined benefits scheme that offers 1/60 of final salary for each year of service with the company.

defined contribution scheme A type of occupational pension that has a fixed contribution rate (and, unlike a *defined benefits scheme,* is not dependent on final salary). At retirement, the pension is used to purchase an *annuity*. It is also known as a money-purchase pension scheme.

deflation A persistent uncontrolled decrease in prices, generally caused by a fall in the level of economic activity within a country. It should not be confused with *disinflation*.

degearing The replacement some of a company's fixed-interest loan stock by ordinary shares.

delayed payment surcharge An extra payment (in addition to interest) that is charged while a debt is outstanding.

del credere agent A person who accepts goods on consignment from exporters, agreeing (in return for an additional commission) to pay for them in the event that the original purchaser defaults.

delinquency The failure to make a payment when it is due.

delivery note In the securities market, a request for the delivery of a security.

delta 1. The rate of change of an option premium with respect to the underlying financial instrument. 2. A stock exchange classification of shares that are traded on the **Alternative Investment Market**. They are generally relatively inactive and stable shares in small companies. *See also* **alpha; beta; gamma**.

DEM (ISO) code Germany – currency Deutschmark. The 1999 legacy conversion rate was 1.95583 to the euro. It will fully change to the euro/cent from 2002.

demand deposit A deposit with a bank, building society or other financial institution that may be withdrawn at a moment's notice. It is also called a sight deposit.

demand loan A loan that can be called for repayment at any time; it has no set maturity date.

demand-pull inflation A theory that inflation is caused by excess of demand over supply, thus pulling up prices. *See also* **cost-push inflation**.

demerger The splitting up of a large company or group of companies into smaller independent ones, or the selling off of a company's subsidiaries. It is generally done to increase the value of the company's shares.

demonetization 1. The process of removing a particular coin or note from circulation and declaring it is no longer *legal tender*. In the UK, the farthing, half-penny, three-penny and sixpenny coins, and the 10-shilling and pound notes, have all been demonetized. 2. The abandonment of the use of a precious metal (gold or silver) as a monetary standard.

denar The standard currency unit of Macedonia.

Denmark currency Danish krøne (DKK) divided into 100 øre.

denomination The face value of something, such as the unitary classification of coinage and banknotes or the nominal value of bills and bonds.

Department of Trade and Industry (DTI) A UK government department that advises and controls business, finance and overseas trade, according to the government's policies.

deposit 1. Money or goods placed with a bank, building society or other financial institution. 2. An initial payment made on an item to reserve it. 3. An initial payment for something being bought on *hire purchase* or by means of a *credit sale* agreement. 4. In insurance, the payment of

Deutschmark

part of a premium before a contract is finalized. 5. An amount an insurance company has to pay the government before being authorized to do insurance business.

deposit account An account with a bank or building society that pays interest, although sometimes notice has to be given before funds may be withdrawn.

deposit bond See *National Savings Deposit Bond*.

deposit receipt An alternative term for a *deposit slip*.

deposit slip A document that records the time and place of a deposit and its value. It is also called a deposit receipt.

depreciation A decrease in value (e.g. of an investment); the opposite of appreciation. In finance it is a progressive decline in the real value of an asset because of use or obsolescence. The concept of depreciation is widely used in accounting for the process of writing off the cost of an asset against profit over an extended period, irrespective of the real value of the asset.

depressed market A market with depressed (weak) prices because supply outstrips demand.

depression A major and persistent downswing of a trade cycle, characterized by high unemployment and the underutilization of other factors of production. A less severe downswing is known as a slump or recession.

deregulation The removal of controls and abandonment of state supervision of private enterprise. A notable instance of deregulation was that of the London Stock Exchange (commonly known as the Big Bang).

derivative Short for derivative instrument, a transferable high-risk security such as a future or an option. Its value is related to that of another investment.

designated market-maker A market-maker who is physically present throughout trading and who maintains two-way up-to-date prices in return for certain concessions from the London International Financial Futures Exchange (LIFFE).

Deutsche Terminborse (DTB) The German futures and options exchange that opened in Frankfurt in 1990.

Deutschmark The standard legacy currency unit of Germany, divided into 100 Pfennig.

devaluation A reduction in the relative value of a currency (by adjusting its exchange rate). It may be relative to an absolute value (such as the gold standard) or to other relative values (such as other currencies).

dies non See *non-business day*.

differential The difference between two values, such as prices or salaries. A dealer may add a differential to purchases, or deduct it from sales, of small quantities (odd lots) of stocks or shares.

dilution Also termed dilution of equity, a deliberate increase in the number of shares on the market, which has the effect of reducing the price of each individual share.

dime The popular term for a US coin worth 10 cents (of a dollar).

dinar The standard currency unit of Algeria (where it is divided into 100 centimes); Bahrain, Iraq, Jordan, Kuwait and Yemen (where it equals 1000 fils); Tunisia (where it equals 1000 millimes); Bosnia-Herzegovina and Yugoslavia (where it equals 100 paras); Libya (where it equals 100 dirhans); and Sudan (where it equals 100 piastres). It is also a subdivision (1/100) of the Irani real.

dip A slight drop in the price of a security after a period of a stable or rising price.

direct debit The practice of debiting a bank account with a sum owed on the authorization of the account holder, but without his or her direct involvement (e.g. by issuing a cheque or making a cash transfer) at the time. The essence is that it is a claim made by a creditor as opposed to a payment made by a debtor. It is a type of banker's order, although the amount to be debited is not specified.

direct investment 1. A company's investment in physical assets (such as machinery and plant). 2. The investment, perhaps by a multinational company, in a foreign company's operations and the consequent influence that may result.

director One of the principals of a company, in a public limited company (plc) appointed by its shareholders. Most companies have a group of directors (the board of directors) who act collectively as the senior management of the company, being responsible to the shareholders for its efficient running and future development. Their duties include the compilation of an annual report and the recommendation of an annual dividend on shares.

direct placement The selling of shares directly to a financial institution or the public without using an underwriter.

discounted cashflow (DCF) 77

dirham The standard currency unit of Morocco (where it is divided into 100 centimes) and the United Arab Emirates (where it is divided into 10 dinars).

dirty float A partly-managed floating exchange rate, in which a central bank continues to intervene in the market for its own currency.

disbursement A payment made on behalf of a client by a banker, solicitor, or other professional person. It is ultimately charged to the client's account.

discharged bankrupt A person discharged from bankruptcy. The debts of the person concerned are judged to have been settled and, if solvent, he or she can begin again.

disclaimer A clause in a contract that states that one of the parties does not take responsibility for some occurrence. For example, the owners of many car parks advertise to motorists that they disclaim any responsibility for loss or damage to cars or anything contained in them

disclosure The revealing of relevant information. 1. A limited company must disclose its financial dealings and position by the publication of annual accounts. 2. The parties to any contract must disclose relevant information. For example, a person holding a life assurance policy must notify the assurers of his or her medical history.

discount 1. The amount by which a new share issue stands below its par value. 2. The price of a share whose price-earnings ratio is below the market average. 3. The amount by which a currency is below par on the foreign exchanges. 4. To make a reduction in the face value of an article (or the price being charged for it), generally in order to make a purchase more attractive to a customer. 5. On financial markets, the charge made for cashing an immature bill of exchange, the discount being proportional to the unexpired portion of the bill. 6. In insurance, a reduction in premium (such as a no-claims bonus).

discount bond A bond selling at a price that is less than its redemption value.

discount broker A broker who acts as an intermediary between those who want to buy and sell bills of exchange.

discounted cashflow (DCF) A method of assessing a company's investments according to when they are due to yield their expected returns, in order to indicate the present worth of the future sum. In this way it is possible to determine preference for one of a number of alternative investments.

discount house An organization whose main activity is discounting bills of exchange.

discounting The act of making a discount. More specifically, it is the practice of selling a debt to an institution at a discount.

discounting back A method of estimating the present value of a future sum, carried out by finding what sum earning x per cent compound interest over the time in question will equal the future sum. The interest rate x is the one in use at the time the calculation is made.

discount market That part of a money market that involves the buying and selling of short-term debt between the commercial banks, the discount houses and the central bank.

discount rate An interest rate applied to future earnings to convert them to present values. It is the cost of capital rate of interest or *hurdle rate* used with a discount factor in calculating a discounted cash flow.

discretionary account (DA) An account into which *discretionary funds* are deposited.

discretionary fund A sum of money left with a stockbroker, to be invested at his or her discretion.

discretionary income The income that remains after meeting the cost of taxes and such necessities as food and accommodation, to be spent at the owner's discretion.

discretionary trust A trust in which the trustees decide the proportionate shares of income to allocate to each beneficiary.

dishonour 1. To refuse to accept or discharge a bill of exchange when it is presented for payment. 2. To fail to pay a cheque when the drawer's account has insufficient funds to cover the amount.

disinflation A policy to curb inflation by the adoption of mild economic measures such as the restriction of expenditure. Other measures include increasing interest rate and the deliberate creation of a budget surplus. It is a mild form of deflation which, by contrast, indicates an uncontrolled fall in prices.

disintermediation The withdrawal of a financial intermediary from a negotiation. The term may also be applied to a flow of funds from lenders to borrowers "off balance sheet" without the intervention of an intermediary (such as a mortgage broker).

disinvestment The withdrawal or sale of an investment. Governments and companies sometimes decide to disinvest from nations whose economic or political complexion offends them.

disposable income That part of a person's income that he or she may dispose of in any way, i.e. what is left after paying for such necessities as accommodation and food.

dissaving The situation in which spending (or consumption) is greater than income; negative saving. It may result in borrowing.

distress borrowing A situation in which a company (or anybody else) is forced to borrow money even when interest rates are high.

distributable profit A company's accumulated realized profits less its accumulated realized losses, available for distribution as dividends. For a public company, this must not result in the net assets being less than the sum of called-up capital and undistributable reserves.

distributable reserves A company's profits that have been retained and which can be distributed as dividends.

distribution 1. Payments made by a company from its profits (such as dividends). 2. The apportioning of a *scrip issue* or *rights issue* of shares. 3. The division of property according to law, such as the distribution of a deceased person's estate.

distribution bond A bond, resembling a *unit trust*, that is sold by a company that deals in life assurance.

diversification 1. The practice of spreading a portfolio of investments over a wide range of securities to reduce losses if one sector of the market enters recession. 2. The extension in the range of goods or services offered by a company into new areas, either material or geographical. By extension the term may also be applied to attempts by local authorities or central government to attract a variety of industries to an area that is heavily dependent on only one industry, particularly one in decline.

divestment The selling off of part of a company, either to reduce costs (and improve profitability) or to concentrate on the remaining parts of the business.

dividend A share in the profits of a limited company, usually paid annually. Dividends are generally expressed as a percentage of the nominal value of a single ordinary share. Thus a payment of 10p on each £1 share (or 10c on each $1 share) would be termed a dividend of 10%. They may also be expressed in terms of the dividend yield, which is the dividend stated as a percentage of the share value.

dividend cover For a company's shares, the ratio of the earnings per share to the dividend per share. A value of less than one indicates that the company is paying dividends out of reserves.

dividend per share (DPS) The expression of a dividend in cents, pence etc. per share rather than as a percentage of the total value of the share. Thus a 10% dividend on a share worth £1 would be termed a "10p per share dividend".

dividend protection A situation in which the strike price of an over-the-counter option is reduced by the amount of any dividend paid on the underlying financial instrument.

dividend warrant An order to a company's bankers to pay a specified dividend or interest to a shareholder or other investor.

dividend yield The ratio of a dividend to the price of the underlying financial instrument, such as the (usually gross) dividend per share divided by the share price.

DJF (ISO) code Djibouti Republic – currency Djibouti franc.

Djibouti Republic currency Djibouti franc (DJF); there is no subdivision.

DKK (ISO) code Denmark – currency Danish krøne.

DMD (ISO) code Dominica – currency East Caribbean dollar.

dobra The standard currency unit of São Tome and Principe.

documentary credit An alternative term for a *letter of credit*.

dog A US colloquial term for a financial product that has a low share of a slowly growing or stagnant market.

dollar The standard currency unit of the USA, divided into 100 cents. It is also the name of the standard currency units of Anguilla, Antigua and Barbuda, Australia, the Bahamas, Barbados, Belau, Belize, Bermuda, the British Virgin Islands, Brunei, Canada, the Caymen Islands, the Cook Islands, Dominica, Fiji, Grenada, Guam, Guyana, Hong Kong, Jamaica, Kiribati, Liberia, Malaysia, the Marshall Islands, Micronesia, Montserrat, Namibia, Nauru, New Zealand, Puerto Rico, Saint Kitts and Nevis, Saint Lucia, Saint Vincent and the Grenadines, Singapore, the Solomon Islands, Taiwan, Trinidad and Tobago, Tuvalu, the Virgin Islands, the West Indies, and Zimbabwe. These currencies are referred to as Australian dollars, Hong Kong dollars, and so on if there is a risk of confusion with US dollars. All are divided into 100 cents. See also *eurodollar*.

Dow Jones Index   81

dollar premium An extra charge, above the official exchange rate, sometimes demanded for the purchase of US dollars.

dolphin An informal term for somebody who buys shares in new issues and then sells for a high profit as soon as trading opens.

domicile A person's place of residence for legal and tax purposes. A person domiciled in the UK, for example, is liable to pay British taxes and is subject to British law.

Dominica currency East Caribbean dollar (DMD), divided into 100 cents.

Dominican Republic currency Dominican Republic peso (DOP), divided into 100 centavos.

donation Money or other asset given by a person or organization (the donor) to another person or organization (the donee).

dong The standard currency unit of Vietnam, divided into 100 xu.

DOP (ISO) code Dominican Republic – currency Dominican Republic peso.

dormant company A company that has not traded during a particular accounting period.

dot com stocks A colloquial description of a company that relies in some way on the Internet to market its products or services.

double auction The normal type of outcry for trading in commodity markets, in which both bids and offers are made in competition with each other.

double bottom In the analysis of share market trends, a price that hits a low point equal to the last low point. The prediction is that once two similar low points have been reached, the price will tend to go up. *See also* **double top.**

double top In the analysis of share market trends, a price that reaches a high point equal to the last high point. The prediction is that once two similar high points have been reached, the price will tend to go down. *See also* **double bottom.**

Dow Jones Index Formal name the Dow Jones Industrial Average, often called simply the Dow Jones, a security price index used on the New York Stock Exchange and issued by the US firm of Dow Jones & Co. (publishers of the *Wall Street Journal*). It is based on the average closing prices of a selection of 30 quoted companies.

downgrade To reduce the status of somebody or something. For example, a person downgrades his or her shareholding by selling part of it.

down payment A deposit, such as part of the price of goods bought on hire purchase or using a credit sale.

downside The amount an investor stands to lose when taking a risk, for example the amount by which a share price may fall, or the amount a person is liable to lose by making a speculative investment.

downstream Describing an economic activity that is in or close to the retail sector, i.e. one that involves the distribution and selling of goods and services. The term is frequently applied to the oil industry, in which context the petrol station is downstream and the oil rig is upstream.

downtick 1. Describing a transaction that is concluded at a lower price than a similar previous transaction. 2. A small and temporary fall in the price of a share. *See also* **uptick**.

downturn The point at which something begins to fall, for example a share price that has been rising and begins to fall, or productivity that is beginning to decline.

DPS Abbreviation of *dividend per share*.

Dr Abbreviation of *debtor*.

drachma Standard unit of Greek legacy currency, divided into 100 lepta.

draft 1. A written order from a customer (the drawer) to a financial institution (the drawee), requesting that money is paid from the customer's account to a third party. 2. The usual US term for a bill of exchange. 3. To draft is to draw up any document, especially a contract.

dragon bond An informal term for a foreign bond issued in the market of one of the so-called dragon countries, such as Indonesia, Malaysia, the Philippines, Singapore or Thailand.

dram The standard currency unit of Armenia.

drawdown A sum of money borrowed or taken against a credit facility (such as a bank loan).

drawee The person or institution to whom a bill of exchange or draft is addressed (e.g. the bank account on which a cheque is drawn).

drawer The person who draws a bill of exchange or draft, i.e. who orders payment (from the drawee).

drip-feed 1. A steady payment of money at regular intervals. It is usually a pejorative term that implies that the recipient is dependent on the payments. It is often applied to foreign aid to underdeveloped countries. 2. *Venture capital* payments made in stages to a start-up company.

drop-dead date The date on which it is expected that a troubled company will run out of funds.

drop-dead fee A payment offered to a bidder by the target of a (usually take-over) bid in an effort to induce the bidder to withdraw.

drop-dead rate The amount demanded by a would-be corporate raider to withdraw a take-over bid.

drop lock A variable-rate bank loan that automatically changes to a fixed-rate long-term bond if interest rates fall bellow a specified level. It effectively converts short-term borrowing into a long-term loan.

DTB Abbreviation of *Deutsche Terminborse*.

DTI Abbreviation of *Department of Trade and Industry*.

dual capacity A stock exchange system that makes no distinction between the functions of stockbrokers and jobbers. One person (called a market-maker) may therefore both buy and sell stocks and shares on the exchange.

dual currency bond A Japanese bond that is denominated in yen but pays interest in a high-yielding currency such as US dollars.

Dubai United Arab Emirates currency dirham (AXD), divided into 100 fils.

due date 1. The date on which a bill of exchange is due to be paid. In the UK, instruments not payable on demand, on sight or on presentation are allowed three *days grace*. 2. The date on which an insurance premium is due to be paid.

Dutch auction A type of auction in which the seller begins by proposing a high price and gradually brings it lower until somebody agrees to buy.

duty Broadly, any tax levied by a public authority, particularly that imposed on imports, exports and certain manufactured goods (such as, in the UK, petrol and diesel fuel and goods that contain alcohol or tobacco).

DZD (ISO) code Algeria – currency Algerian dinar.

E

Eagle A US coin containing from 0.1 to 1 ounce of gold.

early surrender The cashing in of an insurance policy before its maturity date, which often yields less than the amount already paid in (because of loss of bonuses, etc.).

early withdrawal penalty A penalty charged for the withdrawal of funds from a fixed-term investment before the investment matures.

earned income An income received in exchange for labour, rather than derived from investments (in the UK the definition does, however, include some pension and social security payments). It is taxable.

earnest money 1. A part payment (deposit) made for goods or services, showing that the buyer is serious about buying. 2. The *margin* on a futures market.

earnings See *earned income*.

earnings per share (EPS) An *accounting ratio* equal to a company's profit (after deduction of tax, minority interests and any preference dividends) divided by the number of shares issued. It can be used to calculate the *price-earnings ratio*.

earnings yield A hypothetical figure that provides a reliable measurement of the worth of an investment. It is reached by relating a company's divisible net earnings to the market price of the investment. Sometimes, with reference to fixed-interest securities, the term is used interchangeably with flat yield.

earn-out An employee incentive scheme whereby the employee is offered share options that give him or her an interest in the company for which he or she works.

EAS Abbreviation of *Enterprise Allowance Scheme*.

EASD Abbreviation of *European Association of Security Dealers*.

EASDAQ Abbreviation of *European Association of Securities Dealers Automated Quotation System*.

easy money An alternative term for *cheap money*.

ECGD Abbreviation of *Export Credits Guarantee Department*.

econometrics A branch of statistics that uses mathematical models (usually on a computer) to test economic hypotheses, describe economic relationships, and forecast economic trends. It is employed to produce correlated quantitative data rather than to prove economic causation.

economic indicator One of several measurable variables used to study change in an economy. In this context, economists also study production indexes, unemployment trends, the amount of overtime worked and levels of taxation.

ECS (ISO) code Ecuador – currency sucre.

ecu Legacy currency unit of European Union. It is still used in the valuation of the European Monetary Cooperative Fund.

ECU Abbreviation of *European Currency Unit*.

ECU Treasury bill A Treasury bill denominated is in European Currency Units.

Ecuador currency sucre (ECS), divided into 100 centavos.

EEC Abbreviation of *European Economic Community*, now replaced by the *European Union*.

effective annual rate A year's total interest stated as a percentage of the principal at the beginning of the year.

effective date The date on which a contract becomes effective.

effective rate An alternative term for *effective yield*.

effective yield The yield calculated as a percentage of the price of an investment. It is also called effective rate.

EGP (ISO) code Egypt – currency Egyptian pound.

Egypt currency Egyptian pound (EGP), divided into 100 piastres.

EIB Abbreviation of *European Investment Bank*.

EIS Abbreviation of *Enterprise Investment Scheme*.

elephant An informal term for a large corporate entity that is slow but dominant and displays a tendency towards the creation of monopolies. In the USA, large institutional investors who, unlike *contrarians*, tend to move as a herd are also known as elephants.

eligible bank A UK bank that is entitled to discount acceptances at the Bank of England.

eligible bill In the UK, a bank bill that is issued by a bank entitled to discount acceptances at the Bank of England (an eligible bank); it may be rediscounted at the Bank of England. In the USA, it is another term for *eligible paper*.

eligible paper 1. Any first-class security (such as Treasury bills and short-dated gilts) that are acceptable by the Bank of England for rediscounting. 2. In the USA, a banker's acceptance that may be rediscounted at the Federal Reserve Bank.

elves The US banking and stockbroking community centred on Wall Street or, more specifically, the technical analysts who predict changes in share prices.

emalangeni (singular **lilangeni**) The standard currency unit of Swaziland, divided into 100 cents.

embezzlement See *fraud*.

emergency fund A reserve of money held for financial emergencies in an easy-to-access interest-earning account.

emerging market A security market in a newly industrialized country (such as those in Eastern Europe and eastern Asia).

employee buy-out The transfer of ownership of a company to its employees after they have bought all of its shares.

employee share/stock ownership plan (ESOP) A plan that lets employees buy shares (stock) in their own company.

EMS Abbreviation of *European Monetary System*.

EMU Abbreviation of *European Monetary Union*.

endorse To sign one's name on a document, such as a bill of exchange, to certify its validity and transfer its ownership

endorsee A person who signs an endorsement.

endorsement 1. An authenticating signature or explanatory statement on a document. 2. A confirmatory statement. 3. A note attached to an insurance policy detailing an alteration in the original terms.

endowment 1. A gift of money or property to a specific person or organization (and usually for a specified purpose). 2. An *endowment assurance*.

endowment assurance A type of life assurance policy that pays the sum assured on survival to the end of a specified term (the maturity date) or on death, whichever is earlier. A with-profits endowment provides bonuses in addition to the basic sum assured.

endowment mortgage An interest-only mortgage that uses an endowment assurance as a vehicle for repayment of the loan at the end of the term.

enforcement order A court order that deals with default on a loan subject to the UK Consumer Credit Act 1974.

enterprise Any undertaking, but particularly a bold or remarkable one, or the quality of boldness and imagination in an undertaking.

Enterprise Allowance Scheme (EAS) A UK government scheme that was set up to encourage the establishment of new businesses by the unemployed by offering, among other incentives, grants and tax concessions.

Enterprise Investment Scheme (EIS) A UK government scheme established in 1994 that allows tax relief when shares in a company (not quoted on the Stock Exchange) are issued on subscription. It superseded the former Business Expansion Scheme.

enterprise zone A geographical area in which economic activity is promoted by the government. Small businesses are encouraged, and the relocation of industry and firms to enterprise zones is helped by the provision of various incentives.

entrepreneur A person who controls a commercial enterprise – the risk-taker and profit-maker – the person who assembles the factors of production and supervises their combination. The term is also applied to somebody who has a brilliant idea and then finds the money to back it.

EOS Abbreviation of *European Options Exchange*.

EPS Abbreviation of *earnings per share*.

equalization The return on capital invested in a unit trust. All investors in a trust receive an equal sum per unit held, although some may have only invested in the period since the last distribution. The distribution paid on the latter person's stock therefore comprises a dividend and an equalization that brings the return up to par.

equalizing a dividend The transfer of company funds from reserves to make up a dividend payment when there is insufficient profit to do this unaided.

equilibrium price The price of a commodity whose supply matches its demand.

equitable mortgage Also called an equitable charge, a mortgage in which the lender holds the deeds to the property but ownership is retained by the borrower.

equities An alternative term for ordinary shares. Equities entitle their holder to share in the issuing company's profits. Ordinary shareholders bear the ultimate risk, in that they have no entitlements in the event of liquidation.

equity 1. The ordinary share capital (risk capital) of a company. *See equities*. 2. The residual value of the *variation margins* and *initial margins* of a liquidated future. 3. The residual value of common stock over the debit balance of a margin account. 4. The difference between the market value of a property and the debit balance of a mortgage on it. 5 The concept of fairness, of central importance to a branch of law distinct from common law, and as such it has a significant effect on all kinds of contracts, dealings and trusts.

equity capital The capital of a company that belongs to its owners (in many cases the holders of ordinary shares), rather than capital provided by owners of fixed-interest securities.

equity dilution A reduction in the unit value of ordinary shares affected by a *bonus issue*.

equity-linked assurance policy A life assurance policy that has part of its premiums invested in equities. The selling price of the equities becomes the surrender value of the policy.

equity-release scheme Also called a home income plan, a scheme designed for elderly home owners that allows them to receive either regular payments or a lump sum by releasing a part or all of the capital (equity) tied up in their home. The property may revert to the institution providing the money on the death of the borrower.

Eritrea currency birr (ETB), divided into 100 cents.

ERM Abbreviation of *Exchange Rate Mechanism*.

escalating annuity A type of annuity whose payments grow stepwise each year.

escheat The confiscation of property. It is a legal doctrine that states that property or titles revert to the crown in the event that the owner or holder dies intestate and without heirs.

escrow A document held in trust by a third party, for example deeds and titles may be held in escrow until a person reaches the age of majority, or until some specified condition has been met.

escudo The standard legacy currency unit of Portugal and Cape Verde, divided into 100 centavos.

ESOP Abbreviation of *employee stock ownership plan*.

ESP (ISO) code Spain – currency peseta. The 1999 legacy conversion rate was 166.386 to the euro. It will fully change to the euro/cent from 2002.

estate 1. The residual possessions of somebody who has died. 2. Land, most especially a large area of land owned by one person.

estate duty A former UK tax, introduced in 1894, levied on the estate of somebody who died. In 1974 it was superseded by *capital transfer tax*, which was itself replaced by *inheritance tax* in 1986.

Estonia currency kroon, divided into 100 kopecks.

ETB (ISO) code Ethiopia – currency birr.

ethical investment An investment made in a company that is not active in anything that the investor thinks is antisocial or unethical in its dealings. Thus some investors would not put money into companies that deal in or manufacture animal furs, armaments, tobacco products, and so on.

Ethiopia currency birr (ETB), divided into 100 cents.

EU Abbreviation of *European Union*.

EUR (ISO) code European Union – currency euro.

euro The standard currency unit of the European Monetary Union, introduced at the beginning of 1999 (but not adopted then by Denmark, Greece, Sweden or the UK; Greece joined in 2001). Currently only non-cash payments may be made in euros but it will be adopted as normal currency by the participating nations in 2002. *See also* **European Currency Unit**.

eurobond A medium- or long-term bearer bond denominated in a *eurocurrency*. Eurobonds are issued by governments or multinational companies.

90 eurocurrency

eurocurrency The currency of any nation held offshore in a European country, such as eurodollars. The eurocurrency markets deal in very large-scale loans and deposits rather than the purchase or sale of foreign exchange.

eurodollars US dollars held outside the USA, particularly those circulating in Europe. The postwar economic ascendancy of the USA has made the eurodollar an international currency medium.

euronote A type of commercial paper, issued in any *eurocurrency*, that takes the form of a negotiable short-term bearer note.

Eurobond A negotiable debt security issued outside the country of its currency and intended for international distribution.

Eurodeposit A deposit account in any major currency outside the country of that currency.

Eurodollar A dollar deposited with a bank outside the USA.

Eurogiro A pan-European electronic payment system operated by European girobanks.

Euroland A term applied to the EU countries that have accepted the euro as their common and soon-to-be-only currency.

European Association of Security Dealers (EASD) An organization established in 1995 to promote the idea of a Europe-wide stock exchange.

European Association of Securities Dealers Automated Quotation System (EASDAQ) A Europe-wide stock market, established in Brussels in 1966, based on the US National Association of Security Dealers Automated Quotation System (NASDAQ) and catering mainly for high-growth companies.

European Community (EC) A short form of European Economic Community (EEC), now called the *European Union*.

European Currency Unit (ECU) The unit of account in use by the European Economic Community (EEC) from 1979 and now by the European Union (EU). The value of the ECU is calculated by taking a weighted average of the current values of EU member state's own currencies. It exists only on paper, but is used to settle inter-Union debts and in the calculation of Union budgets.

European Economic Community (EEC) An association of originally 12 European nations that were joined by a customs union and committed to the promotion of free trade within the boundaries of the community, now rename the European Union (EU). It was often abbreviated to European Community (EC) and was originally known as the Common Market.

European Investment Bank (EIB) A bank established in 1958 (under the Treaty of Rome) with headquarters in Luxembourg to fund EEC projects through the granting of long-term loans financed through public bond issues.

European Monetary System (EMS) A system established in 1979 for stabilizing exchange rates between EU member states. It can also be seen as a step towards the European Central Bank (ECB) and a single currency as part of *European Monetary Union*.

European Monetary Union (EMU) The ultimate aim to standardize the currency of the EU, the euro. Another objective is to create a deep and liquid capital market in Europe, reducing the cost for issuers and increasing the choice for investors.

European Options Exchange (EOE) An organization established in Amsterdam in 1978 as a market in traded options (mainly in precious metals and currencies). In 1977 it merged with the Amsterdam Stock Exchange to form the Amsterdam Exchanges.

European Union (EU) An association of European nations formerly known as the European Economic Community (EEC) or European Community (EC), and before that the Common Market. It is intended that all factors of production may be moved within the community at will, and remaining customs barriers are expected to be removed at some time in the near future. The EU is committed to a *European Monetary System*, and all that it entails.

European Union currency euro (EUR), divided into 100 cents.

event of default In a loan agreement, a clause that if breached requires repayment of the loan immediately.

evergreen clause In a *letter of credit*, a clause that specifies a regular expiry date with automatic extension.

evergreen funding The gradual supply of capital to a new or recapitalized company.

excess The shares left unsold after a rights issue. They are available for other buyers.

exchange 1. To give one thing and take an equivalent in return. 2. A place where goods or stocks are traded.

exchange arbitrage A method of making a profit from a slight difference between the values of two currencies in terms of a third currency.

exchange broker A person who brings together buyers and sellers on a foreign exchange market (thereby earning a commission).

exchange commission A fee charged for buying or selling foreign currency (i.e. changing one currency into another).

exchange control The control of foreign exchange dealings by the government, either by restrictions on trade or by direct intervention in the market. Exchange controls help a government to exert some influence over the international value of its own currency. In the UK, exchange controls were abolished in 1979.

exchange gain A profit that results from changes in an exchange rate (between buying and selling something).

exchange rate The price at which one currency can be exchanged for another. Such transactions may be carried out on either the spot or forward markets, and are usually conducted either to permit investment abroad or to pay for imports. There is, in addition, considerable *speculation* on exchange rates.

Exchange Rate Mechanism (ERM) An EU regulation that limits variations in the exchange rates of its member states to within cloely defined limits. It is a vital feature of the *European Monetary System*. Britain and Italy left the ERM in 1992.

excise duty A duty levied on home-produced good, either to control consumption and thus influence spending, or to raise revenue. Goods that currently attract excise duty in the UK include alcohol, diesel fuel, petrol and tobacco.

exclusion In insurance, a declared risk that the insurance company will not pay a claim on (for example on a life assurance policy, an exclusion may be death resulting from suicide).

ex-coupon Describing stock that does not give the purchaser the right to the next interest payment due to be paid on it.

ex-dividend (ex div or XD) Describing stock that does not give the purchaser the right to the next dividend payment, or to any dividend payment due within a specified period, generally the next calendar

extended credit 93

month. He or she does, however, have the right to receive subsequent dividends.

execution only Describing the service provided by a dealer in securities that excludes any research, advice or any other service.

executor A person appointed in a will to see that the terms of the will or bequest are carried out.

exercise To make use of a right or an option.

exercise notice A notice issued when the holder of an option wishes to take up his or her right to buy or sell the security for which the option has been agreed.

exercise price The price at which an option may be exercised (also known as the strike price).

ex gratia pension A pension paid by an employer although there is no binding commitment to do so.

exit To leave a market by selling all relevant stocks and shares, or to cease production.

exit charge 1. A charge made to an investor in some unit trusts when he or she liquefies the investment. 2. A charge (to inheritance tax) made when an asset is removed from a discretionary trust.

ex new An alternative term for *ex rights*.

expiry date The date on which an agreement lapses. In insurance, it is the date on which a term assurance ends.

Export Credits Guarantee Department (ECGD) A UK government department, part of the Department of Trade and Industry (DTI), established in 1991 and partly privatized (in 1969) that makes available export credit insurance and guarantees to repay banks that give credit (over two years or more) to exporters.

export duty A tax levied on exports. Because export duties tend to discourage exports and adversely affect the balance of payments, they are seldom used.

ex rights Also known as ex new, a stock exchange term for shares that are sold minus the right to take up *bonus issues*.

extended credit 1. A situation in which a borrower (with a credit card or bank loan, for example) is given more time to pay. 2. Credit that is to be repaid over a very long period of time. In the USA it describes borrowing by a financial institution from the Federal Reserve.

extendible bond A bond whose maturity can be extended if all parties agree.

extension 1. A postponement of the date on which a loan has to be repaid. 2. A prolonging of the life of a documentary credit or other financial instrument.

external bond A foreign bond denominated in the currency of a different country.

external finance Finance that is made available to a company from outside the company (from borrowing, grants or the issue of bonds or shares, for example).

extraordinary items Non-recurrent material items below the line on a company's balance sheet, such as the sale or purchase of premises.

F

face value Also called nominal value, the value or price written on something, such as the denomination of a banknote or the par value of a share.

facility An alternative term for a bank loan or overdraft.

factoring The activity of managing the trade debts of another organization. Commonly, a company sells due debts to a factor at a discount. The factor then makes a profit by recovering the debts at a price nearer their face value. Factoring relieves companies of the burden of administering debts and gives them access to ready cash before payment is due.

fair price provisions (US **fair price amendments**) A clause in a corporate charter whereby a buyer of the company's shares must pay the same amount or make the same consideration for all shares purchased. It is used as a defensive tactic against bootstrapping (*see **bootstrap***).

fair value 1. The value of an asset that could be obtained in an arm's-length transaction between a willing seller and a willing buyer, each acting in his or her own self-interest. 2. The price of a future, option or other derivative equal to that of the underlying instrument (after the deduction of transaction costs).

fallen angel A company, or shares in a company, whose rating has recently fallen significantly.

fall out of bed Describing a sudden fall in a share price, usually because of poor company performance or a threatened take-over.

Fannie Mae The nickname of the US *Federal National Mortgage Association*.

far month For a futures or options contract, the trading month that is farthest distant.

Faroe Islands currency Danish krøne (DKK), divided into 100 øre.

FASB An abbreviation of *Financial Accounting Standards Board*.

FDI Abbreviation of *foreign direct investment*.

FDIC Abbreviation of *Federal Deposit Insurance Corporation*.

Fed See *Federal Reserve System*.

Federal Deposit Insurance Corporation (FDIC) An organization that makes available deposit insurance for US banks. It is part of the Federal Reserve System, employing the US Bank Insurance Fund.

federal funds Deposits held by US federal reserve banks that bear no interest.

federal funds rate The US interest rate at which one federal reserve bank borrows funds from another such bank. It is regulated by the federal reserve.

federal home loan bank A type of US bank that provides secured loans to its savings and loan customers, who must hold stock in the regional bank.

Federal Home Loan Bank Board (FHLBB) In the USA, a regulatory body established in 1933 for savings and loan associations, and which has credit reserves for various mortgage lending institutions.

Federal Home Loan Mortgage Corporation (FHLMC or **Freddie Mac)** A US organization, founded in 1970 and authorized by public charter, that purchases residential mortgages from lenders and then sells them on the open market packages as new securities. Savings organizations throughout the USA own the shares in the corporation.

Federal National Mortgage Association (FNMA or **Fannie Mae)** The US government-sponsored privately-own organization founded in 1938 to purchase residential mortgages from lenders and act as security for them. It finances its activities by issuing shares and various debt securities.

Federal Open Market Committee (FOMC) A committee that determines the monetary policy of the US Federal Reserve System, particularly with regard to its open market operations.

federal reserve bank Any of the USA's central banks, each of which is controlled by a state government.

Federal Reserve Board The organization that controls the growth of US bank reserves and the money supply.

Federal Reserve System (Fed) The US central bank system, under which 12 regional federal reserve banks are governed by the Federal Reserve Board in Washington, appointed by the President. Like the Bank of England in the UK, it sets banking policy and controls the money supply.

FHLBB Abbreviation of *Federal Home Loan Bank Board*.

FHLMC Abbreviation of *Federal Home Loan Mortgage Corporation*.

fiduciary A person or body acting in trust. Anyone holding, say, an investment in trust for another is said to be acting in a fiduciary capacity.

fiduciary loan A loan made without the borrower providing any security.

Fiji currency Fijian dollars (FJD), divided into 100 cents.

fill To carry out a client's order to buy or sell a bond, commodity or shares. If the full amount is not obtained, it is termed a partial fill.

filler A subdivision (1/00) of the Hungarian forint.

fill or kill On a futures market, an order to trade that must be either fulfilled immediately or cancelled.

fils A subdivision (1/100) of the United Arab Emirates dirham, and a subdivision (1/1000) of the dinar in Bahrein, Iraq, Jordan, Kuwait and the Republic of Yemen.

FIM (ISO) code Finland – currency markka. The 1999 legacy conversion rate was 5.94573 to the euro. It will fully change to the euro/cent from 2002.

final dividend A dividend paid at the end of a company's financial year after an **interim dividend** has already been paid.

final salary pension scheme See *defined benefits scheme*.

finance 1. Making funds available (e.g. for investment or consumption), when it equates with lending. It may be short-, medium- or long-term. 2. A general term for the money system, credits, and so on (especially those involving the government).

finance bill An alternative term for *finance paper*.

finance company An alternative name for a *finance house*.

finance house Also known as a finance company or an industrial bank, a company that provides finance (credit), for example to operate hire purchase transactions on behalf of retailers of consumer goods.

finance house base rate The interest rate charged by UK finance houses, equal to the average of the three-month London Inter-Bank Offered Rate (LIBOR), rounded up to the next ½% above.

finance house deposit Funds deposited with a finance house by a large lender such as a bank.

finance lease A lease in which all the risks and rewards of ownership are substantially transferred to the lessee.

finance paper Also called finance bill, a bill of exchange relating to the money owed to a finance house.

Financial Accounting Standards Board (FASB) A private regulatory body, established in 1973, that sets the accounting standards for US public companies.

financial document Any document that can be used like money to make purchases, such as a bill of exchange or cheque.

financial future A future in some financial asset at a specified date and price.

financial institution 1. A bank, building society, finance house or other institution that collects, invests and lends funds. 2. A *financial intermediary*.

financial intermediary A bank, building society, finance house, insurance company or any other business that collects funds (from members, or lenders) to use for making loans (to borrowers) or other investments.

financial market The general market in financial instruments such as the bond market, commodity market, foreign exchange market and stock market. Capital markets deal in long-term debt and equity instruments; money markets in short-term debt.

financial ratio An alternative term for *accounting ratio*.

Financial Services Authority (FSA) A UK organization established in 1997 by the combination of four former self-regulatory organizations (SROs): the Investment Managers Regulatory Organization, the Personal Investment Authority, the Securities and Futures Authority and the Security and Investment Authority. It also regulates building societies, credit unions, friendly societies and the insurance industry. Banking was also planned to come under its remit.

financial statement A document that summarizes a company's activities, assets and liabilities, including the balance sheet and profit-and-loss account.

Financial Times Stock Exchange 100 Index (FTSE or FOOTSIE) An index of shares of the 100 largest UK companies, a weighted average of which is updated every minute during the working day. Then index value of 1,000 was set as the base on 3 January 1984.

Financial Times Stock Exchange 30 Index (FT Index or **FT-30 Index)** An index of changes in prices of 30 major industrial and commercial ordinary shares on the London Stock Exchange, updated hourly during the working day. The index value of 100 was set on 1 July 1935.

financial year A period of 12 months, beginning anywhere in the calendar year, used for company accounting purposes. *The* financial year is the period of 12 months beginning on 1 April to which corporation tax rates apply. See also *fiscal year*.

finder's fee A commission charged by a company or person acting as an intermediary in a transaction.

fineness The purity of gold (e.g. in bullion) expressed as parts per 1,000; thus "980 fine" is 98% pure gold.

fine trade bill A *trade bill* between reputable parties ("good names") that in the money market has a fine rate of discount.

Finland currency markka (FIM), divided into 100 pennia. The 1999 legacy conversion rate was 5.94573 to the euro. It will fully change to the euro/cent from 2002.

firm Strictly, partners trading together, although the term is commonly applied to any business.

firm order An order to buy or sell a security that can be carried out without further confirmation.

first mortgage A residential mortgage that gives the lender (mortgagee) the first charge over a specified property. See also **second mortgage**.

first mortgage debenture A debenture that gives the holder first charge over a company's property.

first notice day On a futures contract, the first day on which notice can be given of intended (or expected) actual delivery.

fiscal agent 1. A person who pays subscribers on behalf of the issuer of a bond. 2. In the USA, the role of the Federal Reserve when it processes payments from and to the government.

fiscal drag An effect during times of inflation in which pay increases push employees into higher tax brackets (giving the government a higher proportion of incomes).

fiscal year (FY) A period of 12 months for the purposes of tax calculations. In the UK the fiscal year runs from 6 April to the following 5 April. *See also* *financial year*.

fixed assets Sometimes also known as capital assets, assets that are used in the furtherance of a company's business, such as machinery or property.

fixed asset turnover An *accounting ratio* equal to a company's sales divided by its average fixed assets, expressed as a ratio to 1.

fixed charge 1. An asset against which a mortgage is secured. 2. A regular payment such as rent or interest on a debenture or loan.

fixed deposit A deposit of funds that has a fixed future repayment date. Early withdrawal may incur a penalty.

fixed exchange rate An exchange rate that the government attempts to control and fix in the short term by instructing the central bank (the Bank of England in the UK) to buy or sell foreign exchange reserves, or by introducing tariffs.

fixed expenses Expenses that are incurred regardless of the level of other activities.

fixed-income investment An investment (security), such as a government or local government bond, that pays a fixed rate of return until maturity or a preference share that pays a fixed dividend.

fixed-interest security A security for which the income is fixed and does not vary. Such securities include bonds, debentures and gilt-edged securities.

fixed loan A loan whose repayment date, and often interest rate, is specified at the outset.

fixed rate Describing a charge or interest rate that does not change (unlike a floating rate).

fixed-rate mortgage A mortgage with an interest rate determined at the beginning of the loan period and fixed for at least the first few years.

fixed trust A unit trust in which investors' money is invested in a set portfolio

fixture Any chattel attached or annexed to land, in which case it becomes part of the property.

FJD (ISO) code Fiji – currency Fijian dollars.

flat market A slow market with very little turnover.

flat yield The yield on a fixed-interest security shown by relating the income from the security to the present market price. It is also known as the running yield. *See also* **earnings yield**.

flexible trust A unit trust in which investors' money is not invested in a set portfolio, but moved (by the fund manager) from one investment to another to maximize earnings.

flex stock option A US option (introduced by the Chicago Board of Trade) that has a choice of expiry date, strike price and terms.

flight capital Capital that is removed from a country that seems to be politically (or economically) unstable, and taken to a more stable environment.

flip The practice of buying and then selling shares (usually in the manner of a *stag*) at high speed in order to make a fast profit.

flip-flop A colloquial term for a perpetual *floating-rate note*.

float 1. Cash or funds used either to give change to customers or to pay for expenses. 2. To sell shares in order to raise share capital and obtain a listing on the stock exchange. 3. To start a new company.

floater 1. A security owned by the bearer, the person who holds it. More formally it is termed a bearer security. 2. A debt instrument used to secure overnight money from a financial institution such as a bank.

floating assets An alternative term for *circulating assets* or current assets.

floating debt A debt that is continually renewed for a succession of short terms.

floating exchange rate Also known as a free exchange rate, an exchange rate that is not in any way manipulated by a central bank, but which moves according to supply and demand.

floating rate A charge or rate of interest for a loan (such as a mortgage) that may change during the period of the loan.

floating-rate note A security issued by a borrower on the *Eurobonds* market that has a variable rate of interest.

floor The trading area of an exchange.

floor broker A member of a commodity market who is authorized to deal on the trading floor. In the USA, a floor broker is a member an exchange who deals in securities, on behalf of clients, on the trading floor. *See also* ***floor trader***.

floor limit The maximum amount of cash that can be withdrawn using a plastic card.

floor trader Somebody who is authorized to trade on the floor of a stock or commodities exchange. *See also* ***floor broker***.

flotation The act of selling shares in a (new) company to raise capital and be listed on the stock exchange.

flotation cost The cost of issuing new shares or bonds, consisting mainly of the earnings of the underwriters and the costs to the issuer.

fluctuation A movement of prices up or down on a market. Downward fluctuation is also known as slippage.

fluctuation limit Upper and lower limits on prices imposed by a commodity exchange. Trading ceases for the day in any commodity that reaches its limit.

FNMA Abbreviation of *Federal National Mortgage Association*.

FOMC Abbreviation of *Federal Open Market Committee*.

FOOTSIE Familiar term for the *Financial Times Stock Exchange 100 Index*.

forced sale A compulsory sale occasioned by a court order or to provide funds to avoid bankruptcy or liquidation.

foreclosure If a property has been mortgaged (i.e. it stands as a security against a loan), the lender may take possession of the property if the borrower fails to pay off the loan. Such an act of possession is known as foreclosure and requires a foreclosure order issued by the court.

foreign bond A bond that is held in one country but denominated in the currency of and issued in another country; in the UK a bulldog bond, in the USA a yankee bond.

foreign crowd Popular term for the members of the New York Stock Exchange who trade in foreign bonds.

foreign direct investment (FDI) Investment in assets overseas or in the overseas operations of a company.

foreign draft A bill of exchange that is payable abroad, or a banker's draft drawn on a foreign branch, usually in the foreign currency.

foreign exchange (**FOREX** or **FX**) The currency of a foreign country, and the buying and selling of such currencies.

foreign-exchange broker A broker who deals in foreign currencies on the foreign exchange market, usually on behalf of commercial banks.

foreign exchange market A market where foreign currencies are traded by foreign-exchange brokers (intermediaries) and foreign-exchange dealers (bank employees). Options and futures on forward exchange rates are also traded.

foreign exchange risk The risk of buying or selling foreign currency (because the exchange rate could change unfavourably between buying and selling).

FOREX Abbreviation of *foreign exchange*.

forfaiting A specialist banking service by which the bank buys foreign debts at a discount without recourse, this removing the risk to the seller of non-payment.

forint The standard currency unit of Hungary, divided into 100 filler.

for the account On the London Stock Exchange, a deal that is to be paid for or settled on the next *account day*.

forward contract The sale or purchase of a financial instrument at the current (spot) price for settlement and delivery at an agreed future date.

forward dating The practice of dating documents in advance, for example an invoice or cheque may be dated some time in the future. It is also known as postdating.

forward discount In a foreign exchange market, the difference between the forward rate and (slightly higher) spot rate.

forward exchange contract An agreement to buy foreign currency at some future date at an agreed rate of exchange.

forward-forward A contract for the purchase at a future date of a financial instrument that matures at a further future date.

forward price 1. The price quoted in a futures deal. 2. A price quoted for goods that are not immediately available or not yet manufactured. It is usually lower than the eventual retail price because it takes into account only the estimated costs of manufacture at some future date.

forward purchase The buying of commodities or securities in advance of delivery.

104 forward-rate agreement

forward-rate agreement 1. A deal in which a currency is bought and sold at a future date at a specified exchange rate. 2. A contract that specifies the rate of interest for a possible future deposit or loan.

founder's shares An alternative term for *deferred ordinary shares*.

franc The standard currency unit of Belgium, Benin, Burkina-Faso, Burundi, Cameroon, Central African Republic, Chad, Comoros, Congo, Cote d'Ivoire, Djibouti, Equatorial Guinea, France and its dependencies, Gabon, Guinea, Liechtenstein, Luxembourg, Madagascar, Mali, Monaco, Niger, Senegal, Switzerland, Togo and Rwanda. In all cases it is divided into 100 centimes. The countries of the French African Community (CFA) all use the CFA franc, which is pegged to the French franc; territories and ex-territories in the Pacific area use the CFP franc. Others are distinguished by their country, such as Belgian franc and Swiss franc.

France currency French franc (FRF), divided into 100 centimes. The 1999 legacy conversion rate was 6.55957 to the euro. It will fully change to the euro/cent from 2002.

franchise A licence bought by a retailer or supplier of services (the franchisee) that entitles him or her to sell the products of a particular manufacturer (the franchisor) under a particular trading name. The system allows the manufacturer to have direct control over who sells the goods or services, and often gives the seller exclusive rights to sell them in his or her area.

franked income Income on which tax has already been paid.

Frankfurt Stock Exchange Germany's oldest, largest and leading stock exchange, founded in 1820. Prices are fixed on an auction basis, with (since 1970) a compterized settlement system. The exchange is operated by Eurex Deutschland GmbH (formerly Deutsche Borse AG).

fraud The illegal practice of obtaining money from people under false pretences, for example fraud is committed if facts pertaining to a contract are purposefully misrepresented. Fraudulently diverting one's company's or employer's money for one's own use is embezzlement.

Freddie Mac The nickname of the *Federal Home Loan Mortgage Corporation*.

free exchange rate An alternative term for *floating exchange rate*.

freehold Describing property or land that is owned outright by its possessor (who may, nevertheless, lease or rent it to a third party). In legal terms it describes an estate "in fee simple absolute in possession".

free issue An alternative term for *scrip issue*.

free market 1. Describing a widely traded security that is plentiful. 2. A market on which the only constraint is the law of supply and demand.

free-standing additional voluntary contribution (FSAVC) An additional sum paid to an independently administered "top up" pension plan with an insurance company.

free stocks On a commodity market, stocks (inventories) that are held by commercial companies as opposed to those that are still held by their producers.

freeze-out A situation in which a company successfully out-performs its competitors, effectively freezing them out of the market.

French Pacific Islands currency CFP (French Pacific Islands) franc (PFF), divided into 100 centimes.

FRF (ISO) code France – currency French franc. The 1999 legacy conversion rate was 6.55957 to the euro. It will fully change to the euro/cent from 2002.

friendly society A society (first coming into existence in 17th-century England, to help to provide working people with some form of financial security) that provides mutual benefits to its members, such as sickness benefit, life assurance and pensions, in return for modest regular subscriptions.

Friendly Society Commission An regulatory organization for friendly societies set up under the Friendly Society Act 1992, due to be absorbed by the Financial Services Authority (FSA).

friendly take-over The purchase of control of a company that is welcomed by the target company's board and shareholders.

fringe benefit An item that is given to an employee as part of his or her payment but apart from wages or salary, for example a company car, health insurance, or goods on discount.

fringes A popular US abbreviation of *fringe benefits*.

front-end loading The initial charges made in an investment plan or insurance policy levied within a short period of commencement, for example one or two years.

front running The illegal private trading by a broker or market-maker

106 frozen assets

who has prior knowledge of a forthcoming large movement in prices.

frozen assets In contrast to liquid assets, frozen assets are those that may not be converted into ready money without incurring loss of some kind, or which may not be converted because somebody has a claim on them or there is an order that they may not be transferred. The latter is also called a frozen fund.

frozen fund See *frozen assets*.

FSA Abbreviation of *Financial Services Authority*.

FSAVC Abbreviation of *free-standing additional voluntary contribution*.

FT Index See *Financial Times 30 Index*.

FTSE See *Financial Times Stock Exchange 100 Index*.

FTSE 100 See *Financial Times Stock Exchange 100 Index*.

FTSE Actuaries All-Share Index An index of shares of 900 companies that between them cover 98% of the market (by value). It is a weighted index, established in 1962.

fully-paid shares Shares whose nominal value has been completely paid for.

fund 1. Money set aside for a specific purpose (for example from which to pay pensions or meet insurance claims), or lent to an institution or government. More specifically, it is the money that the UK government borrows from institutions and the public by issuing various forms of government bonds. 2. To make finance available. See also **unit trust**.

fundamental analysis An analysis of the value of a company's stock, in order to predict movements in its share prices.

fundamentalist An alternative name for a *fundamental market analyst*.

fundamental market analyst In contrast to the way of working of a *technical market analyst*, a fundamental market analyst (or fundamentalist) takes the performance of the company in question as the basis for prediction of share-price movements.

funded debenture interest Interest on a debenture paid in the form of a further debenture rather than in cash.

funded debt Broadly, any short-term debt that has been converted into a long-term debt.

funded pension A type of pension that is paid for by contributions paid in advance. These are invested in a range of financial products (the "fund").

funding The practice of providing money for a specific purpose (*see fund*).

fund manager A person who manages the investment fund of an institution such as an insurance company, pension scheme or trust. He or she makes investment decisions on behalf of investors, and is also sometimes called an investment manager.

fund of funds Also called a managed unit trust, a unit trust organized and managed by an institution to invest in other of its own unit trusts.

funds broker A broker who arranges short-term loans between US banks.

fungible A stock market term describing securities that are in hand, i.e. that have not yet been settled and are therefore interchangeable and substitutable.

futures Contracts that are made for the delivery of, for example, currencies or commodities on a future date. Future markets provide an opportunity for speculation, in that contracts may be bought and sold (with no intention of the traders to take delivery of the goods) before the delivery date arrives, and their prices may rise and fall during that time.

Futures and Options Exchange *See London Futures and Options Exchange*.

Futures Industry Association An organization that represents dealers in the US futures market.

futures market A market that deals in futures and options on bonds, commodities, foreign currencies and shares.

futures option An option to buy or sell a futures contract.

future value The value that a sum of money invested at compound interest will have in the future.

FX Abbreviation of *foreign exchange*.

FY Abbreviation of *fiscal year*.

G

Gabon currency CFA franc (GAF); there is no subdivision.

GAF (ISO) code Gabon – currency CFA franc.

gaijin The name given in Japan to non-Japanese investors (individual or corporate).

gain An alternative term for profit.

gain to redemption The difference between the amount realized by selling stock now and keeping it until maturity.

Gambia currency dalasi, divided into 100 butut.

gambling The act of betting money that a particular uncertain event will happen, involving a high degree of risk. A bookmaker or casino owner euphemistically calls it *speculation*, with the stake as an *investment*. See also **lottery**; **wager**.

gamma 1. The rate of change of an option premium with respect to **delta**. 2. A former stock exchange classification of shares that are rarely quoted on the exchange.

gap A market opportunity (a gap in the market) that nobody else has yet exploited.

gap analysis A method of investigating the difference between a company's expected market potential and the sales actually achieved.

garnishee order A court order made on somebody who owes money to somebody else who has been judged to be a debtor, instructing him or her not to pay the debtor until that debtor has repaid others. If it is issued by the County Court, it is called a garnishee summons.

GATT Abbreviation of *General Agreement on Tariffs and Trade*.

gazetted Describing items published in the *London Gazette* (in Scotland, the *Edinburgh Gazette*), a weekly publication that includes details of company appointments, bankruptcy orders, notices of winding up, changes in company constitutions, and so on. If information is gazetted, it is assumed that everybody in the country has been notified, even if they have never seen or heard of the publication.

gazumping The raising of the asking price for a property after an offer has

gilt auction 109

been agreed verbally or in writing but before the exchange of contracts, in order to take advantage of a better offer or a rising market in property values.

GBP (ISO) code United Kingdom – currency pound sterling.

GDP Abbreviation of *gross domestic product*.

gearing Also called net debt, a company's debt expressed as a fraction of its total assets, that is a measure of its borrowing.

GEMMS Abbreviation of *gilt-edged market-makers*.

General Agreement on Tariffs and Trade (GATT) An international organization, established in 1947 with headquarters in Geneva, Switzerland, and now with more than 100 member countries, whose object is to negotiate on matters of trade policy, notably the reduction of tariffs and other barriers to free trade.

General Index of Retail Prices *See Retail Price Index*.

general lien The right to take possession of assets at will after default.

general partner A partner whose liability for the debts of the partnership is unlimited.

Gensaki The Japanese money market in government securities.

geometric mean An average that is equal to the nth root of the product of a group of n values.

Georgia currency lari.

Germany currency Deutschmark (DEM), divided into 100 Pfennig. The 1999 legacy conversion rate was 1.95583 to the euro. It will fully change to the euro/cent from 2002.

Ghana currency cedi (GHC), divided into 100 pesewa.

GHC (ISO) code Ghana – currency cedi.

Gibraltar currency Gibraltar pound (GIP), divided into 100 pence.

gift tax In the USA, a tax on the value of property given to somebody else. It is paid by the giver. In the UK, gifts made within seven years of the giver's death may qualify for capital transfer (inheritance) tax.

gilt auction A way of selling government stock (gilts) with no set price; bids are accepted from the upper price downwards.

gilt-edged market In general in the UK, the market in *gilt-edged securities*.

gilt-edged market-makers (GEMMS) UK market-makers who trade in government securities on their own account.

gilt-edged security A security that carries little or no risk, in particular government-issued bonds, which are known as gilts for short. In the USA, the term gilt-edged refers to bonds issued by companies with a good reputation for dividend payment and with a good profit record.

gilt repos Introduced by the Bank of England on 1996, a market in (agreed sales and repurchases of) *gilt-edged securities*.

gilts Shortened term for *gilt-edged securities*.

gilt strip Type of gilt-edged stock issued from late 1997 by the Bank of England. It is issued at a discount to compensate for the fact that no interest is paid (until maturity).

Ginnie Mae The nickname of the US *Government National Mortgage Association*.

GIP (ISO) code Gibraltar – currency Gibraltar pound.

glamour sock Shares with a steadily rising price and which are always in demand.

Glass-Steagall Act 1933 A US Act of Congress that separated the activities of commercial and investment bankers.

global bond A fixed-interest security that is issued, mainly by the World Bank, in Asia, Europe and the USA at the same time.

GMP Abbreviation of *guaranteed minimum pension*.

GNMA Abbreviation of *Government National Mortgage Association*.

gnome A remote and detached financial operator, as in the "Gnomes of Zürich", blamed by UK Prime Minister Harold Wilson for the fall in the international value of sterling during the Labour government of 1966-1971.

GNP Abbreviation of *gross national product*.

godfather offer An offer that cannot be refused. In a take-over situation, a godfather offer for the company's shares is made at such a good price that the management of the target company can only accept it.

go-go fund A colloquial term for an investment fund that is being actively traded, producing high capital gains and high market prices.

going concern It is an assumption in company accounting that an organization will continue trading for current plans to be completed. It is also known as the continuity convention.

going naked A situation in which a dealer accepts option money on stock that he or she does not own and therefore cannot deliver in the expectation that it can be bought later at a cheaper price.

going private The removal of a company from stock exchange listing, a process achieved by the company purchasing its own shares. Going private is usually a decision by the principal shareholders that they require more direct control of the company. Its primary purpose is to reduce interference by outside investors and to render the company considerably less vulnerable to take-over bids.

going public To offer shares in a company to financial institutions and the general public, and thereby receive a listing on the stock exchange.

gold See *bullion*.

gold bug An investor who uses gold reserves as a cushion against inflation.

gold card A credit card that offers its holder various additional benefits.

gold coins See *Britannia coins; Krugerrand*.

golden handcuffs A contractual arrangement between a company and its employee whereby the employee has a strong financial incentive (other than the loss of normal salary) to remain with the company, such as a low-interest mortgage or share options that expire if the employee resigns.

golden handshake A gratuitous payment made by a company to an employee who is leaving, or has recently left. Such payment may be made out of goodwill, or to maintain good relations with an ex-employee, or to induce an employee to resign where there are no grounds, or dubious grounds, for statutory dismissal or redundancy.

golden hello A payment other than normal salary paid to an employee on joining a company in order to induce him or her to do so.

golden parachute A term in a contract of employment whereby the employer is bound to pay the employee a substantial sum of money in the event of dismissal or redundancy.

gold fixing An activity that takes place twice a day when the five dealers of gold bullion on the London exchange meet to determine the price of gold (in US dollars).

Goldilocks economy An economy in which there is strong economic growth combined with rising share prices and low inflation.

gold share Also called a golden share, a company share that has special voting rights such that it can outvote all other shares in certain circumstances.

gold standard A historical arrangement whereby the comparative values of national currencies such as the pound sterling or US dollar were determined by a fixed price for gold.

good money Federal funds in the USA that are available immediately.

good-till-cancelled (GTC) Describing an order that remains in force unless it is expressly cancelled. Cancellation is usually dependent upon a satisfactory profit level being reached. It is also known as a resting order or open order.

goodwill The value of a business over and above the book value of its identifiable or physical assets. Or it is the amount paid on acquisition of a business over and above its current market valuation (including any stock). It can refer, for example, to the literal good will of the established customers of a retail business (shop or restaurant) whose benevolent habit (or custom) of using it can be quantified.

gourde The standard currency unit of Haiti.

government bond A fixed-interest security issued by a government agent such as the Treasury. It is also known as a Treasury bond.

government broker A firm formerly nominated by the Bank of England for dealing with new issues of gilt-edged securities, now replaced by a number of market-makers in gilts.

Government National Mortgage Association (GNMA or Ginnie Mae) A US government-owned corporation that guarantees payment on mortgage-backed pass-through securities.

government securities Treasury bills, gilt-edged securities and any other government fixed-interest paper. They are sold as a means of borrowing, often to offset a budget deficit.

government stock Any bond issued by a government, most often central government stock (gilt-edged securities in the UK).

grace period *See cooling-off period; days of grace.*

granny bond A colloquial name for a **National Savings Pensioners Guaranteed Income Bond**.

GRD (ISO) code Greece – currency drachma. The 2001 legacy conversion rate was 340.750 to the euro. It will fully change to the euro/cent from 2002.

Greece currency drachma (GRD), divided into 100 lepta.

Greenland currency Danish krøne (DKK), divided into 100 øre.

greenmail A procedure whereby a person with a sufficient shareholding in a company seeks a sum of money, or the repurchase by the company of his or her shares at an unreasonably high price, in order to induce him or her to refrain from making a take-over bid.

green market A market in a new share issue before subscribers have received their shares.

green pound A notional unit of currency used in the administration of the Common Agricultural Policy of the EU to determine the relative prices (and hence subsidies) of farm produce from the different member countries.

green shoe When a company goes public it may grant its underwriting firm an option on extra numbers of shares. This prevents the underwriter from making a loss if the issue is undersubscribed and the underwriter having to buy shares on the open market to cover a short position.

grey knight In a take-over situation, a third party, acting as a counterbidder, whose intentions towards the target company are not at all clear. Grey knights are normally unwelcome to both the target and the original raider. *See also* **white knight**.

grey market Any semi-legal market, usually for goods that are in short supply; it is one that keeps within the letter if not the spirit of the law. The term is most usually applied to the market dealing in any stock or share whose issue has been announced but which has not yet taken place. Traders therefore speculate on the eventual selling price of the issue when it comes onto the market.

grey pound A colloquial term for the purchasing power of retired and elderly people, who are becoming an increasingly large sector of the population in Western countries.

Groschen A subdivision (1/100) of the Schilling, the legacy currency unit of Austria.

gross dividend The net dividend received by a shareholder plus the value of the tax credit.

gross domestic product (GDP) A measure of the value of goods and services produced within a country, normally in one year. GDP does not take into account the value of goods and services generated overseas. It is sometimes also known as gross value added. *See also* ***gross national product***.

gross earnings Earnings before tax has been deducted.

gross income Income from all sources before tax has been deducted.

gross interest Interest on an investment before tax has been paid.

gross margin Also called gross profit or gross profit margin, the price at which goods are sold minus what they cost, usually expressed as a percentage of the selling price. More formally it is the difference between a company's sales revenue and the cost of the goods sold, ignoring costs of administration, distribution or finance.

gross national product (GNP) A measure of the value of all goods and services produced by a country, including those produced overseas, usually in one year. *See also* ***gross domestic product***.

gross profit An alternative term for *gross margin*.

groszy A subdivision (1/100) of the Polish zloty.

ground rent A payment made, normally annually, by the occupier of a building to the owner of the land on which the building stands (the freeholder). Ground rent is paid only if the building is occupied leasehold.

Group of Five (G-5) Five leading industrial nations (France, Germany, Japan, the UK and the USA), which meet from time to time to discuss common economic problems.

Group of Seven (G-7) Seven leading non-communist nations consisting of the Group of Five countries with the addition of Canada and Italy.

Group of Ten (G-10) Also known colloquially as the Paris Club, the ten countries Belgium, Canada, France, Germany, Italy, Japan, the Netherlands, Sweden, the UK and the USA. These countries signed an agreement in 1962 to increase the funds available to the ***International***

guilder

Monetary Fund and to aid those member countries with balance of payments difficulties.

growth fund A long-term investment that concentrates on capital growth (at a higher risk than a slower-growing but safer investment).

growth stocks Stocks or shares that are expected to provide the investor with a larger proportion of capital growth (*i.e.*, growth in the value of the stock or share) to income (in the form of dividends) than other shares.

GTC Abbreviation of *good-till-cancelled.*

guarani The standard currency unit of Paraguay.

guarantee 1. A promise to pay the debt of somebody else in the event that the debtor defaults (compare with *indemnity*). A document stating that goods or services are of good (merchandizable) quality.

guaranteed equity bond A performance-related lump-sum investment that guarantees the capital and a minimum return, as well as retaining potential for income from the stock market.

guaranteed income bond A life-assurance company bond that guarantees a fixed income and the return of the capital at the end of a fixed term or on the death of the purchaser.

guaranteed minimum pension (GMP) The minimum pension that an occupational pension or personal pension taken out before April 1997 must guarantee a person who has opted out of the State Earnings-Related Pension Scheme (SERPS). After April 1997 new schemes were subjected to a different test of quality.

guaranteed-period annuity A type of annuity that runs for a stated number of years from the initial date even if the annuitant dies in the meantime.

guarantor A person who guarantees, if necessary, to pay somebody else's debt.

guaranty bond A type of surety that protects against loss resulting from the failure of somebody (specified) to do something (also specified).

guilder The standard legacy currency unit of the Netherlands and the Netherlands Antilles, divided into 100 cents.

H

haircut Usually a discount on the market value of a bond. It may also be any discount or deduction from the normal value, or the cutting of the budget for a particular project or operation without harming the project itself.

Haiti currency gourde.

halala A subdivision (1/100) of the Saudi Arabian riyal.

haleru A subdivision (1/100) of the Czech koruna.

hammering A London Stock Exchange term for the announcement of the inability of a member to pay his or her debts. (It was formerly prefaced by three blows of a hammer.)

hammering the market Very active selling of shares by people who think they are overpriced (and due to fall in price).

Hang Seng index An index of share prices quoted since 1964 on the Hong Kong Stock Exchange.

hara-kiri swap A swap that carries no spread but merely increases the market share of the person who initiates it.

hard currency A currency, widely used in international trade, from a country with a stable and prosperous economy. It is thus in high demand and preferred to less stable or legally restricted currencies. Its exchange rate will tend to rise.

hard dollars Dollars traded on the foreign exchange markets, for which demand is persistently high because of a US trade surplus. The value of hard dollars tends to rise.

head and shoulders A pattern that may emerge in a graph of share prices plotted against time, with a maximum between two slightly lower high points. Some analysts believe that it predicts a significant downturn in prices.

heavy shares Shares that command a relatively high price on the stock market.

hedge fund An investment fund that seeks high returns, usually by taking high risks (such as investing in new financial instruments).

hedging A method of protecting against price fluctuations, commonly on the commodities futures market. The term is also used to describe the practice of protecting against fluctuations in exchange rates (by buying forward) to minimize risks and possible losses.

heritable bond Security for a loan in Scotland consisting of a conveyance of land made out to the lender.

Herstatt risk The risk of loss in a currency transaction in which one side of the deal is completed but exchange rates change unfavourably before the other side of the deal can be completed. It is named after a German bank that was caught in this way.

hidden reserve Also called secret reserve, a reserve that is not declared on a company's balance sheet.

high-beta Describing shares that are volatile.

high coupon Describing a bond with a high rate of interest.

high flyer A highly priced speculative share whose price increases sharply in a short time.

high-technology stock Share in a company that is involved in hi-tech activities.

high-yield bond A bond, especially common in the USA, issued by a company with a low credit rating. It is often used to raise funds for a leveraged buyout, secured against the assets of the target company. It is also called a junk bond.

hire purchase (HP) A form of credit, normally extended on consumer goods, whereby the customer takes and uses the goods and pays for them in instalments (with interest) over a period of time. The seller can in theory repossess the goods at any time if the hirer defaults (unlike with a *credit sale*).

historical cost The cost of an asset at the time it was acquired, rather than the current cost of its replacement. It is also called acquisition cost or original cost; some US accountants prefer the term sunk cost.

historical dividend The total dividend paid on a company's shares in the last financial year.

hit bid A bargain in which a dealer sells immediately at a price a buyer is willing to pay, instead of waiting for a possibly better price.

HKD (ISO) code Hong Kong – currency Hong Kong dollar.

holder for value A person who holds a bill of exchange for which a value has at one time been given.

holder in due course A person who has taken up a bill for value before payment is due, and who has no good reason to suspect the title of the previous holder.

holding An investment in a company or in any security.

holding company A company that exists to hold shares in other companies, which are (depending on the level of shareholding) its subsidiaries. An immediate holding company is one that holds a controlling interest in another company, but in turn, the immediate holding company may itself be owned by a holding company.

hold over To defer settlement of a deal on the London Stock Exchange until the next settlement day.

home income plan An alternative term for *equity-release scheme*.

Hong Kong currency Hong Kong dollar (HKD), divided into 100 cents.

Hong Kong stock exchanges See *Stock Exchange of Hong Kong*.

horizontal diversification The diversification into industries or businesses at the same stage of production as the diversifying company. For example, a suit manufacturer might diversify into leisurewear, or a yacht builder into the construction of motor boats. See also ***vertical diversification***.

horizontal spread A combination of a long-call/put option and a short-call/put option with different expiry dates.

hostile take-over bid An attempt to purchase control of a company that is unwelcome to some of the target company's shareholders and directors.

hot issue An issue of shares that are expected to sell extremely rapidly.

hot money An informal term for money obtained illegally (*e.g.*, by fraud or theft). In finance, however, the term is more often used for money that is moved rapidly and at short notice from one country to another to take advantage of changes in short-term interest rates or to avoid imminent devaluation of a currency.

house A business or company. It is also a popular nickname for the London Stock Exchange.

house bill A bill that a company draws upon itself.

HP Abbreviation of *hire purchase*.

hurdle rate In capital budgeting, the rate of interest that a proposal must exceed before it is given consideration; *i.e.*, the required rate of return. It is usually related to the cost of capital, taking into account any risk factors.

hryvnia (plural hryvni) The standard currency unit of the Ukraine.

HUF (ISO) code Hungary – currency forint.

human capital The value of a company's employees.

Hungary currency forint (HUF), divided into 100 filler.

HVF (ISO) code Burkino Faso (formerly Upper Volta) – currency CFA franc.

hyperinflation Inflation (a general increase in price levels) that is running extremely high, also known as galloping inflation.

hypothecation A firm of shippers may borrow money from a bank using cargo it is currently shipping as security. In this case, the bank takes out a lien on the cargo and this is conveyed in a letter of hypothecation. In the USA, hypothecation is putting up securities as collateral on a margin account.

I

IBOR Abbreviation of *inter-bank offered rate*.

IDB Abbreviation of *inter-dealer broker*.

IFA Abbreviation of *independent financial adviser*.

IFMA Abbreviation of *Institutional Fund Managers Association*.

Iceland currency Icelandic krona (ISK), divided into 100 aurar.

idle money Funds that are available but not used to purchase an interest-earning investment.

IDR (ISO) code Indonesia – currency rupiah.

IEP (ISO) code Ireland – currency Irish punt. The 1999 legacy conversion rate was 0.787564 to the euro. It will fully change to the euro/cent from 2002.

illiquidity A situation in which an asset is not easily converted into cash, or in which a person is not able to raise cash quickly and/or easily.

ILS (ISO) code Israel – currency shekel.

IMF Abbreviation of *International Monetary Fund*.

immediate annuity An annuity that begins immediately when purchased.

import duty A government tax levied on imports.

imprest bill An alternative term for a *bill of imprest*.

imputation system A UK tax system, established in 1973, which partly governs the payment of corporation tax. Under this system, a shareholder's dividends are taxed at source, and he or she is issued with a credit for the tax imputed.

inactive stock Shares or other securities in which there is little or no trading.

incentive shares Shares that are issued to a company's employs at less than market price.

incestuous share dealing The dealing in the shares of associated companies in order to win tax concessions. It is often illegal, although not necessarily so.

income-tax schedules 121

inchoate instrument A bill of exchange, cheque or promissory note that is incomplete in some way. Completion of the details may be authorized by the drawer of the financial instrument (for example, the name of the drawee on a bill of exchange may be filled in by a third party).

income Money, goods or services received from an activity. Income may be a return on one of the factors of production – a salary, rent, interest or profit – or it may be a transfer payment made for other reasons, such as (in the UK) unemployment benefit. The definition also includes non-monetary income, such as the benefit a company or individual derives from the possession of assets. For a company it is therefore the amount by which revenue and gains exceed expenses and liabilities (debts).

income bond A type of bond that provides an income rather than capital growth.

income debenture A debenture whose interest can be paid only out of company profits.

income drawdown A method by which income can be drawn from a pension while it remains invested (until the pensioner is 75 years old).

income multiplier A factor that, when applied to a loan applicant's income, determines the maximum amount that a financial institution is prepared to lend.

income shares Shares in a split-level investment trust whose holders receive the income from the assets of the trust. *See also* **capital shares**.

income statement An alternative term for *profit-and-loss account*.

income tax A direct annual tax levied on income, such as on fees, salaries and wages (earned income) and dividends, interest and rents (unearned income). The amount of tax payable varies, depending on the amount of income and its type, as defined by the *income-tax schedules*. In accounting terms it is regarded as an expense or, if not yet paid, a liability.

income-tax month In the UK, a month running from the 6th of one month to the 5th of the next.

income-tax schedules The Inland Revenue's classification of types of income for UK income tax purposes. Schedule A applies to land and property; B to woodlands used as a business enterprise; C dividends and interest from government and public sources; D self-employment (business, trades, professions) and gross interest payments; E wages and salaries from employment (see *pay-as-you-earn*); F distributions by companies.

income-tax year In the UK, the same as *fiscal year*.

inconvertible Describing money that cannot be exchanged for gold of equal value. UK currency has been inconvertible since the country came off the gold standard in 1931.

incorporation The process of setting up a business as a legal entity.

indemnity An undertaking that gives protection against loss or damage. It may be in the form of replacement or repair of property lost or damaged, or the provision of cash to the value of the property.

indenture A deed or instrument to which there is more than one party. It is so called because such deeds were often cut or torn (indented) into portions, one for each party, to prevent forgery and to provide proof of each person's involvement in the transaction. Indentures were formerly widely used to bind an apprentice to his master for the period of his apprenticeship.

independent company A company that operates entirely under its own authority, and is not owned or controlled (in part or in whole) by any other company.

independent financial advisor (IFA) A financial adviser who can give investment advice about the products of any company (*i.e.*, he or she is not tied to only one company as its employee or agent). He or she must offer best advice based on all the products available.

index arbitrage The process of selling stocks at the same time as buying stock-index futures, or vice versa. It is a form of program trading.

indexation A form of *index-linking* that ties income to the retail price index and therefore prevents a fall in real wages during a period of inflation.

indexed portfolio A portfolio (of investments) linked to a stock index, such as the Financial Times Stock Exchange 100 Index (FOOTSIE).

index fund An investment fund that is linked directly to a share index, in that it has investments in shares in that index.

index futures Futures contracts that are based on figures provided by indexes.

indexing See *index number*.

individual savings account (ISA) 123

index-linked annuity A type of *escalating annuity* that is coupled to the rate of inflation.

indexed-linked gilts Gilt-edged securities that have a variable rate of interest adjusted to take account of inflation (using index-linking to the retail price index).

index-linking Also termed indexation, a system of linking costs, prices or wages to the price fluctuations of an economy in order to allow for inflation and to maintain value in real terms. *See also* **index number**.

index number A weighted average that permits the comparison of prices or production over a number of years. The components elected for comparison are weighted according to their importance and then averaged. Figures are compared to those for a base year, selected for its typicality and given the index number 100 or 1000.

India currency Indian rupee (INR), divided into 100 paise. Also 1 lakh = 100,000 rupees and 1 crore = 10 million rupees.

indication-only price A price quoted by a market-maker that indicates what he or she thinks a security is worth although he or she is not prepared to deal in it.

indirect exchange A currency exchange between two countries accomplished via a third country.

indirect investment Also termed portfolio investment, an investment in stocks, shares or other financial security.

indirect taxation A system whereby tax is paid to one person or organization (often to a retailer by a customer), who then pays it to the government. In the UK stamp duty and value added tax are forms of indirect taxation.

individual retirement account (IRA) A US pension scheme that allows people to invest part of their annual income as a tax-free contribution to an interest-earning fund, which must be withdrawn by the pensioner's 70th birthday. Members of company pension schemes are not eligible.

individual savings account (ISA) A tax-free method of saving introduced by the UK government in 1999, when personal equity plans (PEPs) and tax-exempt special savings accounts (TESSAs) lost their tax-free status. A maximum limit of £50,000 applies to an ISA, with limits also on the amount that may be invested each year.

124 Indonesia currency

Indonesia currency rupiah (IDR), divided into 100 sen.

industrials Everyday term for shares in an industrial company, usually manufacturing.

ineligible bill A bill of exchange that cannot be discounted by the Bank of England because it does not bear the signature of an eligible bank (as either acceptor or drawer).

infant industry A newly-established national industry in the early stages of growth.

inflation A persistent general increase in the level of prices. Strictly defined, it includes neither one-off increases in price (occasioned by, for example, a sudden scarcity of one product) nor any other increases caused by real factors. Its causes include an excess of demand over supply and increases in the money supply, perhaps brought about by increased government expenditure, which causes a decline in the real value of money.

inheritance Possessions or titles that pass to one or more people on the death of another.

inheritance tax A tax paid on inheritances by heirs, often calculated in relation to the closeness of the relationship between the heir and the deceased person. In the UK it replaced capital transfer tax in 1986. At the present time, *capital gains tax* covers income from inheritances.

initial charge The charge paid to the fund manager by an investor when he or she first purchases units in a unit trust.

initial margin A deposit that must be paid on selling or buying a contract on a futures market. See also *equity*.

initial public offering (IPO) The US term for the first share offer made by a company going public; a flotation.

initial public offering window (IPO window) The period of time between an announcement of an *initial public offering* and the start of dealing in the shares offered on a stock market. Grey market trading may take place in the IPO window (*see* **grey market**).

injunction A restraining order issued by a court. It instructs a named person to perform a certain duty or forbids him or her to commit a specific act. Failure to comply with an injunction is considered contempt of court.

inland bill A bill of exchange that is both drawn and payable in the UK.

Institutional Fund Managers Association (IFMA)

Any other bill is described as a foreign bill.

Inland Revenue A UK government department whose major responsibility is the collection of various taxes, such as income tax, capital gains tax and corporation tax.

INR (ISO) code India – currency Indian rupee.

inscribed stock A now discontinued way of registering the name of a stockholder, by which the holder was issued with a slip indicating that the holder's name had been registered. This slip did not have the status of a certificate. It was also known as registered stock.

insider A person with special knowledge derived from holding a privileged position within a group or company. It is illegal for the person to use that information in dealing on the stock exchange.

insider dealing Also called insider trading, illegal profitable transactions made on the basis of privileged information available as a result of working inside an organization. Most insider dealing concerns trading in stocks and shares whose value is likely to be affected by the release of news that only a few people are aware of.

insider trading An alternative term for *insider dealing*.

insolvency A state in which total liabilities (excluding equity capital) exceed total assets; it is therefore the inability to pay debts when called to do so. If insolvency is chronic, bankruptcy or liquidation generally follow.

instalment credit See *instalment plan*.

instalment (US **installment**) **plan** A method of purchasing goods or services by paying regular instalments, which may or may not include an element of interest. In the USA installment plan, or installment credit, is the usual term for **hire purchase**.

instant access account A type of building society account from which instant withdrawals may be made (on demand, using a passbook, by cheque or by means of a plastic card).

institutional broker A broker who deals in securities on behalf of financial institutions such as banks, insurance companies, investment trusts, pension funds and unit trusts.

Institutional Fund Managers Association (IFMA) A UK organization established in 1989 to represent institutional fund managers.

institutional investor A corporate rather than individual investor; a company that invests funds on behalf of clients, generally intending to reap profits only in the long term. Institutional investors include banks, insurance companies, investment trusts, pension funds and unit trusts. In the UK, institutional investors hold from 50% to 70% of all negotiable securities.

instrument Broadly, any legally binding document (such as a *financial instrument* or a will).

insurable interest A financial interest, recognizable at law, that the insured has – indeed must have – in the subject matter of an insurance. On some cases, an unlimited insurable interest exists, for example in one's own life or the life of a spouse. In most cases, however, insurable interest is limited to the value of the property or goods insured, or to the extent of liability.

insurance A contract under which the insurer agrees to pay compensation to the insured in the event of a specified occurrence, such as the loss of or damage to property. In return, the insured pays the insurer a premium, usually at fixed intervals, which the insurer invests to finance the business and to make a profit. The premium varies according to the insurer's estimate of the probability that the event insured against will actually occur (a calculation carried out by an actuary). Insurance of a person's life is called assurance. See *life assurance*.

insurance agent A person who sells policies on behalf of an insurance company.

insurance bond A type of bond issued by a life assurance company.

insurance broker A person who arranges and sells insurance. He or she is paid a commission by the insurer to act as an intermediary with the client, arranging policies and processing claims issued by an insurance company.

insurance policy A legally binding document issued by an insurance company that defines the terms of an insurance contract. It details the cover provided (and any conditions or restrictions) and the premium to be paid.

insurance premium A sum paid to an insurance company by a client for cover as defined in an *insurance policy*. It may be paid as a lump sum or in instalments, as one payment or annually, depending on the nature of the policy

insurance tied agent An *insurance agent* who acts for only one insurance company for pensions or life assurance, or for up to six companies for general insurance.

insured A person or company that holds an *insurance policy*; a policyholder.

insurer An insurance company or other person or company that agrees to indemnify somebody against particular risks, usually as defined in an *insurance policy* and for an *insurance premium*. *See also* ***underwriter***.

intangible asset A non-monetary asset that is neither physical nor current. The many examples include brand names, copyright, franchises, goodwill, leases, licences, mailing lists, patents and trademarks. It is sometimes known as an invisible asset.

inter-bank clearing interest rate The interest rate that UK commercial banks charge for short-term loans to each other.

inter-bank market rate *See* ***London Inter-Bank Bid Rate; London Inter-Bank Mean Rate; London Inter-Bank Offered Rate***.

inter-bank sterling market A fairly informal market in which banks lend funds to each other.

inter-company loans market A market in which large companies lend money to each other, established in 1969 to overcome the Bank of England's severe restrictions on bank lending.

inter-dealer broker (IDB) A person who matches deals, usually in gilts, between anonymous buyers and sellers on behalf of two market-makers.

interest A charge made by a lender to a borrower in exchange for the service of lending funds. It is usually expressed as a percentage of the sum borrowed for a specific period (normally a year), termed the interest rate, but it may be paid in kind. Interest is also payment made by a bank or building society to customers who deposit money with them. *See* ***compound interest; simple interest***.

interest cover An *accounting ratio* that is a measure of the interest paid for a company's borrowing in terms of its operating profit. It is equal to the net profit (before interest and tax) divided by the interest charge.

interest holiday A period during which a lender (usually a bank) postpones the requirement to pay interest on a loan (usually made to a start-up business or one in financial difficulties).

interest-only loan A type of loan for which regular interest payments are made until the loan matures, when the whole of the principal also falls due.

interest-only mortgage A mortgage in which the borrower (mortgagee) pays back only interest during the mortgage period because he or she has an investment (such as an endowment) or other asset to repay the capital at the end of the mortgage period.

interest rate Interest charged to a borrower or paid to an investor, usually expressed as a percentage per annum (see *interest*).

interest-rate futures Financial futures purchased as a hedge against an adverse change in interest rates. If interest changes on the hedger's financial instruments produce a loss, the futures contract offsets it.

interest-rate guarantee A protection against future changes in interest rates provided for an investor, for a fee, by a financial institution such as a bank.

interest-rate margin Also called spread, the difference rate of interest (usually the London Inter-Bank Offered Rate, LIBOR) and the rate paid on a debt security, as used for floating rate notes on the Euromarket.

interest-rate risk The risk that the values of investments will suffer because of changes in interest rates.

interest-rate spread The difference between the short-term interest rates in two money markets at any one time.

interest-rate swap The exchange of two interest rate payments in a transaction, in which a borrower of lower creditworthiness benefits from the higher interest rate available to a borrower of higher creditworthiness (who makes a profit on the deal).

interest warrant A cheque issued by the government (through the Bank of England), paying the interest due on a loan.

interim dividend Any dividend other than the *final dividend* declared by a company at the conclusion of each trading year. Interim dividends may be made as a reward for a particularly good economic performance or simple as an effective advance on the final dividend, which will be correspondingly reduced in value. Many UK companies quoted on the stock market make interim dividend payments per annum; it is unusual for a firm to exceed this frequency of interim payments.

interim payment A part-payment made on account.

interim report A short statement published at the end of the first half of a public company's financial year, detailing results fort he previous six months and declaring any *interim dividend*.

International Standards Organization (ISO)

intermediary A person who acts between and deals with two parties who themselves make no direct contact with each other, such as an *insurance broker*. See also *financial intermediary*.

intermediate offer A new share issue that is placed with a financial intermediary, to whom investors may apply through a stockbroker.

internal audit An audit of a company's books that takes place virtually continuously and is undertaken by internal staff, rather than by an external auditor. It is carried out in order to monitor company profitability and to guard against fraud.

internal financing The cash generated within a company's own accounts (such as retained profits) or from its own resources (such as assets or working capital).

internal rate of return (IRR) A discount rate at which, applied to the expected pattern of cash expenditure and income of a capital project, would give a net present value of zero. It may be compared with the return on alternative investments, or on some target rate of return.

Internal Revenue Service (IRS) The US equivalent of the UK's *Inland Revenue*.

International Bank for Reconstruction and Development (IBRD) Part of the World Bank, established in 1945 with headquarters in Washington D.C., to help economic reconstruction in countries after World War II. It makes loans to developing nations or guarantees loans from other sources. The bank's capital comes from the members nations of the International Monetary Fund (IMF).

International Monetary Fund (IMF) An international organization established in 1944 after the Bretton Woods conference, to organize and administer the international monetary system. It was designed to help countries in financial difficulties, especially with their balance of payments. It makes loans and provides financial advisers.

international money order A document that allows the transfer of small sums between countries. An order (denominated in US dollars or pounds sterling) may be bought, and encashed, at a bank. See also *money order*.

International Standards Organization (ISO) An organization that establishes international standards, particularly agreed standard sizes and weights, etc. It includes the three-letter coding (ISO code) for international currencies as included in this dictionary.

intestacy A situation in which a person dies without making a valid will, leaving the estate without a designated heir. If a person dies intestate, the Crown divides the estate between the surviving relatives, making provision first for the spouse, and then for any children. If neither spouse nor children are living, other relatives are entitled to share in the estate. If no relatives can be traced, the estate goes to the Crown.

inter vivos policy A life assurance policy that can be used to cover the potential inheritance tax liability of a *potentially exempt transfer*. It is written as a special type of decreasing-term assurance for the amount of the initial potential inheritance tax liability.

in-the-money option An option to buy shares (a call option) for which the price on the open market has risen above the price fixed (the option's exercise price). Or it is an option to sell (a put option) for which the market price has fallen in relation to the exercise price. An in-the-money option is said to carry *intrinsic value*.

intrinsic value 1. The value of the materials from which an object is made, rather than its market or face value. For example, a coin may be said to be worth so much and is exchanged on the basis of that stated value, but the metal used in minting it (its intrinsic value) may be worth much less. 2. The value (if any) of a traded option that is in-the-money, brought about by a favourable difference between market price and exercise price.

inverse yield curve Describing a plot of interest rate against maturity that slopes downwards left to right (*i.e.*, the longer the maturity, the lower the rate). It happens during times of high inflation that is expected soon to fall rapidly. *See also* **yield curve**.

investment The purchase of something that is expected to increase in value, generally with a view to selling it for a profit at a later date. Although the "something" could be goods or property (real assets), the term most commonly applies to financial instruments such as bonds, commodities, futures, options, shares, stocks, unit trusts and warrants. Interest-bearing accounts in banks and building societies, savings banks, annuities, endowments, pension plans and life assurance policies are also types of investments. All of these and their associated topics are included in the dictionary. To an economist, however, investment covers spending that results in economic growth (such as money spent on the purchase of machinery or the building of plant that will produce goods and services for sale). In this sense, it extends to funds applied to the improvement of the infrastructure, and the term may also be applied to expenditure on human resources.

investment adviser A person who advises individuals or institutions on financial matters related to investment in its widest sense. The function is performed by everybody from a turf accountant to a chartered accountant.

investment analyst A person who studies financial securities and company results with a view to advising about buying and selling shares.

investment bank A US bank that acts mainly as a financial intermediary between investors and companies that want to issue shares. It also carries out many of the functions performed by a UK *merchant bank* or issuing house.

investment bond A type of life assurance policy for which the policyholder pays a single premium which is invested in an asset-backed fund. It pays on-going interest and the investment (along with any growth) is returned at the end of the term.

investment club A voluntary group of private investors who pool their resources and manage their own fund (thus saving the cost of a professional fund manager).

investment company A company that employs its funds to buy securities or shares, as opposed to conducting business on its own account. It is run by a board of directors and so is not the same as an *investment trust*.

investment home loan Also called a buy-to-let mortgage, a type of loan in which the borrowed funds are used to purchase a property that is rented out to provide a source of income (as well as repaying the loan, plus its interest).

investment incentive Any method of encouraging people to invest by lowering the cost or raising the reward, often accomplished via the tax system.

investment income 1. A company's income from outside investments (as opposed to revenue from normal business activities). 2. A person's income from investments.

investment income surcharge Extra income tax that has to be paid on investment income or other *unearned income*.

investment instrument Any medium of investment, including stocks, shares and securities of all kinds, unit trusts and funds, grouped investment media, and so on.

132 Investment Management Regulatory Organization

Investment Management Regulatory Organization (IMRO) A self-regulating UK organization set up under the Financial Services Act 1986 to regulate the activities of people or firms that give investment advice. It reports to the *Securities and Investment Board*, itself due to be absorbed by the Financial Services Authority (FSA).

investment manager An alternative term for a *fund manager*.

investment portfolio A collection of bonds, stocks, shares and other securities held by an individual or an institution that invests on behalf of other people.

investment property A property owned by an investment company, such as an investment trust.

Investment Services Directive (ISD) A directive of the EU, issued in 1966, that deals with cross-border transactions by investment banks and dealers in securities.

investment trust An investment scheme, similar to a *unit trust*, in which a small investor is able to invest in a range of securities through the agency of the scheme's fund managers. *See also* **split-level trust**.

Investors' Compensation Scheme A scheme established in 1988 by the UK Securities and Investments Board to help people who lose money because of default by an investment company authorized under the Financial Services Act. It pays the full loss up to £30,000 and 90% of any further loss up to a total of £50,000 (i.e. a maximum of £48,000 may be paid out).

invisible exports Services (rather than goods) provided to foreign people, organizations and countries. They include banking, shipping and insurance services.

invoice A document that summarizes a business transaction and often doubles as a request for payment. An invoice lists and describes the goods (or services) ordered and details their price, and usually records the dates and times of dispatch and delivery.

invoice discounting The practice of offering a discount on unpaid invoices sold to a *factoring* company, which then tries to claim the money owed on its own account. The size of the discounting reflects the likely difficulty of securing payment.

inward investment An alternative term for foreign investment.

IPO Abbreviation of *initial public offering*.

issuance 133

IQD (ISO) code Iraq – currency Iraqi dinar.

IRA Abbreviation of *individual retirement account*.

Iran currency Iranian rial (IRR), divided into 100 dinars. Also 1 toman = 10 rials.

Iraq currency Iraqi dinar (IQD), divided into 1000 fils.

Ireland currency Irish punt (IEP), divided into 100 pence. The 1999 legacy conversion rate was 0.787564 to the euro. It will fully change to the euro/cent from 2002.

IRR (ISO) code Iran – currency Iranian rial.

IRR Abbreviation of *internal rate of return*.

irredeemable financial security Also termed an undated security, a Consol, preference share or other security that is issued for an indefinite period (and is never repaid).

irrevocable Describing something (for example an order or letter of credit) that is unalterable and cannot be revoked.

irrevocable and confirmed credit Credit facilities that are confirmed by a bank in London on an account held by a non-UK resident.

irrevocable documentary acceptance credit Credit facilities arranged by an overseas customer with a bank in London, who is then presented with a letter of credit to facilitate foreign trade.

irrevocable letter of credit A letter of credit that an issuing bank is obliged to pay to an exporter, when all conditions and terms (which cannot be changed except by agreement of all parties) have been met.

IRS Abbreviation of *Internal Revenue Service*.

ISE/Nikkei 50 Index A share index based on the prices of shares in 50 Japanese companies that are traded on the Tokyo Stock Exchange and on the International Stock Exchange (ISE) in London.

ISK (ISO) code Iceland – currency Icelandic krona.

ISO Abbreviation of *International Standards Organization*.

Israel currency shekel (ILS), divided into 100 agorot.

issuance The procedure of issuing securities, carried out by a company or an issuing house.

issue A quantity of a particular stock or share offered to the public.

issue by tender Stocks and shares may be issued by the process of inviting tenders above a certain stated minimum price and then selling to the highest bidder.

issue date The date from which accrued interest is calculated (e.g. on a security).

issue price The price, including commission, of any issue of securities (i.e. the price at which it is offered).

issued share capital The amount of a company's authorized share capital that has actually been taken up (i.e. sold to investors).

issuing bank A financial institution that administers a new issue of shares.

issuing house A connecting link between those who need capital and those willing to lend it. Often, an issuing house also operates as a share issue underwriter or merchant bank.

Italy currency Italian lira (plural lire) (ITL); there is no subdivision. The 1999 legacy conversion rate was 1936.27 to the euro. It will fully change to the euro/cent from 2002.

ITL (ISO) code Italy – currency Italian lira (plural lire).

Ivory coast (formally Côte d'Ivoire) **currency** CFA franc (CIF); there is no subdivision.

J

Jamaica currency Jamaican dollar (JMD), divided into 100 cents.

Japan currency yen (JPY), divided into 100 sen.

jobber Also known as a stockjobber, a member of the London Stock Exchange who deals in securities with stockbrokers and other jobbers, but not directly with the public. Formerly, the activities of jobbers and stockbrokers were kept separate on the London exchange. Now jobbers have been replaced by market-makers. In the USA, a jobber is any middleman between a wholesaler and a retailer, or a person on a stock exchange who deals in securities that are worthless (e.g. junk bonds). The US synonym for a jobber in the UK sense is dealer.

jobber's turn The profit made in a deal by a jobber.

joint account A bank account in the names of two or more people. The mandate will state who can or has to sign cheques: any one person (the most usual arrangement) or two or all of the account holders.

joint and several The concept by which joint debtors (e.g. two or more partners in a partnership) are responsible for the debt, both jointly and as individuals. Joint and several liability gives the lender the recourse to each of the partners in the debt in the event of default or, of course, to all of them jointly.

joint annuity An alternative term for a *joint-life annuity*.

joint holders If two or more people hold shares jointly, they may have them registered as such but only the first person named receives notices from the company. The holding can, however, be split and registered separately in individual names.

joint-life annuity Also called a joint annuity, a type of annuity that runs until the death of the second person named in the policy.

joint lives policy A life assurance policy involving two people that pays when one of them dies.

joint-stock bank More commonly known as a commercial bank, a UK bank that is a limited company (unlike a private bank, which is usually a partnership).

joint-stock company An alternative name for a *limited company*.

136 joint tenancy

joint tenancy A tenancy in the names of two or more people. If one joint tenant dies, the tenancy continues for the survivor(s).

joint venture A situation in which one (reporting) entity has a long-term contractual interest in another which is controlled jointly by the reporting entity and some other venture. The reporting entity details in its accounts its share of assets, cash flows and liabilities of the joint venture.

Jonestown defence Any form of defensive tactics against a hostile take-over bid that is so extreme as to appear suicidal.

judgement A ruling made by a court in particular case (also spelled *judgment*).

junior mortgage A mortgage, such as a *second mortgage*, that is subordinate to another one.

junk bond Also sometimes called a *high-yield bond*, a bond issued by a company with a low credit rating.

K

kaffir Racist stock exchange nickname for shares in South African mining companies.

kamikaze pricing The practice of deliberately putting a low price on a security with the aim of gaining a greater share of the market.

kangaroo A stock exchange nickname for shares in Australian companies, especially those dealing in tobacco, property or mining.

Kazakhstan currency tenge.

Kenya currency Kenyan shilling (KES), divided into 100 cents.

Keogh plan A US scheme for self-employed people or unincorporated businesses to make tax-deductible contributions to a pension fund. Tax is, however, paid on withdrawals.

kerb market The trading in securities that takes place outside an official exchange.

kerb trading The closing of a deal on a financial futures market after hours. It is so called because originally traders would emerge from the exchange after official trading stopped for the day and remain outside (on the kerb) to close any unfinished business.

KES (ISO) code Kenya – currency Kenyan shilling.

Keynesianism A school of economic thought, named after John Maynard Keynes (1883-1946), an economist who was greatly influential in the late 1930s. Keynesians believe that the best way to bring about economic change is by government intervention in the form of market controls and public investment.

khoum A subdivision (1/5) of the Mauritanian ouguiya.

kickback A form of bribery of a customer who is offered a discount price then charged the original (full) price, for accounting purposes, and later reimbursed the difference.

kick-up A chance offered to holders of bonds to convert them into shares at a profit.

KID (ISO) code Kiribati (formerly Gilbert Islands) – currency Australian dollar.

kina The standard currency unit of Papua New Guinea, divided into 100 toea.

kip The standard currency unit of Laos, divided into 100 at.

Kiribati (formerly Gilbert Islands) currency Australian dollar (KID), divided into 100 cents.

kite Another name for an *accommodation bill*. It is also UK slang for a cheque.

kite flying The raising of money by way of an *accommodation bill*.

kiting Fraudulently issuing a cheque that is not backed by funds in the account.

knight A third party who appears at the scene of a take-over battle. *See also* **grey knight; white knight**.

knock-out A financial option that terminates automatically if the underlying asset's price reaches a predefined level.

know your customer rules Regulations, principally to prevent money laundering, established in the late 1990s to ensure that organizations that accept money on deposit know who is the true beneficiary of any newly-opened account.

kobo A subdivision (1/100) of the Nigerian naira.

Korea (North) currency North Korean won (KPW), divided into 100 zeuns.

Korea (South) currency South Korean won (KRW), divided into 100 chon.

koruna The standard currency unit of the Czech Republic and Slovakia, divided into 100 haleru.

KPW (ISO) code Korea (North) – currency North Korean won.

krona The standard currency unit of Iceland, divided into 100 aurar ,and of Sweden, divided into 100 ore.

krøne The standard currency unit of Denmark, the Faroe Islands, Greenland and Norway, divided into 100 øre.

kroon The standard currency unit of Estonia, divided into 100 kopecks.

Krugerrand A South African coin, minted since 1967, that contains 1 ounce (troy) of pure gold. It is popular with investors who need to overcome restrictions on holding gold *bullion*.

KRW (ISO) code Korea (South) – currency South Korean won.

kuna The standard currency unit of Croatia (Hrvatska).

kuru A subdivision (1/100) of the Turkish lira.

Kuwait currency Kuwaiti dinar (KWD), divided into 1000 fils.

kwacha The standard currency unit of Malawi (divided into 100 tambala) and Zambia (divided into 100 ngwee).

kwanza The standard currency unit of Angola, divided into 100 lwei.

KWD (ISO) code Kuwait – currency Kuwaiti dinar.

kyat The standard currency unit of Myanmar (formerly Burma), divided into 100 pyas.

Kyrgystan currency som.

L

laari A subdivision (1/100) of the Maldives rufiya.

ladder option An option to which the holder can add gains in the price of the underlying security.

Lady Macbeth strategy During a hostile take-over, a strategy undertaken by a party that at first seems to be acting as a *white knight* but subsequently joins the aggressor.

laggard A share that does not keep up with the average price of comparable shares.

lakh 1 lakh = 100,000 Indian rupees.

lame duck A weak individual or company; one ripe for take-over or unable to provide effective competition.

land certificate A document issued by the UK Land Registry to the registered owner of a piece of land. It includes details of any charges (mortgages) that affect the land.

landlord The owner of a property who leases or rents it to a tenant (*see tenancy*).

Laos currency kip, divided into 100 at.

lapsed option An option that is worthless because it has reached its expiry date without being exercised.

lapsed policy An insurance policy that is worthless because premiums have not been paid.

larceny The obtaining goods by trickery (from somebody who did not want to part with them). If the person did intend to part with the goods but was defrauded, the offence is obtaining goods under false pretences.

lari The standard currency unit of Georgia.

last sale The trade in a particular security that occurred most recently. *See also* **closing sale**.

last-survivor assurance A type of life assurance on two people's lives, paid on the death of the second to die. *See also* **tontine**.

last trading day In trading in financial futures, the last day on which

lease 141

trading can take place before delivery.

late charge A fee charge by a lender when a borrower does not make the loan repayments on time.

late-kerb The trading in metals that goes on after hours, usually over the telephone. See *kerb trading*.

lats The standard currency unit of Latvia, divided into 100 santami.

Latvia currency lats (LVR), divided into 100 santimi.

laundering A method of disguising the origin of money by moving it rapidly from one country to another. It thus becomes a complicated business to trace its origins, movements and eventual destination. Counterfeit or stolen money may be laundered, although more usually the money represents the proceeds of crime.

law of large numbers The principle (in insurance) whereby the insurer benefits due to large numbers of homogeneous exposure being insured. It states that the actual number of events that occur will tend towards the expected number, where there is a large number of similar situations.

LBMA Abbreviation of *London Bullion Market Association*.

LBO Abbreviation of *leveraged buy-out*.

LBP (ISO) code Lebanon – currency Lebanese pound.

L/C Abbreviation of *letter of credit*.

LCE Abbreviation of *London Commodities Exchange*.

LCH Abbreviation of *London Clearing House*.

leading indicator A measurable variable (such as housing production) that moves in advance of the indicated item (such as the level of employment). The behaviour of the stock market is often a leading indicator of economic activity.

LEAPS Abbreviation of *long-term equity anticipation security*.

lease A contract that gives temporary possession of property, sometimes in areas where prices are appreciating so rapidly that it is not in the owner's best interest to sell. Buildings are the most common subjects of a lease, although it is also possible to lease land and other possessions, such as vehicles and machinery. Long-term leases are often mortgaged, bought and sold. See also *ground rent*.

142 lease-back

lease-back An arrangement by which a property is sold on condition that it is immediately leased back to the original owner. Capital tied up in the property is thereby released for other uses.

lease financing A type of off-balance sheet financing in which goods (for example, machinery) are leased rather than being purchased outright. Lease financing is therefore generally thought of as a form of disguised borrowing.

leasehold Describing a property that is held under a lease agreement.

lease-purchase A method by which lease payments may be put towards the purchase of the leaseheld property.

Lebanon currency Lebanese pound (LBP), divided into 100 piastres.

legacy See *bequest*.

legacy currency A currency used as a national currency before the country's adoption of the euro, e.g. the Deutschmark in Germany.

legal charge Another term for a *mortgage*.

legal tender Currency; coins or notes that may be offered, and not refused, as a medium of exchange (to pay for goods or services). In the UK this means any number of Bank of England banknotes; up to £10 in £2, £1 and 50p coins; other "silver" (cupro-nickel) coins to the value of £5; and bronze coins up to 20p. Notes issued by the Bank of Scotland are not legal tender in England and Wales. Strictly neither are cheques, credit cards and so on legal tender.

lek The standard currency unit of Albania, divided into 100 qindars.

lender of last resort A central bank that is prepared to lend to the banking system as a whole, including to commercial banks. In the UK the lender of last resort is the Bank of England. It must be prepared to advance money to discount houses that have insufficient funds to balance their books, preventing their bankruptcy. It therefore gives confidence to the markets and helps to prevent a damaging run on the banks. By acting as a lender of the last resort, the Bank of England is able to influence the money supply and interest rates.

lending The temporary grant of money, goods, equipment, people and so on, made on the understanding that the thing lent, or its equivalent, will be returned, often with an additional (*interest*) payment. The lending of money is generally termed a loan. The act of taking up a loan is borrowing (termed negative saving by economists).

leveraged company 143

lepta A subdivision (1/100) of the Greek drachma.

Lesotho currency loti (plural maluti) (LSM), divided into 100 lisente.

lessee A person who is granted a lease.

lessee deposit A deposit that is paid by the lessee on a rented property, intended to cover the lessor against damage or loss and returnable on termination of the lease.

lessor A person who grants a lease.

letter of administration See *administrator*.

letter of allotment A means by which shares are allotted. It may be used as proof of ownership and entitles the holder to a certificate for the number of shares stated in the letter. It should not be confused with an *allotment note*.

letter of credit (L/C) A letter from a bank that authorizes another bank to pay the sum specified to the person named in the letter. It is also referred to as a documentary credit.

letter of identification An alternative term for a *letter of indication*.

letter of indication Also called a letter of identification, a letter from a bank to a depositor who has been issued with a *letter of credit*. It is used with the latter as proof of the bearer's signature and identity.

letter of intent A document that outlines some intended action sent to establish intent in the eyes of the law.

letter of regret A letter informing an applicant that he or she has been unsuccessful in applying for a new share issue.

leu (plural **lei**) The standard currency unit of Moldova (formerly Moldavia) and Romania, divided into 100 bani.

lev The standard currency unit of Bulgaria, divided into 100 stotinki.

level-term assurance A type of life assurance with a fixed value but increasing annual premiums.

leverage An alternative, and mainly US, term for *gearing*.

leveraged buy-out (LBO) The buy-out of a large company by a smaller one, the capital for which has been borrowed from a friendly source, secured on the assets of the company being bought.

leveraged company A company that is seriously in debt.

levy A duty applied by EU countries to imports of agricultural products from countries outside the Union (thus bringing their prices in line with inter-EU prices).

LIA Abbreviation of *Life Insurance Association*.

liabilities A company's or person's debts. Long-term (or deferred) liabilities are usually distinguished from current liabilities, which are payable within 12 months, as are secured debts from unsecured debts.

Liberia currency Liberian dollars (LRD), divided into 100 cents.

LIBID Abbreviation of *London Inter-Bank Bid Rate*.

LIBOR Abbreviation of *London Inter-Bank Offered Rate*.

Libya currency Libyan dinar (LYD), divided into 1000 dirham.

licensed dealer A dealer who is not a member of the Stock Exchange but is licensed by the UK Department of Trade and Industry (DTI) to deal in securities and give investment advice.

licensed deposit taker (LDT) An organization authorized by the Bank of England to accept deposits from the public (but not allowed to call itself a *bank*), such as a commercial bank, finance house or savings bank. It is, however, subject to the Bank's credit controls.

licensing The practice of allowing a person or company to use a copyright or patent in return for a royalty, usually calculated as a percentage of value or a fee per unit sold.

Liechtenstein currency Swiss franc (CHF), divided into 100 centimes.

lien The right to possession of property until such time that an outstanding liability has been paid. A banker's lien gives a bank the right to retain or sell the property of a debtor in lieu of payment.

life annuity A type of annuity for which payment ceases when a specified person dies (who need not be the annuitant).

life assurance An insurance policy for which the policyholder pays a premium and when the person whose life is assured dies, payment is made to the named *beneficiary*. Policies can be for a specific term or for the whole of life. An insured person who survives for the whole term of a with-profits term policy shares in the assurance company's profit and so such a policy can be considered to be a type of investment.

life assured The person whose death results in payment under a life assurance policy.

limited partner 145

Life Assurance and Unit Trust Regulatory Authority (LAUTRO) A former UK self-regulating organization (SRO) that governed the trading and operation of unit trusts, replaced by the Personal Investment Authority in 1994.

life assurance premium relief Income tax relief in respect of personal life assurance premiums (or those of one's spouse), on policies taken out before 14 March 1984. It is no longer available on policies taken out after that date, but continues to be available at a rate of 12.5% for those policies effected before the date, as long as they are not varied.

life insurance See *life assurance*.

Life Insurance Association (LIA) A UK organization, established in 1972, of some 23,000 life assurance intermediaries.

life of another policy A type of life assurance in which the policyholder (the person to whom the proceeds are paid) or guarantee is not the person whose life is assured.

life office A company that provides life assurance.

life policy A life assurance policy that contains personal details of the insured, the premium payable, and the amount to be paid by the assurance company when the assured reaches a certain age or dies.

life table A statistical table of life expectancies at different ages, used by assurance companies in calculating premiums.

LIFFE Abbreviation of *London International Financial Futures Exchange*.

lilangeni (plural **emalangeni**) The standard currency unit of Swaziland, divided into 100 cents.

limited A short form of *limited company (Ltd)*.

limited company (Ltd) Also called a limited liability company, a company formed from a group of people whose liability is limited to the extent of the investment they have made (usually to purchase shares in the company), although occasionally limited liability is limited by guarantee to a certain amount as specified in the company's memorandum. *See also public limited company*.

limited liability See *limited company*.

limited partner A partner whose liability for the debts of the partnership is limited in law to the sum he or she invested in it. A limited partner does not generally share in the management of the firm. He or she may, however, offer advice and examine the books of account. See *limited partnership*.

limited partnership A partnership in which one or more of the partners has only limited liability for the firm's debts. In each limited partnership there must be one general partner with unlimited liability. A limited partnership is therefore unpopular and a public limited company is preferred, because all shareholders in such a company have only limited liability.

limited payments policy A type of life assurance for which premium payments cease when the assured reaches a certain age (often 65 years).

limit order On a stock exchange commodity exchange, an instruction given by a client to his or her stockbroker which specifies the maximum price the broker is authorized to pay to buy a shareholding, or the minimum price at which it can be sold. It is also the US term for a stop loss order.

limit price The price specified in a *limit order*.

limit up/down The maximum and minimum limits within which the price of some commodity futures and financial futures are permitted to fluctuate in one day's trading.

line The acceptance risk of an underwriter. Also, in reinsurance, it is the retention limit under a surplus reinsurance treaty.

line of credit A facility for a loan made available by a creditor on condition that he or she uses the money to buy goods or services from the creditor. A bank may establish a line of credit for a customer to draw down money in stages, in which case it is similar to an overdraft facility.

liquid assets Assets that consist of cash or can readily be converted into cash. They are also known by various other names, such as liquid capital, quick assets and realizable assets.

liquid assets ratio The ratio of the total assets held by a company to the value of assets that may be converted to cash without loss.

liquidate The closing out or cancelling a futures contract where the contract's owner has assets available for sale on the prescribed date, usually achieved by selling the assets.

liquidation The winding-up of a company, so-called because the company's assets are liquidated – converted into cash money – in order that outstanding creditors may be paid (in whole or, more usually, in part). The company thereby ceases to exist as a legal entity. In the USA the term is also used to denote payment of a debt.

liquidator A person who officially oversees the winding up of a company, acting as a receiver and manager. See *liquidation; receivership*.

liquidity The ease with which an asset can be converted into cash. Cash deposits in current bank accounts may be quickly withdrawn and are said to be highly liquid; money in most deposit accounts is slightly less liquid because notice must usually be given before withdrawal. Of a company, liquidity is the availability of cash (or near cash) to meet its debts and take advantage of investment opportunities.

liquidity index A method of measuring a company's liquidity in terms of the number of days it would take to convert current assets into cash.

liquidity preference An economist's term for a person's preference for holding on to money rather than investing it.

liquidity ratio Also called the acid-test ratio or quick ratio, an *accounting ratio* equal to a company's current assets (ignoring stock and long-term trade debts) divided by its current liabilities.

liquidity trap A situation in which people prefer to hold onto money rather than invest it because interest rates are so low.

lira (plural **lire**) The standard legacy currency unit of Italy, San Marino and the Vatican City, divided into 100 centesemi; the standard currency unit of Turkey and the Turkish Republic of North Cyprus, divided into 100 kurus; and Malta, divided into 100 cents.

Lisbon Stock Exchange (LSE) Properly Bolsa de Valores de Lisbon, Portugal's stock exchange, founded in 1769, which uses a computer-linked trading system (TRADIS). It principal market index is the BVL General Index (which includes all listed shares).

lisente A subdivision (1/100) of the maluti (Lesotho).

listed company A company whose shares are listed on a stock exchange.

listed security A security recognized for quotation and trading on a stock exchange.

listing The *flotation* of a company on a stock exchange; the sum of the actions that permits securities to be traded on a stock market. The issued shares are then listed in the exchange records and their price fluctuations recorded and published.

litas The standard currency unit of Lithuania, divided into 100 centai.

Lithuania currency litas, divided into 100 kopecks.

Little Board A colloquial name for the *American Stock Exchange*.

LKR (ISO) code Sri Lanka – currency Sri Lankan rupee.

Lloyd's A short form of *Lloyd's of London*.

Lloyd's of London An incorporated association of insurers that specializes in marine insurance. Formally established by Act of Parliament in 1871, the Corporation developed from a group of 17th-century underwriters who met at Edward Lloyd's coffee house in London. Lloyd's supervises about 20,000 individual insurers ("names") grouped into syndicates, each of which has unlimited liability and accepts a fraction of the risk of business brought to them by one of more than 200 registered brokers. Lloyd's involvement in marine insurance currently comprises less than half the total business transacted by Lloyd's underwriters. Following disastrous losses between 1988-1994, limited liability companies are now allowed to become "corporate names".

LME Abbreviation of *London Metal Exchange*.

loading In insurance, 1. An extra sum added to a premium for a risk that is egarded as greater than normal for the type of policy. 2. The part of a premium that funds costs and profits.

loan Also called an advance, a sum of money borrowed by one person or organization from another on condition that it is repaid, generally for a specified time and often at an agreed rate of interest. See also **lending**.

loanback A loan made by a pension fund to a contributor to that fund. Loanback pensions are secured not against the total value of the contributions to date, but against some other asset, although the maximum available loan is generally equal to the total value of the accumulated contributions. The loan becomes an asset of the borrower's pension plan and interest payments are, therefore, part of the income of the plan.

loan capital An alternative term for *borrowed capital*.

Loan Guarantee Scheme A UK government scheme to support small businesses whereby it guarantees 70% of a company's overdraft (for a premium of 3%); the bank accepts the risk for the other 30%.

loan rate The rate of interest charged for a loan.

London Clearing House (LCH) 149

loan stock An unsecured security issued in respect of loan funds made available to a company by investors. It is similar to a debenture (which is, however, secured).

loan to value (LTV) The sum of money a lender is prepared to advance (by way of a mortgage), expressed as a percentage of the value of the property used as security for the loan.

local authority bond A bond issued by a local government authority, also known as a municipal bond.

local currency The currency of a foreign country with which an exporter or trader is dealing.

local taxation A tax levied on people, businesses or their property in a particular area. The chief local taxes in the UK are business rates and council tax.

lock-up On financial markets, an investment expected to yield profit only in the long term, and in which the capital will therefore be "locked up" for some time.

lock-up option In a situation in which a company is being threatened with an unwanted take-over, a defensive tactic whereby the target company promises to sell its most attractive assets to a *white knight*.

Lombard rate The interest rate used by the German central bank (the *Bundesbank*) in lending to German commercial banks.

London acceptance credit The credit of an exporter with a London bank or accepting house, on which bills of exchange may be drawn (within specified limits of amount and timing). The lender may requite security for such an arrangement.

London bank export credit A similar arrangement to London acceptance credit, although any bills of exchange are drawn on the foreign buyer and collected by the bank.

London Bankers' Clearing House An organization established in the 1770s that clears cheques drawn against UK clearing banks.

London Bullion Market Association (LBMA) An organization established in 1987 by members of the gold and silver bullion market, who deal on a forward, options or spot basis. Five of the members are responsible for the daily fixing of the price of gold (always expressed in US dollars).

London Clearing House (LCH) An organization established in 1888 that clears futures, options and other forward contracts.

150 London Commodities Exchange (LCE)

London Commodities Exchange (LCE) A market that deals in cocoa, coffee, rubber, spices, tea and other commodities. In 1996 it merged with the *London International Financial Futures and Options Exchange*.

London Derivatives Exchange A financial exchange organization established in 1990 by the merging of the London International Financial Futures Exchange and the Traded Options Market.

London Foreign Exchange Market A market that deals in sterling and various foreign currencies, using contracts that are made verbally (using telephones or other electronic means) and later confirmed in writing.

London Fox The shortened name of the *London Futures and Options Exchange*.

London Futures and Options Exchange (London Fox) A commodity market established in 1987 that deals in futures and options. The Baltic International Freight Futures Exchange merged with London Fox in 1991.

London Inter-Bank Bid Rate (LIBID or **LIBBR)** The rate of interest that banks use to buy from and sell funds to each other. *See also* **London Inter-Bank Offered Rate**.

London Inter-Bank Mean Rate (LIMEAN) An average of the *London Inter-Bank Bid Rate* and the *London Inter-Bank Offered Rate*.

London Inter-Bank Offered Rate (LIBOR) The rate of interest that commercial banks offer to lend money on the London inter-bank market. Along with the minimum lending rate, it has a significant effect on bank interest rates.

London International Financial Futures and Options Exchange (LIFFE) A financial futures market established in 1982 for dealing in options and futures contracts within the European time zone. Originally the London International Financial Futures Exchange, its name changed in 1992 when it merged with the London Traded Options market (LTOM). A further merger in 1996 with the London Commodity Exchange (LCE) gave it unique status in the financial world.

London International Financial Futures Exchange *See* London *International Financial Futures and Options Exchange*.

London Metal Exchange (LME) A market established in 1877 to deal in non-ferrous metals, including aluminium, copper, lead, nickel, tin and zinc.

London Securities and Derivatives Exchange (OMLX) An exchange established in 1990 (as a means of avoiding local tax) to deal in Swedish futures and options. The tax has been repealed but the exchange continues to operate in London.

London Stock Exchange (LSE) An organization established in London's Threadneedle Street in 1773 (hence its nickname: the Old Lady of Threadneedle Street). Today it is third in size in the world (after New York and Tokyo) but still the largest in Europe, especially since the large increase in trade in non-UK shares. All trading is done electronically using computer screens and telephones.

London Traded Options Market See *London International Financial Futures and Options Exchange*.

long bond A bond with more than 15 years to maturity.

long end of the market The part of the bond market that deals in issues of long-term bonds.

long hedge A hedge against a fall in the interest rate on the futures market.

long position The position taken by a bull speculator, who acquires quantities of stock or commodity in excess of the amount contracted for, in the expectation that the price will rise and permit the surplus to be sold at a profit.

longs Fixed-interest securities with redemption dates more than 15 years in the future. It is also a US term for securities that somebody has bought and actually owns.

long tap Long-term government securities issued in unlimited numbers.

long-term A period normally exceeding 15 years, but more loosely applied to stocks issued for an indefinite period of time or in perpetuity. In the City, the phrase "long-term" is loosely applied to any period over one year.

long-term equity anticipation security (LEAPS) A long-term (two- to five-year) equity option that is traded over the counter on US exchanges.

long-term liability A debt that need not be repaid in the next three years.

loophole Any circumstance that permits the evasion of a custom or rule, but especially a legal inexactitude that offers an escape from a contract.

loss A disadvantage, forfeiture of money or goods, or negative profit (the amount by which expenses of a transaction or project exceed income).

152 loss ratio

loss ratio In insurance, the value of all claims expressed as a percentage of total premiums for a period. The figure is used as a guide to the profitability of the business when considering rates.

Loti The singular (plural maluti) of the standard currency unit of Lesotho.

lottery A game of chance in which participants buy numbered tickets. Winning tickets drawn at random entitle their owners to a prize. Usually there are millions of tickets at a modest price, buyers being willing to accept a large chance of losing their ticket money for a very small chance of winning a great deal of money. *See also* **gambling;** *National Savings Premium Bond.*

low-beta Describing shares that are relatively stable.

low-cost endowment mortgage An insurance policy that repays capital on a mortgage while also providing death benefit and long-term savings in the form of a tax-free lump sum on maturity (although not usually guaranteed).

LRD (ISO) code Liberia – currency Liberian dollars

LSE Abbreviation of *London Stock Exchange*.

LSM (ISO) code Lesotho – currency maluti.

LTV Abbreviation of *loan to value*.

LUF (ISO) code Luxembourg – currency Luxembourg franc. The 1999 legacy conversion rate was 40.3399 to the euro. It will fully change to the euro/cent from 2002.

lump sum A sum of money paid all at once, as opposed to being paid as a series of separate sums (instalments).

Lutine Bell A bell that hangs in the underwriting room at Lloyd's of London. It was formerly rung before the announcement of important news, such as that concerning the fate of a missing ship. It was recovered from the *Lutine*, a ship that sank in 1799 and which was insured at Lloyd's for £1.4 million.

Luxembourg currency Luxembourg franc (LUF), divided into 100 centimes. The 1999 legacy conversion rate was 40.3399 to the euro. It will fully change to the euro/cent from 2002.

LVR (ISO) code Latvia – currency lat.

Lwei A subdivision (1/100) of the Angolan kwanza.

LYD (ISO) code Libya – currency Libyan dinar.

M

Macedonia currency denar.

macroeconomics The study of broad or aggregate economics. It concerns itself with the relationship between such major aggregates as prices, incomes, total consumption and total production, together with interest and exchange rates, savings and investment.

MAD (ISO) code Morocco – currency Moroccon dirham.

Madagascar currency Malagasy franc (MGF); there is no subdivision. Also 1 ariary = 5 Malagasy francs.

made bills Bills of exchange traded in the UK but drawn and payable overseas.

Madrid Stock Exchange One of four stock exchanges in Spain (the others are at Barcelona, Bilbao and Valencia), which since 1995 have been interlinked by an order-driven computer trading system. Its principal market index is the IBEX-35.

main market The market in stocks and shares on the London Stock Exchange's official list (and thus excluding unlisted securities).

majority interest A shareholding that gives the holder control of a company, i.e. a holding of more than 50%.

major market index (MMI) A US futures contact established in 1983 by the Chicago Board of Trade based on the Dow-Jones Industrial Avergae of the USA's 20 largest companies. It was transferred to the Chicago Metals Exchange in 1993.

major trading currency One of the leading currencies in which most international trade is conducted, such as the US dollar, the Canadian dollar, the Japanese yen and the main West European currencies.

making a market *See making a price.*

making a price The action of a stockbroker or market-maker when he or she quotes a bid price or offer price for a stock or share. It is also termed making a market.

makuta A subdivision (1/100) of the zaire (Zaire Republic).

Malawi currency Malawian kwacha (MWK), divided into 100 tambala.

154 Maldives currency

Maldives currency rufiya, divided into 100 laari.

Malta currency Maltese lira (MTL), divided into 100 cents.

maluti The standard currency unit of Lesotho, divided into 100 lisente.

managed account An investment account that is managed for a depositor by a bank's investment department.

managed bond An investment in a *managed fund*.

managed fund A fund that is set up by a life office, unit trust or investment company which is made up of a range of securities and managed by a fund manager. The spread of investments and the extent of a fund manager's expertise means that this type of fund usually offers a lower risk for a small investor.

managed futures fund A mutual fund that deals in derivatives.

managed unit trust An alternative term for a *fund of funds*.

management The control and supervision of a company, asset or operation; or the group of people who control and administer a company, as distinct from the workforce.

management buy-in The take-over of a company by a group of managers outside it (who purchase shares in order to gain a controlling interest).

management buy-out (MBO) The purchase of a company by its own managers, one of the most common forms of buy-out.

management fee A charge levied on an investor in a *managed fund*.

managing trustee A trustee who buys and sells investments to make gains for the benefit of the beneficiaries of a trust.

manat The standard currency unit of Azerbaijan and Turkmenistan.

M and A Abbreviation of *mergers and acquisitions*.

Mareva injunction A court injunction that prevents the transfer of funds overseas until a case concerning them has been heard in the UK courts.

margin 1. The proportion of the total cost of a product or service that represents the producer's profits. 2. When trading commodities or financial futures, the proportion of the contract that is put up. 3. The proportion of the total price of a share paid by the purchaser to his or her stockbroker when the broker buys securities on credit. The practice is more common in the USA than in the UK, where most dealing is done on account. 4. The price added by lenders to the market rate of interest to provide a profit.

margin account An account held by a broker on behalf of an investor which allows the investor to purchase securities on credit.

margin call A broker's request for more funds from an investor who has not paid the full price for an investment.

margin dealing In futures trading, if an adverse price movement more than eradicates a party's margin, the balance of the deficit is called upon, often cancelling the bargain.

margin loan A loan commonly made on limited security. For example, a group of several lenders may advance money secured on property to 75% of its value. A margin loan would then be secured on the remaining 25%. It would carry a higher risk and therefore attract a slightly higher rate of interest. It is also known as a top-up loan.

margin trading Investing in the stock market using (hopefully cheap) borrowed funds.

markdown A reduction in the selling price of goods, either below their marked up price (*see marking up*) or, in desperate times, below the retailer's purchasing price. The valuation of a security can also be marked down.

market 1. A place where goods and services are bought and sold. 2. The actual or potential demand for those goods or services. 3. An abstract expression denoting any area or condition in which buyers and sellers are in contact and able to do business together.

marketable loan A loan that can easily be transferred from one person to another.

marketable security Any security that is easy to sell.

market capitalization Also termed market valuation, the value of all the issued shares of a company at current market prices, equal to the share price multiplied by the number of shares issued.

market clearing price The price for all goods or services that will find buyers in a given market.

market forces The forces of supply and demand, which together determine the prices of goods and services on the open market.

market if touched (MIT) An instruction to a broker to sell shares as soon as the price reaches a designated level.

market index *See index number.*

market instrument Any short-term debt instrument (for raising a loan).

market leader A company that has the largest share of a particular market. Individual products that have the largest share of a market are called brand leaders.

market-maker A market principal who encourages dealing by varying the price of stock to promote its sale or purchase. The term is used especially with reference to the stock market.

market order An order to buy or sell securities on the stock market or a financial futures exchange at the best obtainable market price.

market price Also called market value, the price at which something is traded on the open market.

market rate The base interest rate charged for a loan. A spread is added to give the interest rate for a variable-rate loan.

market risk 1. A part of the total risk inherent in buying stock, which depends on market movements as a whole rather than on the particular characteristics of the stock itself. For example, during a market crash, the share prices of many sound companies whose earning prospects remain unchanged may fall in line with less sound stock. This illustrates the market risk, rather than the specific risk inherent in stock market dealings. 2. The risk that the price will change taken by a market trader in a long or short position. For example, a holder of securities (not hedged by the sale of futures) loses if the price falls; a seller of futures who does not actually hold them loses if the market rises.

market share The fraction of all sales in a given market (usually expressed as a percentage) that are held by one company or by one brand.

market tending The control of a market's stock index, by intervention buying and selling.

market timer A US investment manager who operates by moving his or her investments from one instrument to another depending on market prices.

market to market Following an earlier calculation of the value of a portfolio of securities, a second calculation using current market prices to determine whether a profit or loss has resulted in the meantime.

market value An alternative term for *market price*.

mean price 157

markings On the London Stock Exchange, the number of deals that have taken place in one working day.

marking up The upward adjustments of a price (say, by a retailer) to allow for a profit margin. The retailer's mark-up is equal to gross profit.

mark to market On a financial futures exchange, the adjustment of a customer's account to allow for profits or losses on his or her open contracts during the previous day's trading.

mark-up See *marking up*.

markka The standard legacy currency unit of Finland, divided into 100 pennia.

MAT Abbreviation of moving annual total. See *annualize*.

matched bargain A deal made by finding a client who wishes to sell a particular stock and one who wishes to buy that same stock.

matched sales technique A method of getting round foreign government-sanctioned price controls by linking the purchase of a price-controlled item with one that is not subject to such controls.

maturity The date, specified in advance, on which a financial instrument may be exchanged for its cash value.

Mauritania currency ouguiya, divided into five khoums.

Mauritius currency Mauritian rupee (MUR), divided into 100 cents.

maximum fluctuation Also known as maximum slippage, the upper limit to which a price may rise during one day's trading. It is fixed in advance as a percentage of the current price, and trading in a contract is halted for the rest of the day if the maximum fluctuation price is reached.

maximum slippage An alternative term for *maximum fluctuation*.

MBO Abbreviation of *management buy-out*.

mean Also called arithmetic mean, the average. Of a group of values it is the sum of all the values divided by the number in the group.

mean deviation A measure of statistical dispersion equal, for a group of values, the sum of the differences between each value and the arithmetic mean, divided by the number in the group.

mean price The arithmetic mean of two specified prices, such as the highest buying and lowest selling prices of a security. It is also called the middle-market price and is usually the one quoted on the Stock Exchange's daily listing.

158 median

median A statistical average used as an alternative to the arithmetic mean when there are a few extreme values in a group of numbers. It is obtained by putting the group of numbers in ascending order and nominating the middle one as the median (or the average of the two middle ones if there is an even number in the group).

medium bond A bond with between 5 and 15 years to maturity.

medium-dated gilt A gilt-edged security with a redemption term of between 5 and 15 years.

medium-dated stock Stock with a redemption term of between 5 and 15 years.

medium of exchange An economist's term for *money*.

medium-term note (MTN) Euro commercial paper with several years' maturity.

megamerger A merger between two very large companies to form a gigantic corporation.

meltdown A sizeable financial crisis; a severe crash. The term is taken from the nuclear power industry, where a meltdown in a reactor would trigger a major disaster.

memorandum of association A document that has to be registered and filed at Companies House in the UK, giving details of a company's particulars and aims. It is accompanied by the *articles of association*, which sets up the internal regulations of the company's operations and states, among other things, the powers of the directors.

merchant bank A bank that originally specialized in financing trade, but today offers long-term loans to companies, venture capital, management of investments and underwriting of new share issues. Merchant banks also function as *acceptance houses*. See also **venture capital**.

merger The fusion of two or more companies, as distinct from a take-over of one company by another. Mergers may be undertaken for various reasons, notable to improve efficiency of two complementary companies by rationalizing output and taking advantage of economies of scale, and to fight off unwanted take-over bids from other large companies. The companies involved form one new company and their respective shareholders exchange their holdings for shares in the new concern at an agreed rate.

minimum fluctuation   159

mergers and acquisitions (M and A)   The field of arranging mergers between companies or take-overs of companies, or the department within a large organization that is formed to carry out this function.

metical   (plural **meticais**) The standard currency unit of Mozambique, divided into 100 centavos.

Mexico currency   Mexican peso (MXN); there is no subdivision.

Mexican Stock Exchange   The Bolsa Mexicana de Valores, founded in 1894 in Mexico City and now the largest in Latin America.

mezzanine finance   Money lent to a small and growing, but financially viable, company. It is so called because the risk of making the loan falls between that of advancing venture capital and the safer course of putting the finance into established debt markets.

MGF   (ISO) code Madagascar – currency Malagasy franc.

microeconomics   The study of the individual components of an economy in isolation. It examines the choices open to specific people, companies and industries and has been developed to enable the study of subjects such as utility, price mechanisms, competition and margins.

middleman   An individual or corporate dealer that acts as an intermediary between two parties (to a trade), a service that usually earns a commission.

middle price   The price of a commodity or security that is halfway between the bid (buying) and offer (selling) prices quoted on a market. The prices published in the financial press are generally middle prices.

Midwest Stock Exchange   An exchange established in 1882 as the Chicago Stock Exchange to deal mainly in securities of banks, energy companies and railway companies. It became the USA's second largest exchange and adopted its present name in 1948, but declined in size and reverting back to its original name in 1993.

Milan Stock Exchange   The Borsa Valori, an important Italian exchange established in 1991 by the merger of 10 previous national exchanges and administered by the Commissione Nazionale per la Società e la Borsa. All trading has been screen-based since 1994.

mill   One-tenth of a (US) cent.

millimes   A subdivision (1/1000) of the Tunisian dinar.

minimum fluctuation   Also known as the basis point, the lower limit to which a price may fall in one day's trading on an exchange. As with the maximum fluctuation, it is fixed in advance and trading is halted for the day if the minimum fluctuation is reached.

minimum lending rate (MLR) The minimum rate at which the Bank of England, acting in its capacity as lender of the last resort, is willing to discount bills of exchange and at which it offers short-term loans. It has a direct effect on bank interest rates.

minimum payment The minimum amount that a borrower is required to pay on revolving credit such as a credit card (or late payment charges may accrue).

minority interest A shareholding that does not give the holder control of a company, i.e. less than 50% of the shares.

minority shareholder A person who holds a *minority interest* in a company.

MIRAS Abbreviation of *mortgage interest relief at source*.

MIT Abbreviation of *market if touched*.

MLR Abbreviation of *minimum lending rate*.

MMC Abbreviation of *Monopolies and Mergers Commission*.

MMI Abbreviation of *major market index*.

MNC Abbreviation of *multinational company*.

MNE Abbreviation of multinational enterprise; see *multinational company*.

mock auction An auction that is in some way illegal. This may occur in several ways: when goods are sold for a price lower than that of the highest bid; when some goods are given away in order to attract bidders; when those who have not already bought lots are excluded from bidding; and when all or part of the agreed price is returned privately to the bidder.

mode Statistical average equal to the number that occurs most frequently in a group of numbers; a measure of central tendency.

model code The Stock Exchange code of conduct that sets out guidelines for share dealings by company directors. It specifies, broadly, that directors should not engage in questionable dealings in their company's stock, and in particular forbids share dealings within two months preceding a company announcement of profit, loss, dividend, a proposed merger, take-over, sale of assets, and so on.

money-center bank 161

modern portfolio theory A theory of stock valuation developed in the early 1980s. It values stocks by estimating their future earnings discounted back to the present.

moengoe A subdivision (1/100) of the Mongolian tughrik.

Moldova (formerly Moldavia) currency leu (plural lei), divided into 100 bani.

momentum In finance, the rate at which a price increases or decreases.

Monaco currency French franc (MCF), divided into 100 centimes. It will adopt the euro/cent from 2002.

monetary control A method used by a government to control the money supply through its central bank (in the UK the Bank of England).

monetary inflation A type of inflation caused by an increase in the money supply.

monetary policy Any government policy of how to regulate the money supply (and its effects on employment, industrial growth, inflation, and so on).

Monetary Policy Committee A committee of the Bank of England, established in 1997, that sets UK interest rates (formerly a function of the Treasury).

monetary system A system that controls the exchange rates of a group of countries, or a system that a single country uses to control its own currency exchange while ensuring that there is enough money in circulation for internal use.

money A medium of exchange; any generally accepted token (e.g. coins or banknotes) that may be exchanged for – used in payment for – goods or services.

money at call Loans that may be called in at short notice, and which therefore attract only low rates of interest.

money broker A dealer in short-term loans and securities on the money market. On the London Stock Exchange, six firms act as money brokers, channelling borrowed stocks from institutions onto the market, thereby enhancing the liquidity of the gilt-edged securities (gilts) and equity markets in particular.

money-center bank In the large financial centres of the USA, a major bank that acts as a clearing bank for the smaller banks of the area.

money laundering See *laundering*.

moneylender A person licensed by the government to lend funds to others. The term is, however, used informally to describe anyone lending money independently of banks and other financial institutions, often at high rates of interest, and as such carries negative connotations.

money market A market operated by banks and other financial institutions to facilitate the short-term (up to one year) borrowing and lending of money, and trading in financial securities; it is also sometimes known as the discount market. In the UK, the Bank of England is the lender of last resort. A wider money market includes also the markets in bullion and foreign exchange. See also *financial market*.

money-market fund 1. A fund into which individual small savings are accumulated for investment in the money market, adopted particularly in the USA to get round the controls on interest rates that could be paid by banks. 2. A type of *unit trust*, sometimes called a money-market unit trust, in which income is invested in high-yield, short-term instruments of credit.

money-market instrument A financial product traded on the money market, including certificates of deposit and other short-term instruments.

money-market unit trust See *money-market fund*.

money order A document that can readily be turned into cash by the payee (the person named on the order). In the UK, a money order scheme is run by the Post Office (obviating the need to send cash or cheques through the post). See also *international money order; postal order*.

money-purchase pension scheme A pension plan that is based, like all personal pensions, on contributions to the pension fund rather on salary immediately before retirement. At retirement, the pension fund is used to purchase an annuity.

money runner An informal US term for a person who invests in markets throughout the world, probably creating *hot money* in the process.

money supply The total amount of money available at short notice in a given country. There are several categories of money supply, designated M0, M1, M2 and M3.

M0 is defined as notes and coins in circulation in bank tills, plus the operational balances that banks place with the Bank of England. M0 is the narrowest category and is sometimes called narrow money.

M1 is defined as notes and coin in circulation and money deposited in bank current accounts. It is the best gauge of money immediately available for exchange.

M2 is an obsolete definition of the money supply. It includes notes and coins in circulation and in bank accounts, together with funds saved in deposit accounts maintained with the clearing banks, National Giro Bank, Bank of England banking department and discount houses.

M3 is defined as M2 plus interest-bearing non-sterling deposit accounts held by British residents, and other certificates of deposit. M3 is the broadest definition of the money supply and may also be known as broad money. A subsidiary measure, £M3, excludes non-sterling deposit accounts.

Mongolia currency tughrik, divided into 100 moengoe.

Monopolies and Mergers Commission (MMC) A UK government organization that monitors take-overs and mergers (in the public and national interest) and acts as a watchdog over monopolies and restrictive trade practices.

monopoly Strictly, an industry with only one supplier. The term is also applied more widely to an industry controlled ("monopolized") by one company, which produces a sufficient proportion of the total output of that industry to effectively control supply and therefore price.

monopsony An industry in which there are many manufacturers but only one customer for the goods produced. By controlling demand the customer can, in theory, set the price. Monopsonies generally evolve to serve nation states; the market for warships, for example, is a virtual monopsony in that the vessels produced are purchased only by the government of the nation concerned, or by other governments that have its approval.

monthly investment plan A scheme for saving money run by many banks and other financial institutions in which monthly contributions are credited to an interest-earning deposit account or used to buy shares in a trust.

moral obligation An obligation, usually to perform some service or complete some transaction, that cannot be enforced in law but which is nevertheless met out of honour.

moratorium A grant of an extended period in which to repay a loan, or a period during which the repayment schedule is suspended. Usually, it refers only to the repayment of capital, and interest payments may still be required.

Morgan Stanley Capital International World Index (MSCI Index) A world index of the prices of shares, based on more than 1300 shares from 19 countries. It thereby covers about 60% of the share market value on stock exchanges throughout the world.

Morocco currency Moroccon dirham (MAD), divided into 100 centimes.

mortgage The transfer of the deeds to a property as security for the repayment of a debt. For example, a building society that provides a loan for the purchase of a house takes legal possession of the property until the loan and interest have been repaid. The lender is the mortgagee; the borrower is the mortgagor. A mortgage is also called a legal charge.

mortgage bond 1. A certificate stating that a mortgage has been taken out and that a property is secured against default. 2. A bond (with specified interest rate and a maturity date) financed by a mortgage, popular in Continental Europe for making house purchases.

mortgage debenture A debenture secured by the mortgage of a property or other asset owned by the institution concerned.

mortgage guarantee insurance See *mortgage indemnity guarantee*.

mortgage indemnity guarantee A single-premium insurance to cover a mortgagee (lender) for the amount of a mortgage in excess of a certain sum, usually 75% of the value of the property, should the mortgagor (borrower) default on the loan. See also **mortgage protection policy**.

mortgage interest relief at source (MIRAS) A former UK government scheme that gave income tax relief on mortgage interest payments, now phased out.

mortgage protection policy A type of life assurance (taken out by a mortgagor) that covers the outstanding debt on a repayment mortgage. The sum assured decreases during the term of the mortgage but premiums remain level throughout the repayment term.

Mozambique currency metical (plural meticais), divided into 100 centavos.

MSCI Index See *Morgan Stanley Capital International World Index*.

MTL (ISO) code Malta – currency Maltese lira.

MTN Abbreviation of *medium-term note*.

multi-component Euronote facility A facility that allows Euronotes to be issued in a mixture of currencies of the issuer's choice.

multinational Concerning more than one nation, particularly with regard to the dealings of large companies.

multinational company (MNC) Also called a multinational enterprise (MNE), a company that has facilities, such as those for production and marketing, in various countries other than its country of origin.

multinational corporation A corporation that has operations and offices in more than one country.

municipal bond Also called a local authority bond, a bond issued by a local authority, generally regarded as being a safe investment.

municipal revenue bond See *revenue bond*.

muster roll A register of the holders of a given security.

mutual Describing a company or organization owned by its depositors or members but which does not issue stocks or shares. In the UK, many insurance companies and (formerly) building societies have this status. The conversion of status of such organizations to incorporation as a limited company (which can issue shares) is termed demutualization. In the USA, mutual savings banks have mutual status.

mutual fund An alternative US term for a *unit trust*.

mutual life assurance company A life assurance company that is owned by its policyholders. It has no shareholders and so all the profits available as surplus are distributed to with-profits policyholders in the form of bonuses.

mutual organization See *mutual*.

MUR (ISO) code Mauritius – currency Mauritian rupee.

MWK (ISO) code Malawi – currency Malawian kwacha.

MXN (ISO) code Mexico – currency Mexican peso.

Myanmar (formerly Burma) **currency** kyat (BUK), divided into 100 pyas.

MYR (ISO) code Malaysia – currency ringgit.

N

naira The standard currency unit of Nigeria, divided into 100 kobo.

Nakasone bond A Japanese government bond issued in non-Japanese currency.

naked Describing a security, particularly a derivative, that is not covered or hedged against various risks.

naked debenture An alternative term for an *unsecured debenture*.

naked option An option to buy shares in which the seller of the option (the option writer) does not already own the shares. In this instance, the option writer hopes to buy back the option before it is exercised and so avoid having to supply the shares. If the option is exercised and the market price of the shares has risen, the option writer makes a loss. An option writer who sells naked options is known as a naked writer.

naked writer *See naked option*.

name A member of a *Lloyd's of London* syndicate, who underwrites insurance business. The liability of a name is unlimited.

name day On the London Stock Exchange, the day before *account day*, on which sellers of securities are supplied with the names of those who have bought from them during the last account.

NAPF Abbreviation of *National Association of Pension Funds*.

narrow market A market in which there is a shortage of goods or services for sale, particularly of a particular company's shares on a stock market.

NASD Abbreviation of *National Association of Security Dealers*.

NASDAQ Abbreviation of *National Association of Security Dealers Automated Quotation System*.

NASDIM Abbreviation of *National Association of Security Dealers and Investment Managers*.

National Association of Pension Funds (NAPF) An organization that represents firms that provide *occupational pensions*.

National Association of Security Dealers (NASD) A US national self-regulatory organization that regulates the *National Association of*

nationalization 167

Securities Dealers Automated Quotation and the over-the-counter (OTC) market.

National Association of Security Dealers and Investment Managers (NASDIM) A former UK organization established in 1979 (as the Association of Licensed Dealers) that represented licensed security dealers, who have since become members of various self-regulating organizations (SROs). NASDIM ceased to exist in 1987.

National Association of Securities Dealers Automated Quotation (NASDAQ) A US computer-based system, established in 1971, that deals with orders and provides information for the US over-the-counter (OTC) market. More than 500 market-makers deal in actively traded securities of more than 4000 US companies.

National Development Bonds Former UK government bonds, introduced in 1964 and available through the Post Office or Trustee Savings Banks. The last issue has now matured, and no further interest is payable.

National Insurance A tax levied in the UK, nominally to pay for social security benefits and retirement pensions. It is paid by employers, employees and self-employed persons.

National Insurance Contributions (NICs) Payments made by those with earned income in the UK into the *National Insurance Fund*, from which various benefits are paid. There are five classes of contributions: Class 1, primary contributions from employees, secondary contributions from employers; Class 1A, payable by employers on the taxable value of cars and fuel provided to employees; Class 2, flat-rate contributions paid by the self-employed; Class 3, voluntary flat-rate contributions paid by those who want to top up their contribution record; Class 4, profit-related contributions paid by the self-employed when profits exceed a dertain amount.

National Insurance Fund A UK government fund into which the self-employed, employees and their employers pay regular contributions. The fund is administered by the Department of Social Security (DSS) and provides contributors to the fund with state pensions and various social security benefits, including invalidity benefit, unemployment benefit, maternity benefit, sickness benefit and widow's benefit. It also funds the income support system and related benefits such as housing benefit and family credit, which are payable to non-contributors.

nationalization A government policy whereby industries previously in private ownership are bought by the state and subsequently controlled by the government. *See also privatization.*

168 National Market System (NMS)

National Market System (NMS) A computerized real-time US system, established in 1975, that provides information about the prices of stocks.

National Savings Bank (NSB) A UK government savings bank established as the Post Office Savings Bank in 1861. It changed its name in 1969 but is still operated through the Post Office, where savers may deposit and withdraw money and invest in National Savings Certificates etc.

National Savings Capital Bond A five-year £100 bond offered since 1989 by the National Savings Bank aimed at non-tax payers, who receive 7.75% compound interest if the bond if left for the full term.

National Savings Certificate A tax-free five-year certificate issued by the National Savings Bank through Post Offices and High Street banks. Investors receive 4.5% interest plus an index-linked bonus if the certificate is left for the full term.

National Savings Children's Bonus Bond A tax-free bond issued by the National Savings Bank for a child under 16 years old. It continues to earn interest at 7.85% until the child is 21 years old, during which time a bonus is added every five years. The bond is aimed at parents and grandparents as a means of investing on behalf of the child.

National Savings Deposit Bond A now defunct premium interest-rate bond for lumps sums of between £100 and £100,000 that was available from 1983 to 1989. They earned interest, even after 1989, until they had been held for 10 years.

National Savings First Option Bond A fixed interest rate savings tax-paid (= FIRST) bond issued by the National Savings Bank. For a minimum investment of £1000, an investor receives a guaranteed interest of 4.8% for the first year, increasing by 0.3% each year. The "option" is to cash in the bond after any 12-month period.

National Savings Income Bond A bond issued by the National Savings Bank, aimed at non-tax payers because the interest (6.5% or 6.75% variable for over £25,000 worth) is paid gross every month and can therefore constitute a regular income.

National Savings Pensioners Guaranteed Income Bond A bond similar to the *National Savings Income Bond* issued by the National Savings Bank to non-tax payers aged 65 and over. For a minimum investment of £500 the bonds pay an interest of 7.75% gross, fixed for five years and paid monthly. They have become known colloquially as granny bonds.

National Savings Premium Bond A stake in the form of a lottery run by the UK government through the National Savings Bank since 1956. The bonds cost £1 each – bought in multiples of ten – and carry no interest, but each week and month tax-free prizes (equivalent to 5.2% of the money paid in) are awarded to the holders if bonds selected by a random number generator out of the interest accumulated on all premium bonds. They are not transferable, but may be redeemed at any time at their face value.

National Savings Stock Register An organization run for the UK Department of National Savings that enables people to buy gilt-edged securities (gilts) by post without having to employ a stockbroker. Interest is paid before tax, although it remains taxable.

National Securities Clearing Corporation A US clearing house, established in 1977, owned jointly by the American Stock Exchange, the National Association of Security Dealers and the New York Stock Exchange.

National Stock Exchange (NSE) The national exchange of India and the second largest in the country, founded in 1994 as an alternative to the Bombay Stock Exchange. It operates a nationwide automated clearing and settlement system.

natural monopoly A type of monopoly that arises where such is the scale of business operations that is sensible to have only one supplier of the service (such as nationalized or privatized energy and water utilities).

NEF (ISO) code Niger Republic – currency CFA franc.

natural rate of interest The interest rate at which the demand for and supply of loans is equal.

NAV Abbreviation of *net asset value*.

NBV Abbreviation of *net book value*.

nearby delivery In the commodity market, indication that delivery will be made in the next calendar month.

nearby futures Futures contracts that are closest to maturity. In the USA they are known as nearbys.

nearest month In the trading of commodity futures and options, the expiry dates that are closest to the present.

near money A liquid asset that can be transferred immediately (such as a bill of exchange or cheque), although not as liquid as cash. It is also known as quasi-money.

negative cashflow A cashflow in which the outgoings are greater than income.

negative equity An asset that is currently worth less than the money borrowed to pay for it. An all-too-common example is a house whose current market price is less than the remaining value of the mortgage taken out to buy it.

negative income tax (NIT) A system of taxation by which those earning less than a specific income receive tax credits to bring their income in line with a guaranteed minimum income.

negative interest A charge made by a bank or other financial institution for holding funds for a certain time.

negative pledge A contractual undertaking by a borrower not to use the same assets to obtain another loan elsewhere (without the lender's permission).

negotiable Transferable, or subject to adjustment by negotiation.

negotiable instrument A document that may be freely exchanged, usually by endorsement, and which entitles the bearer to a sum of money. Negotiable instruments include bills of exchange, certificates of deposit and promissory notes.

negotiable security A security that is easily passed from one owner to another by delivery. In the UK, very few securities are negotiable in this way.

negotiation fee A bank's charge for arranging a loan.

Nepal currency Nepalese rupee (NPR), divided into 100 paisa.

net That which remains after all deductions and charges have been made.

net assets The difference between a company's assets and its liabilities (sometimes termed owners' equity).

net asset value (NAV) The amount that, in theory, each share would be allocated if a company ceased trading, sold its assets, and shared the proceeds. It is the ratio of the company's shareholders' funds to the number of shares issued.

net cashflow In any accounting period, the difference between cash entering a company and cash leaving it. See *cashflow*.

net change For any bond, commodity, mutual fund or stock, the difference between the closing price from one day to the next.

net current assets The difference between current assets and current liabilities, equal to a company's working capital.

net debt *See gearing.*

net dividend The dividend paid on a company's shares after the tax credit has been deducted.

net interest Any interest paid on a deposit or investment after deduction of income tax at source (such as interest paid into a tax-payer's account at a building society).

net loss For a given accounting period, the amount by which all expenses and losses exceed all revenues and gains; sometimes called negative net income.

net margin The difference between the selling price of an item and the total cost of making and selling it.

net present value (NPV) In a discounted cashflow, the present value of cash outflows from a company less the present value of cash inflows. The worth of a future project can be assessed by discounting all future cashflows to the present to see if a desired rate of return would be achieved. A negative NPV would indicate that the project is not viable.

net profit The amount of a company's income that remains after deducting all expenses.

net profit ratio An *accounting ratio* equal to a company's net profit divided by its sales.

net profit percentage An *accounting ratio* equal to a company's net profit (before interest and tax) divided by its sales, multiplied by 100.

net realizable value (NRV) The amount that could be obtained for an asset (less direct selling costs). Or the sales value of a company's stock (less cost of sales). Both may be less that actual cost.

Netherlands Antilles currency Netherlands Antilles guilder (ANG), divided into 100 cents.

Netherlands currency guilder (florin) (NLG), divided into 100 cents. The 1999 legacy conversion rate was 2.20371 to the euro. It will fully change to the euro/cent from 2002.

net worth The value of a company after liabilities have been deducted from the true market value of its assets.

net yield The yield (on an investment) after tax has been deducted.

new issue An issue of shares by a company that is seeking listing on a stock exchange for the first time. The term may also apply to the issue of equities or loan stock by an existing listed company in order to raise additional capital.

new issue market The part of the money market, principally the stock exchange, that supplies long-term capital to a company (see *new issue*). It is also known as the primary market.

new listing A security that has just begun trading on an exchange.

new sol The standard currency unit of Peru, divided into 100 centimos. It is also known simply as the sol.

new time On the London Stock Exchange, the last two days of an account. Transactions conducted in new time are settled at the end of the next account; for this reason, new time is effectively part of the next account period.

New York Cotton Exchange (NYCE) New York's oldest commodity exchange, dating from 1870. In addition to commodities, it and its subsidiaries trade in financial futures and options.

New York Futures Exchange (NYFE) A US subsidiary of the New York Stock Exchange, established in 1979 in competition with the domination of futures trading by the Chicago exchange.

New York Mercantile Exchange (NYMEX) A US commodity market established as the Butter and Cheese Market of New York in 1872. It changed its name to the New York Metals Exchange in 1887. It adopted its present name after merging with the Commodity Exchange (COMEX) in 1994. The NYMEX division deals mainly in futures in crude oil and oil products (including petrol), palladium and platinum; the COMEX division deals in other metals, such as aluminium, copper, gold and silver; it also trades in coal.

New York Metals Exchange See *New York Mercantile Exchange (NYMEX)*.

New York Stock Exchange (NYSE) The biggest stock exchange in the world, established in 1792, which trades in stocks, shares, bonds, warrants, rights and options. More than 2000 companies and 5000 securities are listed. Situated in Wall Street, it is colloquially called Big Board (after the huge illuminated display of share prices on the floor of the exchange).

New Zealand currency New Zealand dollar (NZD), divided into 100 cents.

NGN (ISO) code Nigeria – currency naira.

ngultrum The standard currency unit of Bhutan.

ngwee A subdivision (1/100) of the Zambian kwacha.

NIC Abbreviation of *National Insurance Contribution*.

niche marketing The practice of selling in a sector of the market that caters for a well-defined and usually small group of customers.

niche player A generally small financial institution that deals with a specialized sector of the market (*see niche marketing*).

NIF Abbreviation of *note issuance facility*.

Niger Republic currency CFA franc (NEF); there is no subdivision.

Nigeria currency naira (NGN), divided into 100 kobo.

Nikkei Average A short form of *Nikkei Stock Average*.

Nikkei-Dow Jones Average The former name of the *Nikkei Stock Average*.

Nikkei Stock Average A share index of the Tokyo Stock Exchange, published since 1949, based on the 225 major equities quoted on the market. It is determined by the newspaper group Nihou Keizai Shimbun, commonly called Nikkei.

nil basis A way of calculating earnings per share (after tax) that assumes there is no distribution of profits as dividend.

nil paid A new issue of shares for which the issuing company has yet to be paid. The term is most commonly applied to rights issues.

NIT Abbreviation of *negative income tax*.

NL Abbreviation of *no liability*.

NLG (ISO) code Netherlands – currency guilder (florin). The 1999 legacy conversion rate was 2.20371 to the euro. It will fully change to the euro/cent from 2002.

NMS Abbreviation of *National Market System and normal market size*.

no-brainer A fund that tracks the performance of a stock index. Its manager buys all the stocks listed on a major index, and hence no discretionary investment decisions are required.

NOK (ISO) code Norway – currency Norwegian krone.

174 no liability (NL)

no liability (NL) The Australian equivalent of a *public limited company (plc)*.

no-load share A share sold at net asset value with no commission charge.

no-load fund A form of US unit trust that employs no salesman and therefore pays no commission or distribution costs. An investor thus avoids paying a commission on shares purchased, the only expense remaining being a relatively modest management fee.

nominal capital Another term for *authorized capital*.

nominal exchange rate A currency's exchange rate expressed in terms of current prices (with no allowance for inflation).

nominal interest rate A rate of interest expressed in terms of current prices (with no allowance for inflation).

nominal partner A partner who lends his or her name to a firm, but who has invested no capital and does not take an active part in the organization. He or she remains liable for the partnership's debts.

nominal price The price of a security expressed in terms of current prices (with no allowance for inflation).

nominal value An alternative term for *face value*.

nominee A person or institution in whose name assets are transferred but who has no beneficial interest in the asset concerned.

nominee shareholder Usually an institution that acquires shares in a company on behalf of somebody else (the beneficial owner). This enables the true shareholder's identity to be concealed and is often used when a person wishes to build up his or her shareholding prior to a take-over bid.

non-acceptance The refusal to accept a bill of exchange by the person on whom it is drawn.

non-amortizing mortgage A mortgage in which a lump sum has to be paid at the end of the mortgage period to pay off the outstanding principal and interest. It is also called a balloon mortgage.

non-assenting bond A bond whose issuer has plans for a financial reorganization but which has not been approved by the bondholder.

non-bank An organization that transacts financial business outside the commercial banking system. See *licensed deposit taker*.

non-business days Sundays and bank holidays when most financial institutions are closed for business. They are not included in days of grace, and bills of exchange that fall due on a non-business day are postponed until the following day. The Latin form of non-business day is dies non.

non-contributory pension An occupational pension scheme in which the employee makes no contribution. The employer is responsible for paying all the necessary contributions and offers the pension scheme as a benefit to its employees.

non-cumulative preference share A type of preference share for which unpaid interest (dividend) is not carried over until the next year.

non-equity investment Any investment in securities except in company shares (equities).

non-forfeiture clause A clause in a life assurance policy that allows it to continue even though premiums have not been paid. Usually the surrender value is used to pay the premiums for a set period, or until the value is exhausted.

non-interest-bearing note Another term for a *zero-coupon bond*.

non-marketable security A security that cannot be traded on the Stock Exchange (i.e. there is no secondary market), such as annuities, certificates of deposit and the various National Savings products.

non-participating policy A type of life assurance policy in which there is no additional bonus from an investment element.

non-participating preference share Type of preference share in which holders are paid a dividend before ordinary shareholders but do not receive additional dividends in a very profitable year.

non-performing asset The part of a company's capital that is currently yielding no return, and on which none is expected. Fixed assets are generally classified as non-performing.

non-performing loan A loan whose interest payments are very overdue (usually taken to be 90 or more days in the USA).

non-profit insurance *See without-profits policy.*

non-qualified Describing an employee share option plan in which the gain made by the employee (i.e. the difference between the grant price and the market price) is taxed as income and not as a capital gain.

non-qualifying policy A type of life assurance policy that does not satisfy the qualification rules (regarding tax). Before 1984, a non-qualifying policy would not have qualified for premium relief. The effect of holding a non-qualifying policy now is that policyholders who are higher-rate taxpayers when payment is made may be subject to 17% tax on any gain made on the policy. Basic-rate taxpayers, however, have no liability.

non-recourse finance A type of loan that relies for its repayment and servicing on the profit made by the object for which the money was borrowed (and not on any other assets of the borrower).

non-voting share A company share whose holder is not entitled to vote at the annual general meeting (AGM).

normal market size (NMS) A method of classifying shares, introduced in 1991, equal to 2.5 times the average daily customer turnover last year divided by the price of the share. It has replaced the classification into alpha, beta, gamma and delta shares.

Norway currency Norwegian krone (NOK), divided into 100 ore.

note issuance facility (NIF) A type of medium-term credit guarantee in which a bank provides funds to an issuer of promissory notes before the notes are actually issued; the guarantor usually buys any unsold notes.

note of hand An alternative tem for a *promissory note*.

note purchase facility An alternative tem for a *note issuance facility*.

notice day In commodity markets, the day when notice must be given of the intention to supply a commodity (under contract to be delivered that month).

notice deposit Any type of deposit account for which notice of withdrawal must be given (or a charge or loss of interest incurred).

noting and protest The first two stages in dishonouring a bill of exchange. The bill is first "noted", or witnessed, by a *notary public*, who thereby testifies to its existence but not necessarily to its validity. It is then presented again, and if refused for a second time it is protested by being returned to the notary, who then testifies to its refusal. Noting must be completed within one working day of the bill's first being dishonoured.

novation The making of a contract between the parties to an original contract and a third party in which it is agreed that the third party shall replace one of the original parties.

NPR (ISO) code Nepal – currency Nepalese rupee.

NPV Abbreviation of *net present value*.

NRV Abbreviation of *net realizable value*.

NSB Abbreviation of *National Savings Bank*.

NSE Abbreviation of *National Stock Exchange*.

NYCE Abbreviation of *New York Cotton Exchange*.

NYFE Abbreviation of *New York Futures Exchange*.

NYMEX Abbreviation of *New York Mercantile Exchange*.

NYSE Abbreviation of *New York Stock Exchange*.

NZD (ISO) code New Zealand – currency New Zealand dollar.

O

obligation A debt; or a debt instrument (such as a bond).

OBSF Abbreviation of *off balance sheet finance*.

OBU Abbreviation of *Offshore Banking Unit*.

occupational pension A pension in a scheme set up by an employer for the benefit of its employees, or certain categories of employees. It can be contributory, where the employee pays a set percentage contribution as well as the employer, or non-contributory, where the employer pays the full amount. It can be insured with an insurance company responsible for collecting premiums and paying benefits, or self-administered, with trustees who are responsible for all administration. Such schemes may be final salary or money purchase, and either contracted-in or contracted-out (of the sate pension scheme).

odd lot A collection of stocks and shares that is so small and varied that they inconvenience the broker who agrees to sell them, and which he or she will therefore buy at only a low price. In the USA, an odd lot of fewer than 100 shares are dealt at a higher commission rate than larger quantities.

OEIC Abbreviation of *open-ended investment company*.

off balance sheet finance (OBSF) A type of company finance such that some or all of it (and associated assets) do not appear on the company's balance sheet. Although legally allowable, the practice can give a very distorted view of a company's financial status.

offer A statement that one party is willing to sell something, at a certain price and under certain conditions. If a particular buyer is unwilling to buy at the offer price or under the conditions of the offer, he or she may make a bid against the seller's offer.

offer by prospectus In contrast to an *offer for sale*, an offer by a company to sell shares or debentures directly to the public by issuing a prospectus, instead of selling shares to an issuing house.

offer for sale An offer by a company to sell its shares to an issuing house, which then publishes a prospectus and sells shares to the public.

offer for sale by tender An offer by a company to sell its shares to people who tender for them, at a price above a stated minimum.

offering circular A document that in the USA contains information regarding offers of shares exempt from Securities and Exchange Commission regulations and regulation.

offer period During a take-over, the length of time an offer for shares must remain open (at least 21 days).

offer price The price at which a market-maker is prepared to sell a security. The equivalent US term is asked price.

offer to purchase An alternative term for *take-over bid*.

Official List Formally the Stock Exchange Daily Official List (SEDOL), the official publication of the London Stock Exchange which appears daily at 5.30 p.m. detailing price movements and dividend information for almost all the securities quoted on the exchange.

official price Also known as the settlement price, on the London Metal Exchange it is the price attained in the day's first trading session, then used as a basis for most world trade for the following 24 hours.

official quotation A figure quoted daily for almost all securities on the *Official List* of the London Stock Exchange.

offshore Describing business carried out (in, e.g., London) between foreigners in foreign-denominated currency. The term is also used to describe a business that operates from a tax haven.

offshore banking unit (OBU) A foreign bank that deals in eurocurrency and foreign exchange settlements, located in a tax-favourable offshore banking centre.

old-age pension The popular name for the UK state retirement pension, paid to women over 60 years old and men over 65. Strictly, the term describes a state pension that is paid to people over the age of 80 years.

Old Lady A popular name for the Bank of England.

Old Lady of Threadneedle Street The Bank of England, which is situated in Threadneedle Street in the City of London. It is a popular term of endearment dating from the 19th century.

oligopoly An industry in which there are many buyers but few sellers. Such conditions give the producer or seller a certain amount of control over price, but leave him or her especially vulnerable to the actions of competitors.

Oman currency Omani rial (OMR), divided into 1000 baiza.

OMLX Abbreviation of *London Securities and Derivatives Exchange* and *Options Market London Exchange*.

OMR (ISO) code Oman – currency Omani rial.

on-balance-sheet financing The obtaining company funding, using internal or external sources, that shows up on the company's balance sheet.

on call Describing a repayment that must be made whenever the lender requires it (without notice).

on demand Describing a bill of exchange that is payable to the bearer immediately on presentation, such as an uncrossed cheque.

one-month money Money placed on the money market that cannot be withdrawn without penalty for one month.

one-year money Money placed on the money market that cannot be withdrawn without penalty for one year.

on-floor Describing transactions that are conducted and concluded on the floor of an exchange in the usual manner.

on-the-close order An order to buy/sell a specified number of shares at a price that is nearest the day's closing price.

on-the-open order An order to buy/sell a specified number of shares at a price that is nearest the day's opening price. The order is cancelled immediately if the trade cannot be made at that price.

open credit A type of credit extended by a financial institution that requires no security (because of the high creditworthiness of the borrower).

open-end credit An alternative term for *revolving credit*.

open-ended investment company (OEIC) A type of pooled investment fund (similar to an investment trust or unit trust) that issues shares and has no fixed share capital.

open-end fund Alternative term for a US *unit trust*.

opening price The price of a share at the beginning of a day's business on a stock exchange. This may differ from the previous evening's closing price, generally because the price has been adjusted to take into account events that have occurred overnight and the performance of other exchanges.

opening range On a financial futures market, the highest and lowest prices recorded at the opening.

opening sale The sale of an option contract where the seller becomes in effect the writer of the option by assuming responsibility for its performance.

open market A market in which goods are available to be bought and sold by anybody who cares to. Prices on an open market are determined by the laws of supply and demand.

open-market option The right to buy an annuity from the retirement fund of a personal pension scheme from any insurance company or friendly society in the market.

open order An alternative term for an order *good-till-cancelled*.

open outcry A trading method for commodities or securities in which dealers shout out buy or sell offers on the main floor of the exchange. Potential buyers or sellers also shout, and eventually one of each type get together to make a trade.

open position The exposed position of a speculator who has bought or sold without making any hedging transactions, and who therefore gambled that the market will rise or fall as he or she predicted.

operating margin A company's *operating profit* expressed as a proportion of price or operating costs.

operating profit/loss Profit/loss made by a company through its main activity, calculated by taking operating costs away from trading profit (or adding operating expenses to its trading loss). It excludes interest on loans, returns on other investments, or any other extraordinary items.

opportunity cost Revenue foregone by using an asset for one purpose rather than another. For example, a company owning a building which it uses as storage space could rent it to someone else. That rent is the opportunity cost of the building.

option An investor may pay a premium in return for the option to buy (a call option) or sell (a put option) a certain number of securities at an agreed price (known as the exercise price), on or before a particular date. The dealer may exercise his or her option at any time within the specified period and normally does so at an advantageous time depending on market prices. Otherwise the dealer may allow the option to lapse.

option dealing The buying and selling of options, which usually involves buying or selling goods or shares at some future date and at a prearranged price.

option money A premium paid in return for an option.

option price The market price of an option at any particular time.

Options Clearing Corporation A New York clearing house for over-the-counter derivatives.

options date The date on which a child's assurance is terminated or converted to a whole life assurance or endowment assurance in the child's name (often set at the date of the child's 18th birthday).

Options Market London Exchange (OMLX) An options market, established in 1989, that trades in Norwegian and Swedish equities and derivatives, to which wood pulp futures were added in 1997.

option to purchase shares An option to buy shares in a company, often to its employees, by a specified date and at a predetermined price (which generally has to be paid up front).

option writer A person who sells call options, thereby agreeing to supply shares, or a person who sells put options, agreeing to buy shares.

oral contract See *verbal contract*.

ordinary shares Company shares whose holders are the owners of the company. They are entitled to a dividend (at the discretion of the directors) after other preferential payments have been made. Ordinary shares are sometimes classed as either voting or non-voting shares, and are often also known as equities.

OSE Abbreviation of *Oslo Stock Exchange*.

Oslo Stock Exchange (OSE) Norway's major exchange, dating from 1819, which trades in commodities, options and securities using an electronic dealing system.

OTC market Abbreviation of *over-the-counter market*.

outcry market On commodity markets, trading is recorded from the outcries of the traders on the floor, although deals are sealed by private contract. Markets on which trading is carried out in this noisy manner are known as outcry markets and the style of trading is known as open outcry.

out-of-the-money option An option to buy shares (call option) for which the current price is lower than when the price was fixed. Equally, an option to buy (put option) for which the market price has risen above the agreed exercise price. In either case, the dealer makes a loss if he or she exercises the option.

outright forward A single sale/purchase in a forward currency contract (as opposed to a *forward-forward* or *swap* sale/purchase).

outright purchase/sale In the USA, the purchase or sale of financial instruments in the money markets by the Federal Reserve, not for immediate resale and therefore affecting the reserves of the banking system.

outright transaction In a foreign exchange market, a forward transaction that is not linked to a spot transaction.

outside broker A stock and share dealer who is not a member of any exchange.

outstanding Describing an account or bill that has not been paid.

overbought If there are many buyers on a market, prices (e.g. of shares) are pushed to artificially high levels and the market is said to be overbought.

overdraft If a bank customer withdraws more money from a bank account than is actually deposited with the bank, the excess is a bank overdraft. An overdraft facility must normally be agreed in advance with the bank and interest on the overdraft is charged on a day-to-day basis. It attracts high rates of interest and is ideally used only for short-term borrowing. An unauthorized overdraft attracts even higher interest (and the displeasure of the bank).

overexposure An overabundance of risk. For example, if a stockbroker is paid a salary largely dependent on the performance of the company and maintains a substantial shareholding in that company, he or she is overexposed to the possibility of a downturn in the company's business.

overheating Describing an unhealthy economic situation in which bank borrowing, balance of payment deficit, prices and wages are all rising.

overnight loan A bank loan to a discount house, secured by bills of exchange and repayable the next day.

overriding commission A commission paid to a broker in return for finding underwriters to an issue of shares.

oversold Describing a market in which there are too many sellers, with the result that prices fall to an artificially low point, too rapidly.

oversubscribed Describing the situation in a sale of shares by application and allotment where the number of shares applied for exceeds the number of shares available. The distribution is then often made using a ballot. Such shares often sell at a premium (over the issue price) when the market opens.

over-the-counter (OTC) market A market on which securities not listed on any stock exchange may be bought and sold. In practice, the OTC market is operated by a limited number of market-makers, often on the basis of matched bargains.

overvalued currency A currency that trades on foreign exchange markets at a price that makes exports uncompetitive, usually leading to a balance of trade deficit.

P

pa'anga The standard currency unit of Tonga, divided into 100 seniti.

packing The practice of adding, to the payments on a loan, charges for services such as insurance etc. without the borrower requesting them, or indeed fully understanding what he or she is buying. The practice is illegal.

pac-man defence A method of defending against a hostile take-over bid, in which the target company makes a tender offer for the shares of the aggressor (named after an early US computer game in which pac-man gobbled up his attackers).

paid-in capital In the USA, owners' equity in a company, i.e., the total amount invested during and since its incorporation.

paid-in surplus In the USA, excess received by a company over and above the par (standard) value of its issued shares.

paid-up policy A life assurance policy where, before the end of the term of the policy, the assured has stopped paying premiums. The policy continues with a reduced sum assured (its surrender value being invested in a single-premium whole life policy) but no further premiums are paid.

paid-up share capital The capital obtained by a company for a share issue in which the shares are fully paid.

painting the tape A method of creating an impression of activity around a share, by reporting fictitious transactions. It is illegal.

paisa A subdivision (1/100) of the Indian, Pakistani and Nepalese rupee; and of the Bangladeshi taka.

Pakistan currency Pakistani rupee (PKR), divided into 100 paisa.

paper Colloquial term for any type of security or loan, particularly a short-term loan such as a Treasury bill. Most paper is negotiable (commercial paper) and can be bought and sold like any other commodity.

paper bid A take-over bid in which the bidder offers its own shares (not cash) in payment for the target company's shares.

paper company A company established, often with little capital, merely for financial purposes.

186 paper currency

paper currency An alternative name for *paper money*.

paper money Any *legal tender* in the form of a document, with a stated value but with no intrinsic value (such as a banknote).

paper profit/loss An apparent increase/decrease in the value of an asset or investment, not realized until it is sold.

Papua New Guinea currency kina (PGK), divided into 100 toea.

par Equal to the face value, or to current rate of exchange.

para A subdivision (1/100) of the Bosnia-Herzegovina and the Yugoslavian dinar.

Paraguay currency guarani.

parallel market A market outside the normal one for a particular financial instrument (such as American depositary receipts).

par bond A bond that trades at par (usually related to the new issue price).

parcel A block of shares that change hands in a single deal, or bargain.

parent company A company that owns or part-owns, but more importantly controls, one or more subsidiary companies.

Paris Bourse France's principal and, since 1991, only stock exchange (incorporating those at Bordeaux, Lille, Lyons, Marselles, Nancy and Nantes). It has had an electronic trading system (*Cotation Assistée en Continue* (CAC), based on Totonto's Computer-Assisted Trading System (CATS)) since 1988, later upgraded to SUPERCAC.

Paris Inter-Bank Offered Rate (PIBOR) French equivalents of the UK's *London Inter-Bank Offerred Rate*.

parity Equality (in value).

parking The practice of placing funds in a high-interest account while deciding what other medium to invest in.

par-priced Describing a security that is trading at its par value.

participating loan A syndicated loan, for which there are two or more lenders. The lead bank or manager arranges the loan and its terms using agreed contributions from the other banks or lenders.

participating preference share A type of *preference share* that has additional rights to a further share of profits after dividends have been allotted to ordinary shareholders.

particular lien The right to take possession of specified assets in the event of a default. A particular lien relates only to the debt arising over which the lien is held.

partly-paid Describing securities and shares for which the full nominal value has not been paid and on which the holder is liable to pay the balance either on demand or on specified dates. Formerly, it was common for a company to call up only a part of the nominal value of each share, retaining the right to demand the balance when it became necessary to increase its capital. This gave the company access to extra capital without the need to issue new shares. The term also applies to new issues in which the issue price is to be paid in instalments.

partner A person engaged in a business enterprise jointly with, and generally with the same status and responsibilities as, another or others. See *partnership*.

partner's drawing A payment to a partner, which is charged against his or her share of revenue.

partnership A formal business association, in the UK normally formed between two to twenty partners. The partners are jointly liable for the debts of the partnership, so that if one partner dies or decamps, the remaining partners are responsible for any debts.

partnership at will Partners are normally bound by a formal agreement; if not, the partnership is termed a partnership at will, and may be broken at any time by any partner.

part payment An interim payment or instalment.

par value An alternative term for *face value* or nominal value.

passbook A book issued by a building society or savings bank in which deposits and withdrawals are recorded.

passed dividend A dividend that is not paid in a particular year (because the company has insufficient funds).

passing a name The act of providing a seller with the name of a potential buyer. A broker often "passes a name" in this way, but rarely guarantees the buyer's solvency when doing so.

passive income The income a company receives from its operations in a *tax haven*.

passive management A form of mutual fund management, increasingly popular in the USA, in which a fund's investments are selected automatically to match the exact performance of a stock index.

patent An authorization that grants the addressee the sole right to make, use or sell an invention for a specified period of time. Applicants for a patent must establish the novelty of their invention.

pawnbroker A person who lends money secured against goods, called a pledge, and issues a formal receipt for them. Loans are normally made for a period of six months and seven days and, if not repaid in that time (with interest), the pawnbroker is entitled to sell the pawned goods.

payables An informal term for a company's short-term debts (debtors).

payable to bearer A bill of exchange on which the payee or, if the bill has been endorsed, the endorsee is not named. The bill is payable to the bearer.

payable to order A bill of exchange payable to an existing payee or order and not endorsed in blank. Only a bill payable to a payee or "bearer", a fictitious payee or endorsed in blank will be payable to bearer and therefore transferable by delivery without endorsements.

pay-as-you-earn (PAYE) A system of income tax collection in the UK in which tax is deducted from current earnings at source (formally schedule E). The employer is responsible for collecting the tax, and the employee receives only net wages. A similar system is called pay-as-you-go in the USA.

payback period The time that elapses before a new project's or investment's revenue equals its initial cost. In the USA it is also called payoff or payout.

pay day Account day; a colloquial term for the day on the London Stock Exchange when settlements are due.

PAYE Abbreviation of *pay as you earn*.

payee A person or people to whom money is paid (in the case of a cheque also called the drawee).

payer A person who authorizes payment (in the case of a cheque also known as the drawer, the person who signs it).

paying agent A bank or other institution that pays capital or interest to holders of bonds, for which the agent may charge a fee.

pension 189

payment for honour supra protest The payment of a bill of exchange (that is not paid and is protested) by somebody who is not named on the bill.

payment in kind A payment, generally of wages, made in goods or services rather than in money. Payment of total wages in kind was made illegal in the UK in the 19th century, but part-payment in kind still occurs (for example, luncheon vouchers and the use of a company car are payments in kind).

payment on account Part payment of an outstanding debt, usually coupled with an agreement to repay the balance by a specific date. For long-term contract work, payment on account (also called progress payment) denotes a stage payment for work completed by a certain specified time.

pay-out ratio A US term for a dividend expressed as a percentage of the available company profit, known in the UK as dividend cover.

peculation Embezzlement, particularly the appropriation of public money or goods by an official.

PEG Abbreviation of *price-earnings growth factor*.

pegging the exchanges The maintenance of a fixed currency exchange rate, by government intervention in the markets. Pegging the exchanges is generally resorted to in order to prevent an unfavourable rise or fall in the value of a currency.

penalty clause A clause in a contract stating that if one party breaks the contract (e.g. by late delivery of goods) it will be liable to pay a penalty, usually in money.

pence A subdivision (1/100) of the pound sterling, the Gibraltar pound, and the legacy currency the Irish punt.

pennia A subdivision (1/100) of the Finnish markka.

penny shares/stock Shares/stock in a company that are traded in low denominations (usually under 50p). Penny shares are often highly volatile.

pension A regular payment, made weekly, monthly or annually to a person after he or she retires from full-time employment, generally for the rest of the pensioner's life. Retirement pensions are provided by the state in the UK; private pensions include personal annuity schemes (personal pensions) and occupational pensions.

P

pensionable age The age at which somebody is entitled to draw a *pension*. See also *retirement age*.

pension fund A pool of money, contributed by employers and employees, which is invested and from which pensions are paid.

pension holiday A moratorium in an employer's contributions to a company pension scheme because the pension fund is in surplus.

pension mortgage A type of mortgage in which the borrower pays back only interest while funding a pension plan that will provide a lump sum to pay off the capital as well as providing a pension at retirement.

pension plan An alternative term for *pension scheme*.

pension scheme A system set up to pay its members a pension over and above any entitlement for a state pension. It may involve a personal pension, or a company pension that is topped up by additional voluntary contributions (AVCs).

PEP Abbreviation of *personal equity plan*.

PER Abbreviation of *prices/earnings ratio*.

PE ratio See *price-earnings ratio*.

per capita Latin for "by the head". It usually indicates that a sum will be divided equally among a group of people. Thus *per capita* income is calculated by dividing the total income received by a group by the number of people in the group; it is thus the average income.

percentile For a range of numbers or values, the nth percentile is the value below which n per cent of them fall. The 50th percentile is the *median*.

per diem Latin for "by the day". It usually applies to allowances, rental or charges made on a daily basis.

perfect competition An idealized situation in a market in which all rival products are the same (so the buyers have no preference), there are many small buyers and sellers (so that none can on its own control price) who all try to maximize profit and can leave or join the market whenever they like, and buyers pay only the lowest price.

perfecting the sight The act of supplying the full details demanded on a *bill of sight*.

performance bond Also known as a contract bond, a bond delivered by a contractor to a public authority for a sum in excess of the value of a contract, and which is to be paid in the event of a breach of contract. It is therefore a form of guarantee.

performance fund A type of unit trust that invests in high-growth stocks with the aim of making higher-than-average returns (when the stocks are traded).

permanent interest-bearing shares (PIBS) A type of high fixed-interest building society investment redeemable only with the winding-up of the society.

per mille Per thousand, equal to 0.5%.

perpetual annuity The payment of a constant annual amount in perpetuity.

perpetual debenture A debenture that may not be repaid on demand.

perpetual floating-rate note A type of *floating-rate note* that is not to be repaid, i.e. it has no maturity and is mainly used as an investment instrument.

personal annuity scheme A type of contributory pension for self-employed people or those not in an occupational pension scheme.

personal equity plan (PEP) A UK government scheme, dating from 1987, that encouraged people to invest in equities (such as stocks and shares). The investments can include unit trusts and investment trusts. The growth and proceeds from a PEP were completely free of income and capital gains tax, but they lost their tax-free status in 1999, when *individual savings accounts (ISAs)* were introduced.

Personal Investment Authority (PIA) A UK self-regulatory organization (SRO) established in 1993 that oversees businesses that deal with private investors. It took over responsibilities from the Financial Intermediaries, Managers and Brokers Regulatory Association (FIMBRA) and the Life Assurance and Unit Trust Regulatory Organization (LAUTRO). In 1997 it was itself incorporated into the Financial Services Authority (FSA).

personal loan A generally unsecured loan made (usually by a bank but now increasingly by registered brokers) to a private individual. This form of loan is generally fairly modest and intended for some specific purpose, such as the purchase of a car.

personal pension scheme Also called a personal pension plan (PPP), an arrangement that allows somebody to contribute part of his or her earnings to an insurance company or other pension provider, which invests the money in a pension fund. The lump sum that becomes available on retirement purchases an annuity, which provides the pensioner with regular (taxable) payments. It is therefore a money purchase scheme.

personal tax Income tax levied on earned and unearned income.

PET Abbreviation of *potentially exempt transfer*.

petrocurrency Money (usually US dollars) paid to the exporters of petroleum in exchange for their product. After the OPEC countries markedly increased prices, the amount of petrocurrency in circulation exceeded the oil-exporting countries' economies to absorb it. As a result, much of it was invested in the world's financial markets, where it helped to offset the trade deficits caused by the OPEC price rises.

petrodollars Petrocurrency denominated in dollars.

Peru currency Peru new sol (PES), divided into 100 centavos.

PES (ISO) code Peru – currency Peru new sol.

peseta The standard legacy currency unit of Spain (including the Canary Islands) and Andorra.

pesewa A subdivision (1/100) of the Ghanaian cedi.

peso The standard currency unit of Argentina, Chile, Colombia, Cuba, the Dominican Republic, Guinea-Bissau, Mexico, and the Philippines, divided into 100 centavos; and or Uruguay, divided into 100 centesimos. The latter is also known as the peso Uruguayo.

Pfennig A subdivision (1/100) of the German legacy currency the Deutschemark.

PFF (ISO) code French Pacific Islands – currency CFP (French Pacific Islands) franc.

PGK (ISO) code Papua New Guinea – currency kina.

Phillipines currency Phillipines peso (PHP), divided into 100 sentimos.

PHP (ISO) code Phillipines – currency Phillipines peso.

physical Short for physical commodity, any traded commodity that, unlike a *future*, is available for immediate (or very early) delivery.

PIA Abbreviation of *Personal Investment Authority*.

piastre A subdivision (1/100) of the Egyptian, Lebanese and Syrian pound, and of the Sudanese dinar.

PIBOR Abbreviation of *Paris Inter-Bank Offered Rate*.

PIBS Abbreviation of *permanent interest-bearing shares*.

PINC Abbreviation of *property income certificate*.

pink sheet A daily US publication, by the National Quotation Bureau, that lists bid and offer prices of brokers who deal in American Depositary Receipts (ADRs) and over-the-counter stocks (OCTs).

pit On a commodity exchange, the equivalent of a stock exchange trading floor. It derives its name from the nickname for the floor of the Chicago Commodities Exchange; the term now applied to the floor of any open outcry exchange.

pitch The area in which a trader operates.

pit trader A dealer on the floor of a commodity market or stock exchange that trades by open outcry.

PKR (ISO) code Pakistan – currency Pakistani rupee.

placement Another term for *placing*.

placing The process of issuing shares through an intermediary, usually a stockbroker or syndicate. The intermediary "places" the shares with clients, frequently institutional investors, or with members of the public. A certain proportion of any share quoted on the London Stock Exchange must be made available to the public through the Exchange.

plain vanilla A colloquial term for the most basic form of a financial instrument (with no added bells and whistles).

playing the market The practice of buying securities on a rising market and then selling quickly to make a modest profit.

PLC (also **plc**, **Plc**) Abbreviation of *public limited company*.

pledge A transfer of personal property from a debtor to a creditor as security for a debt. Legal ownership of the property remains with the pledger. *See also* **pawnbroker**.

ploughed-back profit An alternative term for *retained profit*.

plus tick An alternative name for *uptick*.

point The unit of price in which stocks are traded. One point usually equals £1 or $1.

poison pill A technique used by companies facing a hostile take-over bid to make their stock as unattractive as possible to the aggressor. Stock may be diluted by new issues and company articles changed to require the approval of a greater proportion of the shareholders for the take-over. Expensive subsidiaries may be purchased to reduce the attractiveness of the company's balance sheet, and provision is often made for *greenmail* payments and for *golden parachutes*.

Poland currency zloty (PLZ), divided into 100 groszy.

polarization Under the terms of the UK Financial Services Act, a regulation that does not allow financial intermediaries to act as advisers about financial products and at the same time sell their own products. They must act either as independent advisers, recommending the best product for their client from all those available, or as tied agents, selling only their own products – i.e. they must polarize.

policyholder A person who has an insurance policy; it is usually, although not necessarily, the insured person (the insured).

policy loan A loan from a life office against the security of an endowment policy. The loan is limited to 90% or 95% of the surrender value accrued.

political risk In trading in securities, the risk that an investment may be harmed by changes in government policy towards such things as currency controls, interest rates, quotas, state ownership, tariffs, taxation and so on. Devaluation of a country's currency is not normally regarded as a political risk.

Ponzi scheme A scheme in which depositors are paid interest by using capital from the later depositors. It is fraudulent (and therefore illegal), named after a 1920s US swindler named Charles Ponzi.

pool An organization of insurers and reinsurers through which particular risks are written. Premiums, losses and expenses are shared in agreed proportions, usually fairly small percentages. Pools exist for extremely hazardous risks such as nuclear risk.

pooled investment An investment in which many small amounts paid by individuals are pooled together to spread the risk and gain the advantages of economies of scale. Examples include *unit trusts* and *investment trusts*.

pooled pension fund A collection of pension funds under the management of one fund manager.

portable pension A pension that can be taken from job to job, employment to self-employment, and vice versa without any loss of rights. The term is used to describe an advantage of a personal pension or free-standing additional voluntary contributions.

portfolio A selection of securities held a person or institution. Portfolios generally include a wide variety of stocks and bonds to spread the risk of investment, and the contents of the portfolio are generally managed – that is, continually adjusted in order to maximize income or growth.

portfolio insurance Protection for a portfolio of investments provided by financial futures and options. Decisions about buying and selling these are made by the fund manager.

portfolio investment An alternative term for *indirect investment*.

portfolio manager See *portfolio*.

Portugal currency Portuguese escudo (PTE), divided into 100 centavos. The 1999 legacy conversion rate was 200.482 to the euro. It will fully change to the euro/cent from 2002.

position In general terms, the place of a dealer or investor (in terms of financial commitment) in a fluctuating market. See also *long position; open position; short position*.

postal order An order for the payment of money up to the value of £20 that can be purchased at any UK post office and encashed at a post office or paid into a bank account. A commission called poundage (95p on a £20 order) is paid by the person who buys the order. See also *money order*.

post-date To affix some future date to a financial instrument, most commonly a cheque, thereby preventing the occurrence of actions or transactions concerning that document before the specified date.

postdating An alternative term for *forward dating*.

potentially exempt transfer (PET) The transfer of a gift from one person to another, or certain types of trust (disabled, accumulation and maintenance or interest in possession) that does not attract inheritance tax immediately. Tax is paid only if the donor dies within 7 years of making the gift and then on a sliding scale. Once the donor lives for 7 years, the gift becomes fully exempt. See *inter vivos policy*.

pot is clean A term indicating that all the shares allocated during an issue for offer to institutional investors have been taken up.

pound The standard currency unit of Cyprus, divided into 100 cents; Egypt, Lebanon, Sudan and Syria, divided into 100 piastres; and the Falkland Islands, Gibraltar and the United Kingdom, divided into 100 pence. See also *punt*.

pound cost averaging The lower average cost per share that results from investing a fixed sum of money regularly in a share, compared with buying a fixed number of shares at the same frequency (because more shares are purchased at low prices than at high prices). In the USA it is termed dollar cost averaging (equal to a constant dollar plan).

pound sterling The standard currency unit of the United Kingdom, so called to distinguish it from other currencies called the pound (*see pound*).

PPP Abbreviation of personal pension plan (*see personal pension scheme*).

PPP rate See *purchasing power parity exchange rate*.

preauthorized payment The US equivalent of a UK banker's order or direct debit.

precious metal Gold, silver, platinum or palladium, held as bullion by many central banks and in the form of coins or jewellery by some investors. Most investment vehicles for precious metals are, however, in the form of paper: commodities, futures, options and shares in mining companies.

predator A company that is attempting a hostile take-over bid for another company, also called an aggressor.

pre-emption The right to purchase shares before they become generally available, usually offered in the case of new issues to existing shareholders. Rights of pre-emption are often proportional to the value of an existing holding.

preference shares Also known as preferred stock, preference shares offer the shareholder preferential claims to dividends, usually at a fixed rate, and a prior claim to ordinary shareholders on the company's assets in the event of liquidation. The market price for the preference shares tends to be more stable than that of ordinary shares. Preference shareholders may not vote at meetings of ordinary shareholders. Preference shares fall into five categories: cumulative, non-cumulative, redeemable, participating and convertible. They are known as preferred stock in the USA.

preferential creditor A creditor who gets paid in preference to others in

pre-tax profit 197

the event of a company's liquidation (such as the Inland Revenue, for taxes outstanding, and Customs and Excise, for VAT).

preferential debt In bankruptcy or liquidation, a debt owed to a *preferential creditor*.

preferred stock A US term for *preference shares*.

preliminary statement An announcement of a company's full year results made a month or two before publication of its annual report.

pre-market Describing trading in commodities before the main market opens.

premium In general, any price, payment or bonus valued higher than the norm; the opposite of discount. More specifically, it is the difference in price between the offer price of a new share issue and the price at which it begins trading, if the latter exceeds the former. The term is also used to describe the positive difference between the face value and redemption value of any stock or bond.

premium bond In the UK, a short form of **National Savings Premium Bond**. In the USA, it is a bond whose selling price is higher than its face value or redemption value.

premium income The income that an insurance company receives from premiums on insurance policies.

pre-placement An activity that occurs before a share has been placed (*see placing*).

pre-preferential debt In bankruptcy or liquidation, a debt that ranks before even preferential debts (such as money held on trust by a bankrupt).

pre-refunding The practice of issuing shares to re-fund (i.e. pay for debts that are about to mature), not immediately before maturity of the old issue, but in advance of it, in order to take advantage of favourable interest rates.

present value An assessment of the current net cost or value of future expenditure or benefit. Most frequently it is used to measure return on capital investment.

president The chief executive of a US company, equivalent to a managing director in the UK.

pre-tax profit A profit calculated before allowance is made for tax (such as corporation tax and capital gains tax).

Prevention of Fraud (Investments) Act 1939

Prevention of Fraud (Investments) Act 1939 UK legislation that requires dealers in shares to be licensed (unless a member of a stock exchange) and banning the making of misleading statements about or unsubstantiated claims for shares (as was once done by share pushers).

price The cost of purchasing a unit of goods or services. Very broadly, prices are generally set by the manufacturer and retailer, taking into account all fixed costs and variable costs and allowing for a profit margin.

price-earnings growth factor (PEG) The ratio of the predicted *price-earnings ratio (P/E ratio)* of a share to is anticipated growth rate in *earnings per share*, devised to help in choosing investments (the higher, the better).

price-earnings ratio (PE ratio) A method of deciding whether a share is expensive or not compared with those of other companies obtained by calculating the ratio between the share price and the earnings per share.

price index A series of numbers that represent average prices over a period of time, relative to a base (usually 100 or 1000) assigned to the first period. *See also* **share index**.

primary capital The capital that is used in the start-up of a business.

primary commodity A commodity that is essential to a nation, such as food, fuel and raw materials for industry.

primary dealer A regulated dealer in US government securities, or a market-maker in UK gilt-edged securities (gilts) and Treasury bills.

primary efficiency ratio An alternative term for *return on capital*.

primary market The market in new security issues, also known as the new-issues market.

prime lending rate A referential interest rate charged in the USA for short-term loans made to people or organizations with a high credit rating. It is approximately equivalent to the banker's base rate in the UK.

prime rate Alternative term for prime lending rate.

principal 1. In finance, the original sum invested or lent, as distinct from any profits or interest involved. 2. A person who gives instructions to an agent.

principal-only bond A bond, issued at a discount, on which no interest is paid. The full face value is paid on maturity.

private bank A UK bank that is usually a partnership (unlike a commercial or joint-stock bank, which is a limited company).

private company A privately-owned company whose shareholders' liability may be limited or unlimited. See *private limited company*.

private equity An investment in an unlisted company by an institutional investor.

private limited company A company with share capital of at least £50,000 whose shares are not available to the general public through the medium of a stock exchange (i.e. it is unlisted), and whose members do not exceed 50 in number. The shareholders' liability is limited the value of their shareholding. See also *public limited company (plc)*.

privately held Describing a company, capital or other possessions that are in the hands of a person or a group of people.

private placement An alternative term for *private placing*.

private placing The sale of the whole of a new issue of shares to a financial institution.

private property Assets that a person holds as part of his or her personal wealth.

privatization The practice of offering shares in previously state-owned industries or enterprises for sale to the general public. British Aerospace, British Rail and British Telecom are privatized companies in the UK. It may also be called denationalization.

probate The acceptance of the validity of a will by a proper authority. A will that has not been probated has no legal force. A grant of probate is the document issued by the probate registry to confirm that the will is valid.

probate value The value of a person's assets at the time of his or her death.

profit The surplus money, after all expenses have been met, generated by a firm or enterprise in the course of one accounting period.

profit-and-loss account An annual summary of a company's financial operations, required by law to be submitted by every trading company.

It has three sections: the trading account, the profit-and-loss account and the appropriation account. The profit-and-loss section of the account takes the profit or loss figure from the trading account, and after accounting for income not concerned with trading and expenses such as those incurred in administration, deducts tax from the final profit or loss figure.

profit margin The gross profit, usually expressed as a percentage of net sales, or as a simple net profit. A company's policy generally specifies some profit margin below which it is hardly worthwhile producing goods.

profit-sharing The distribution of some or all of a company's profits among its employees as a bonus. The distribution may be in the form of cash or shares.

profit-sharing scheme A scheme in which a trust holds shares granted to employees as a share in the company's profits. The shares cannot be sold for two years and attract income tax if sold within five years (although capital gains tax is payable).

pro forma invoice A form of invoice that is submitted before goods are despatched and used to confirm an order and to advise of despatch.

projection An estimate of future developments made on the basis of, or projected from, a knowledge of past and present events.

promissory note A document stating that a person promises to pay a certain sum of money on a certain date. It is also known as a note of hand.

property Legally property is divided into real and personal property. Real property may be defined as land and buildings held freehold. Personal property consists of other personal possessions. More specifically, property is sometimes defined as something that appreciates in value or yields an income.

property company A company that develops and owns property. It may let properties, develop new ones or convert existing ones (in order to sell them).

property enterprise trust A type of mutual fund that invests solely in *enterprise zone* properties in order to gain tax advantages for its investors.

property income certificate (PINC) A share in the ownership of a building that can be traded. It provides income from rents and, if property values rise, an opportunity for growth.

proprietary company (Pty) An Australian limited company.

proprietorship ratio An *accounting ratio* equal to the shareholders' equity in a company divided by its total sources of finance, multiplied by 100.

prospectus A document that describes a proposal, for example issued to prospective shareholders by a company intending to make a public issue of shares, giving details of past and present performance and of prospects.

protected bear An alternative name for a *covered bear*.

protectionism A policy based on self-interest, for example one that shields an industry from overseas competition, usually by the imposition of selective or general quotas and tariffs.

proxy An authorization given by a voter to another person to allow that person to vote on his or her behalf, for example a shareholder may give somebody proxy to vote at a company meeting that he or she is for some reason unable to attend.

PTE (ISO) code Portugal – currency Portuguese escudo. The 1999 legacy conversion rate was 200.482 to the euro. It will fully change to the euro/cent from 2002.

Pty Abbreviation of *proprietary company*.

public 1. Describing something that is the hands of the people and, as such, managed or controlled by the government. 2. Something that is open to everybody.

public limited company (plc or PLC) A UK company whose shares are available to the general public through a stock exchange.

puisne mortgage A mortgage that is not protected by the deposit of the property's title deeds. The lender may instead register the property with the Land Register or the Land Charges Register, which ensures that any transaction involving the property must have the approval of the lender.

pula The standard currency unit of Botswana, divided into 100 thebe.

pule A subdivision (1/100) of the afghani.

pullback After a period during which market prices have been fluctuating erratically, the movement or return to a more recognizable and predictable trends.

punt The standard legacy currency unit of Ireland, divided into 100 pence.

punter A colloquial term for a gambler or speculator. See *gambling; speculation*.

purchased life annuity A type of annuity that pays an income for life (after a specified date) in return for the payment of a single premium.

purchasing power The ability of a particular monetary unit to buy goods and services – "what you can get for your money".

purchasing power parity exchange rate Known as a PPP rate for short, an exchange rate that is based on the same "basket" of goods in each country.

pure endowment assurance A type of life assurance that pays an agreed amount if the policyholder survives to a specified date. No payment is made if the assured dies before that date.

put *See* **put option**.

put band The period for which a *put option* is valid.

put option An option to sell shares, commodities or financial futures at an agreed price on or before an agreed future date.

put-through A stock exchange dealing procedure used in cases of very large orders, where a stockbroker finds both a seller and a buyer and is therefore able to "put the shares through the market" in a single quick transaction.

pya A subdivision (1/100) of the Myanmar (formerly Burmese) kyat.

pyramid selling Also known as a pyramid investment scheme, the practice of selling distributorships, or the right to sell them. The pyramid seller makes his or her profit from the sale of franchises and leaves the franchisee to dispose of the goods. In a typical system, each franchisee must guarantee to purchase a certain quantity of goods, which he or she then disposes of by recruiting distributors. Those at the bottom of the pyramid usually have to sell to their family and friends.

Q

QAR (ISO) code Qatar – currency Qatar rial.

Qatar currency Qatar rial (QAR), divided into 100 dirham.

qindarka A subdivision (1/100) of the Albanian lek.

qualification period With certain insurance policies, the period of time that must elapse before an insurance company will meet a claim by the policyholder.

qualified acceptance An acceptance of a bill of exchange that imposes certain conditions. The liability of any endorsers is cancelled if the holder refuses to take up the qualified acceptance.

qualified endorsement An endorsement phrased in such a way as to limit the endorser's liability. *See*, for example, *without recourse*.

qualified report Also termed a qualified audit report or qualified opinion, an auditor's report in which he or she qualifies the financial statements (because he or she does not sanction the way in which some matters are treated or because the scope of the audit has been limited for some reason).

qualifying life assurance policy A type of life assurance policy, which has to meet various conditions, whose proceeds are free from tax liability. Policies effected before 14 March 1984 are eligible for *life assurance premium relief* if qualifying.

qualifying shares A fixed number (or percentage) of shares that a person must hold before he or she is entitled to a position on the board of directors or to a bonus issue.

quality of bills of exchange One of the three grades of bills of exchange: trade bills, agency bills or bank bills.

quantitative fund management A method of making investment decisions based on mathematical analysis of the market.

quantity discount A reduction in price made available to the purchaser of at least a stated minimum quantity of goods.

quanto option An option on a foreign security that is guaranteed to be free from exchange rate risk.

quasi-equity Loan stock or a debit instrument that offers its holder rights and befits similar to those offered to holders of shares. See also *mezzanine finance*.

quick ratio An alternative term for **liquidity ratio**.

quid pro quo Literally, this for that. The principle of quid pro quo underlies all contracts in that a contract is an agreement to exchange something such as services in return for something else, such as cash.

quiet time The time between the registration of a new share issue and its being offered for sale.

quotation spread The difference between the offer price and the bid price on a security. It is also known as the bid-offer spread.

quoted company A company that has received a listing on a stock exchange.

quoted currency A rate of exchange is determined by relating two currencies. The base currency is assigned the numerical value one; the other is the quoted currency. Thus if the exchange rate between sterling and the Deutschmark is quoted at 3.5, sterling is the base currency and the Deutschmark is the quoted currency.

quoted investment An investment in shares or debentures that are quoted on an official exchange.

quoted price The price of a security as it is quoted on an exchange. The quoted price may fluctuate from day to day, or even minute to minute.

quote driven Describing a stock market that reacts (in terms of prices) to the quotations of market-makers rather than to the number and flow of incoming orders.

R

raider A person or group that initiates a hostile take-over bid by buying quantities of the target company's shares.

rally A rise in market price of a share (or of market prices in general) when prices have stagnated or consistently fallen, usually followed by a further fall.

ramp To artificially push up the price of a share (usually by buying them and thus making them look sought after). It is illegal for a company to buy its own shares for this purpose.

rand The standard currency unit of South Africa, divided into 100 cents.

random walk theory A theory of stock movements developed in the 1950s and 1960s, which states that share prices move in a random way, and so their movements up or down cannot be predicted.

range The difference between the highest and lowest prices (of a commodity, security, etc.) during a given period of time.

RAP Abbreviation of *retirement annuity policy*.

rate of collection of debtors An *accounting ratio* equal to a company's average trade debtors divided by its credit sales, multiplied by 365 (to express the result in days).

rate of exchange Also called exchange rate, the rate at which various currencies are exchanged for each other. See **exchange rate**.

rate of interest See *interest*.

rate of payment of creditors An *accounting ratio* equal to a company's average trade creditors divided by its credit purchases, multiplied by 365 (to express the result in days).

rate of return The amount of money made on an investment (in the form of interest or dividend), normally expressed as a percentage of the amount invested. The revenue a company receives for investing resources in some commercial activity is also known as its rate of return. See also **accounting ratio**.

rate of return of gross assets An *accounting ratio* equal to a company's net profit (before interest and tax) divided by its average gross assets, multiplied by 100.

rate of return on shareholders' equity An *accounting ratio* equal to a company's earnings for equity shareholders divided by the average shareholders' equity, multiplied by 100.

rate of stock turnover An *accounting ratio* equal to a company's cost of goods sold divided by its average stock held. It can be multiplied by 365 to express the result in days.

rating A method of classifying various financial instruments, based on an assessment of whether payments of capital and interest will be made when they are due. For example, Standard & Poor's ratings in the USA range from triple A (AAA), the best, to D (the worst: a debt that is in default).

rating agency An organization that rates the quality of issuers of securities or commercial paper (*see* **credit rating; rating**).

reaction A fall in market prices after a period of continuous price rises. It is the opposite of a *rally*.

real The standard currency unit of Brazil (also called cruzeiro real), divided into 100 centavos.

real-estate investment trust (REIT) A publicly-quoted US trust that issues bonds against a package of commercial property as security.

realignment The effectively a devaluation of a currency occurring under a fixed exchange rate system when one country's currency gets out of line (thus favouring its exports).

real income Income after taking into account inflation. For example, a 10% pay rise when inflation is running at 6% is worth only 4% in real terms.

real interest rate The interest rate after taking into account the effects of inflation. For example, if an investment pays 5% interest and inflation is running at 4%, the real interest rate is only 1%.

real investment An investment in tangible assets rather than in paper assets such as securities and so on.

realized profit/loss The profit/loss that results from selling an investment or security (before which it is only a paper profit/loss).

real profit/loss A profit/loss adjusted to take into account inflation.

real property Property that consists of freehold land (as opposed to personal property).

real value The value of something after taking into account the effects of inflation.

rebate A sum of money returned to a payer because he or she has paid too much (such as a tax rebate), or a discount on the price of something.

recapitalization A euphemism for an injection of cash into a company that has insufficient of its own to continue trading safely.

receiver An official into whose hands a company with financial difficulties is placed to ensure that, as far as possible, creditors are paid.

receivership A company's state when a *receiver* is called in.

recession A stage in a trade cycle in which the decline in economic activity accelerates, causing investment values to fall, companies to have to deal with adverse trading conditions, and unemployment to rise and so income and expenditure to fall. A recession may end in a depression unless there is a recovery.

Recognized Investment Exchange (RIE) A market that has been authorized by the UK Securities and Investment Board to carry out investment business. Its individual members must also be authorized, in accord with the Financial Services Act.

Recognized Professional Body (RPB) An organization of which membership is sufficient to comply with the terms of the UK Financial Services Act with regard to investment activities and giving financial advice, without having to belong to a Self-Regulatory Organization (SRO).

recourse The right to claim from the seller of a financial instrument, such as a bill of exchange, if its commitment is not honoured.

recourse agreement In hire purchase transactions, an agreement that enables the seller to repossess goods in the event of the purchaser being unable to make the payments required.

recovery An upturn in the financial position of a company, a market or the economy in general.

recovery shares When a company's performance is improving after a period of difficulty, its share price is likely to go up. Shares in such a company are known as recovery shares (or stocks).

redeemable preference shares Preference shares for which the issuing company reserves the right to redeem (but only out of distributable profits).

208 redeemable security

redeemable security A security (stocks or bonds) that is repayable at par value at a specified date or dates (or in the event of something specified happening).

redemption The repayment of an outstanding loan or debenture stock by the borrower.

redemption date The date on which a loan or debenture is to be repaid. Redemption dates (plural) are those on a stock which is redeemable at par. In the case of UK Treasury stocks, the precise date of repayment is decided by the government.

redemption fee A premium paid to shareholders who surrender redeemable shares when asked to do so by the issuing company.

redemption price Also termed the call price, the price at which forms of indebtedness (e.g. bills of exchange or bonds) are redeemed by the institution or government that issued them.

redemption yield Also called yield to maturity, for bonds with a fixed redemption date, the yield taking into account capital gain upon redemption plus the dividend, related to the market price of the bond.

red herring On Wall Street, an initial prospectus for a share issue, circulated before the price has been fixed and the issue has been ratified by the appropriate regulating authority.

rediscounting The discounting of a bill of exchange that somebody else (such as a discount house) has already discounted.

REF (ISO) code Reunion – currency French franc. It will adopt the euro/cent from 2002.

refinance credit Credit for a foreign buyer who does not wish to pay cash and who cannot obtain credit from the UK exporter, which is made available at a foreign bank in London. The deal is concluded using a sight draft (to pay the exporter) and a bill of exchange on the buyer (paid into the foreign bank).

refinancing The taking out of a loan (at one rate of interest) to pay back other borrowing (at a higher rate of interest), known as refunding in the USA. Early repayment of a debt, however, may incur a penalty.

reflation Government action that attempts to boost a country's economy. It is done by increasing the money supply, usually by reducing interest rates and taxation.

refund 1. To return goods or money. 2. To retire an existing issue of bonds by selling a new issue.

refunding An alternative (US) term for *refinancing*.

regional stock exchange A smaller stock exchange that deals in shares of local companies as well as those listed on the main exchange. Only Germany and Switzerland still maintain significant regional exchanges.

registered bond A bond that is registered in the name of the holder. It may be transferred to another holder only with the consent of the registered holder.

registered equity market-maker A member firm of the American Stock Exchange that is allowed to trade on its own account, often buying and selling to stabilize an imbalance in a security.

registered investment adviser A US financial adviser who is registered with the Securities and Exchange Commission. He or she passes on the client's instructions to a stockbroker, in return for a percentage of the broker's commission.

registered office A UK company's official "residence" as registered with Companies House in Cardiff, and the address to which legal documents have to be delivered. It need not be on the company's premises (it may, for example, be at the offices of its accountants or auditors). It is the keeping place of the company's register of members (the share register, listing the names of shareholders and so on).

registered security A security whose holder is registered with its issuer. See *registered bond*.

registered stock An alternative term for *inscribed stock*.

register of debentures A list drawn up by a company of those people who hold debentures.

registrar A person who keeps a register. In business finance the registrar is the company or person who keeps the register of members (the share register).

Registrar of Companies A person who keeps a record at Companies House in Cardiff of all UK joint-stock companies. The registrar also holds their memorandums of association and copies of the annual report and accounts.

regressive tax A tax that decreases proportionately as a person's income increases, *e.g.*, an indirect tax such as value added tax.

regulated loan A loan of £15,000 or less, regulated by the UK Consumer Credit Act 1974, that is not exempt under the 1974 Finance Act

(which exempted loans for the alteration, improvement, purchase or repair of a private dwelling)

reimbursement The act of paying back somebody for his or her out-of-pocket expenses.

reinsurance The transfer of an insurance (or part of the risk covered) from one insurance company to another for a premium, not necessarily with the knowledge of the policyholder.

REIT Abbreviation of *real-estate investment trust*.

remaining monthly balance The amount still owing on a monthly statement (for, *e.g.*, a credit card), which usually attracts further interest.

remortgage Effectively to move a mortgage from one lender to another, using the funds provided by the second lender to pay off the first.

renewable increasable convertible term assurance (RICTA) A term life assurance contract that incorporates renewable, increasable and convertible options.

renewable term assurance A term life assurance contract for 5 years, with the option to renew at the end of the term for a further 5 years without medical evidence.

renewal notice A document sent by an insurance company to the insured reminding him or her that the next premium payment on an existing policy is due.

rent Money paid for the occupation or use of something for a period of time (such as a building, factory, office, car or television set). *See also lease*.

rent back To sell property (offices, factory space, etc.) on the understanding that the new owner will lease back the property to its original owner. It is a way of raising capital by realizing property assets without having to vacate the premises.

rentier A person whose income consists of dividends and interest (from investments), rather than wages or salary; somebody of independent means.

repackaging The practice of dividing a security into different parts and selling them as separate financial instruments (such as repayment of principal and payment of interest).

retail price index (RPI) 211

repatriation The act of transferring capital from overseas to the home market.

replacement cost For a given asset, the current market price of another similar asset. See also *replacement value*.

replacement value The amount aid by an insurance company to replace an insured item exactly as it was when lost or damaged. It is the item's replacement cost.

REPO Abbreviation of repossession, or of *repurchase agreement*.

reporting dealer Official US term for a *primary dealer*.

repurchase Situation that occurs when an issuer buys its own securities. It is most frequent in unit trust holdings.

repurchase agreement (REPO) A transaction between a bond dealer and a bank. The dealer sells government securities while at the same time agreeing to buy them back at a specified time at a price high enough to allow the bank a profit margin. In this way, the repro may be looked upon as a form of loan.

required rate of return The return (profit) an investor requires before he or she will commit money to an investment.

rescheduling of a loan An agreement between the lender and borrower to change the timing of repayments (interest or capital, or both) of a loan.

reserve price The minimum price for shares sold by tender. It is also a general term for the lowest price at which somebody is prepared to sell something or accept a bid at auction.

residential mortgage A mortgage on residential property, the commonest type of mortgage (and at one time the only type available through a building society).

restrictive endorsement An endorsement on a bill of exchange that limits the power of the endorsee to negotiate the bill.

retail price The price at which goods or services are actually sold through a retailer (higher than the wholesale price because of the retailer's mark-up).

retail price index (RPI) Formally called the General Index of Retail Prices, an analysis of trends in UK retail prices, expressed as an index number and used to evaluate changes in retail prices with reference to inflation (and thus a measure of the cost of living). It is usually related to a basket of particular goods and services. In the USA it is called the consumer price index (CPI).

retained benefits The pension benefits that have accrued in respect of a previous period of employment or self-employment. It includes deferred pensions, trasnfer plans and personal pensions.

retained earnings That part of a company's post-tax earnings not distributed to shareholders, and thus retained by the company to finance its day-to-day activities and any future expansion. Retained earnings are added to reserves and thus appear on the company's balance sheet. They are also called retentions, retained income, retained profits or ploughed-back profits.

retained income Alternative term for *retained earnings*.

retentions An alternative term for *retained earnings*.

retirement age The age at which somebody ceases full-time employment, generally at his or her own choice or sometimes written into a contract of employment. It is not necessarily the same as *pensionable age*. See also *old-age pension; state pension*.

retirement annuity policy (RAP) An individual pension arrangement that was the forerunner of the personal pension before July 1988. Existing RAPs can still be increased but no new ones could be established after that date.

Retirement Pension Forecast and Advice (RPFA) A service of the UK Department of Social Services that provides advice to people about their forecast state pension entitlements.

retiring a bill The act of withdrawing a bill from circulation by having the acceptor pay it, either on or before the due date.

return The profit and income from transactions or investments. The term is also used for a document (usually describing a financial situation) sent to an authority, such as a tax return.

return on assets (ROA) The revenue that results from employing (fixed) assets, a measure of how well a company is using them.

return on capital (ROC) Also called return on capital employed (ROCE), a measure of how well a company's capital is used, equal to 100 times the trading profit (before tax and interest) divided by the average capital employed.

return on capital employed (ROCE) See *return on capital*.

return on equity (ROE) A measure of a company's performance equal to 100 times its pre-tax profit divided by the shareholders' funds (share capital and reserves).

return on investment (ROI) A mainly US term for *return on capital employed* or *return on equity*.

return on sales (ROS) A measure of a company's performance equal to 100 times its pre-tax profit divided by the number of units sold.

Reunion currency French franc (REF), divided into 100 centimes. It will adopt the euro/cent from 2002.

revaluation A practice by means of which a company puts a new value on its fixed assets, because the nominal values and real values of such assets as property and machines have changed significantly.

revenue bond Also called municipal revenue bond, a type of bond that is popular as a source of finance with US local authorities, in which the money (principal and interest) comes from the earnings of a project that the loan helps to finance.

reversal A change in the fortunes of a company and/or its shares (from being profitable to being unprofitable, or vice versa).

reverse arbitrage The practice of paying off a bank loan by borrowing from the money market.

reverse auction A method used to reduce the number of bonds at issue by the issuer inviting holders to offer prices at which they may be bought back.

reverse mortgage A financial arrangement in which a home owner uses the equity in the home to finance the receipt of regular payments. The lending organization retains its share in the equity when the home is eventually sold.

reverse take-over The purchase of control of a public company by a smaller, private company. This is often done in order that the private company may obtain a listing on a stock exchange.

reverse yield gap A situation in which low-risk assets provide greater returns that high-risk assets.

reversionary annuity An alternate term for a *contingent annuity*.

reversionary bonus In life assurance, a bonus paid to the holders of a with-profits policy, related to the profitability of the assurance company.

revocable credit A credit facility extended by a banker who is willing to take bills of exchange, but ones that are revocable (i.e. repayable) at any time.

revolver The US term for *revolving credit*.

revolving credit Also called open-end credit, a type of lending made by a bank that is automatically renewed at the start of each period (or as soon as the sum is repaid). For example, a bank may arrange to lend a company a certain amount each month. It will stop any borrowing above that limit once it is reached, but allow borrowing to go on at the start of the next month. The US term for this arrangement is revolver.

rial The standard currency unit of Iran, divided into 100 dinars; Oman, divided into 1000 baiza; Qatar, divided into 100 dirham; and the Republic of Yemen, divided into 1000 fils.

rider 1. An addition to a document that follows logically from what has gone before. 2. An additional benefit added to a life assurance policy, e.g. a disability rider.

RIE Abbreviation of *Recognized Investment Exchange*.

riel The standard currency unit of Cambodia.

rigging the market Any action that influences a market, by overriding market forces. For example, it may be done by one dealer buying a substantial number of shares or a significant quantity of a commodity, thus pushing up the market.

rights issue The practice of offering existing shareholders the opportunity to buy more shares (i.e. subscribe more capital to a company), in order to raise additional capital. Rights issues act as a protection for the shareholder in that the total number of shares issued increases without decreasing the percentage holding of each shareholder.

ring In general, a group of people who get together in order to illegally rig the market, for example by acting in concert to push prices up or down. A ring is also a method of trading on the London futures market or metals exchange (*see* ***ring trading***).

ringgit The standard currency unit of Malaysia, divided into 100 sen. It is also known as the Malaysian dollar.

ring trading Method of trading in commodities in which dealers assemble around a ring, calling out their bids and offers. It is thus a type of outcry market.

risk The amount a buyer or seller potentially stands to lose by a transaction. There are various identifiable risks in financial trading, including **credit risk, exchange rate** risk, **interest rate** risk and **political risk**. People who do not (want to) take risks are described as risk-averse.

risk arbitrage The practice of buying into a take-over bid in the expectation that share prices will rise.

risk capital An alternative term for *venture capital*.

riskless deal A transaction that guarantees a profit to the dealer (e.g. buying a commodity or security on one market and selling it on another market at a higher price). *See also* **round tripping**.

risk premium In the currency markets, the difference between the forward exchange rate and the expected future spot rate.

risk reversal A combination of selling a call option and simultaneously buying a put option, to minimize potential loss.

riyal The standard currency unit of Saudi Arabia, divided into 100 halalas.

ROA Abbreviation of *return on assets*.

ROC Abbreviation of *return on capital*.

ROCE Abbreviation of *return on capital employed*.

rocket scientist A colloquial term for a mathematician who uses statistical methods (and computers) to analyse financial markets.

ROE Abbreviation of *return on equity*.

ROI *See* *return on investment*.

ROL (ISO) code Romania – currency leu (plural lei).

rolled-up coupon A coupon (representing the interest payment on a security or other financial instrument) that is reinvested in the instrument rather than being passed to the holder.

roller coaster A colloquial term to describe violent swings in the prices of shares or other securities over a short time.

rolling over The practice of carrying over debts into the future rather than paying them at the due date, by arrangement with the lender (usually for an additional fee).

roll-up fund An offshore investment that reinvests interest so that it becomes part of the capital, thus providing potential tax advantages.

Romania currency leu (plural lei) (ROL), divided into 100 bani.

Roosa bonds Bonds that were issued by the US Treasury in the early 1960s. They were denominated in currencies other than US dollars and held as non-marketable securities by central banks (to help to finance the federal deficit).

ROS Abbreviation of *return on sales*.

rouble (US **ruble**) The standard currency unit of Belarus (also known as Belorussia, Byelorussia) and Russia, divided into 100 kopecks; and of Tajikstan, divided into 100 tanga.

round lot A number of (possibly mixed) shares or bonds traded at the same time, as a lot; some stock exchanges specify a minimum number, depending on how actively the shares are trading. The commission charged on a round lot is generally slightly less than on an *odd lot*.

round tripping 1. On a futures market, the practice of buying and then selling the same investment, or vice versa. 2. The practice of a creditworthy company that borrows money using a bank overdraft and then lends it on the money market at a profit.

round turn An entire futures transaction from start to finish.

royalty A sum paid to an inventor, originator or author, or owner of something from which a product may be made (such as an oilfield), and calculated as a proportion of the income received from the sale of the product.

RPB Abbreviation of *Recognized Professional Body*.

RPFA Abbreviation of *Retirement Pension Forecast and Advice*.

RPI Abbreviation of *retail price index*.

rufiya The standard currency unit of the Maldives, divided into 100 laari.

running ahead The personal trading in a share by a broker immediately before following a client's instructions to do the same. It is illegal in the USA.

running margin The difference between the interest rates on borrowed money and an investment bought with it.

running yield An alternative term for *flat yield*.

rupee The standard currency unit of India, Pakistan and Nepal, divided into 100 paisa; and of Mauritius, the Seychelles and Sri Lanka, divided into 100 cents.

rupiah The standard currency unit of Indonesia, divided into 100 sen.

Russel 2000 The New York Stock Exchange index of share prices of smaller companies.

Russia currency rouble, divided into 100 kopecks.

S

safe haven currency A national currency that is secure politically.

salary Money paid to an employee, normally expressed as so much per year (per annum, p.a.), but usually paid monthly by cheque or directly into the employee's bank account.

sale Formally, the act of transferring goods or services from one person to another, accompanied by the exchange of money (the price).

sale and leaseback A sale of property where the buyer agrees to lease the property back to its former owner. In this way, the seller is able to turn the property into liquid capital while at the same time remaining *in situ*.

sales tax A type of indirect tax levied as part of the retail price of something. See also ***value added tax***.

Samurai bond A bond denominated in yen and issued by a non-Japanese company in Japan.

sandbag A defensive tactic for a take-over bid in which the target company agrees to negotiate a take-over, but lengthens the talks in the hope that a ***white knight*** might ride by in the meantime.

S and L Abbreviation of *savings and loan association*.

S & P 500 See *Standard and Poor's 500*.

santimi A subdivision (1/100) of the Latvian lats.

São Tome and Principe currency dobra.

SAR (ISO) code Saudi Arabia – currency Saudi Arabian riyal.

satang A subdivision (1/100) of the Thai baht.

Saudi Arabia currency Saudi Arabian riyal (SAR), divided into 100 halalas.

savings Money (income) set aside and not spent, often invested in a way that pays interest or makes a profit (although it can just be hidden under the mattress). Savers generally seek a "safer" investment than an ordinary investor, who may be prepared to take more risk. In corporate terms, savings are retained profits. See also ***speculation***.

savings account An account with a bank, building society or savings bank

SDR-linked deposit 219

in which people invest personal savings and earn interest. Often notice of withdrawal must be given.

savings and loan association (S & L) The US equivalent of a UK building society, also known as a building and loan association.

savings bank A bank in which (relatively small amounts of) personal savings can be deposited and interest received. The usual equivalent US term is thrift institution. See also **National Savings Bank**.

savings bonds US government bonds issued at a discount to their par value, which is their maturity value. They provide a capital gain and interest on maturity.

savings certificate See *National Savings Certificate*.

savings-related share option scheme A scheme in which a company offers its employees the chance to purchase shares in the company with money that is regularly deducted, usually before tax, from their pay.

SBIC Abbreviation of *small business investment company*.

schedule See *income-tax schedules*.

Schilling The standard currency unit of Austria, divided into 100 Groschen.

SCM Abbreviation of *small companies market*.

scorched earth A defensive tactic for a hostile take-over bid in which the target company sells its most attractive assets, or initiates adverse publicity about itself in an effort to make it seem a less desirable acquisition.

scrip issue The practice of issuing extra shares to existing shareholders free of charge. It is done by transferring reserves into the company's share account. In this way, the company increases its capitalization while at the same time reducing its share price and increasing the number of shares on the market. It is also known as a bonus issue, capitalization issue or free issue. The usual US term is stock dividend or stock split.

SDP (ISO) code Sudanese Republic – currency Sudanese dinar.

SDR Abbreviation of *special drawing right*.

SDR-linked deposit A type of private bank deposit in *special drawing rights*.

220 SEAF

SEAF Abbreviation of *Stock Exchange Automatic Execution Facility*.

seasonal variations The statistical variations that occur during a particular season. They are often taken into account when calculating e.g. unemployment figures and trends. In these cases the figures are said to be seasonally adjusted.

seat A membership of an exchange (for commodities or securities), which may be bought or sold.

SEATS Abbreviation of *Stock Exchange Alternative Trading Service*.

SEAQ Abbreviation of *Stock Exchange Automated Quotations System*.

SEC Abbreviation of *Securities and Exchange Commission*.

secondary market A market in securities that have been listed for some time, rather than in new issues. Secondary market trading occurs on a stock exchange.

second mortgage A remortgage on a property that is already mortgaged. The inevitable high risk (because the first mortgagee holds the security) results in high interest rates, and a second mortgage may not be granted unless the property has sufficient value to act as security for both loans.

second-tier market A market for shares in companies that do not have a listing in the main market (i.e. an *unlisted securities market*).

secured creditor A creditor (such as a bank) hat has a legal charge on one of the debtor's assets.

secured liability A debt in which the lender is safeguarded because the borrower has put up sufficient assets as security in the event of non-payment.

secured loan A loan secured by specified assets that revert to the lender if the loan is not repaid. It generally attracts lower interest than an unsecured loan.

securities *See security*.

Securities and Exchange Commission (SEC) A government organization founded in 1934 that regulates the securities market (brokers and stock exchanges) in the USA. It also controls auditing practices and the financial reporting of companies.

Securities and Futures Authority (SFA) A self-regulatory organization (SRO) established in the UK in 1991 to regulate the conduct of people who deal in debentures, futures, options and shares. It was formed by combining the functions The Securities Association (TSA) and the Association of Futures Brokers and Dealers (AFBD). It is itself due to be absorbed by the Financial Services Authority (FSA).

Securities and Investment Board (SIB) A UK financial watchdog, set up in 1986 by the Department of Trade and Industry to oversee the UK's deregulated financial markets. Its functions are to pass to the Financial Services Authority. The US equivalent is the *Securities and Exchange Commission*.

Securities Association, The (TSA) A former UK self-regulatory organization, established in 1986, for dealing in securities. It was formed from the London Stock Exchange and the International Securities Regulatory Organization (ISRO), and in 1991 merged with the Association of Futures Brokers and Dealers (AFBD) to form the *Securities and Futures Authority*.

securities swill An informal US term for securities that are worth virtually nothing.

securitization A tendency of companies to use security markets to raise finance rather than taking loans (borrowing) from the more traditional financial intermediaries such as banks.

securitized paper A financial instrument created by converting a bank loan into a negotiable security.

security 1. Anything (usually property or a financial instrument) pledged as personal *collateral* against a loan by the actual borrower, or the document that sets out the terms of such collateral. 2. Any financial instrument that is traded on a stock exchange and that yields an income, usually in the form of interest. It represents a loan that will be repaid at some time in the future, and a key attribute is that it should be saleable. Such securities include bills of exchange, bonds, debentures, gilt-edged securities, options, shares, stocks and unit trusts. Also included are assurance policies (but not insurance policies).

SEDOL See *Official List*.

seedcorn capital The minimum capital needed to start a new business. See *front money*; *venture capital*.

seed money An alternative term for *front money*.

SEHK Abbreviation of *Stock Exchange of Hong Kong*.

SEK (ISO) code Sweden – currency Swedish krona.

self-administered pension scheme A pension scheme that is administered by a company itself, rather than be insured or third-party administered. Often larger schemes are administered "in house", although trustees may call in investment consultants or actuaries to give advice on certain aspects.

self-assessment A system, in place since 1996/7, that enables certain UK taxpayers (such as the self-employed) to calculate their own liability for income tax and capital gains tax when making an annual tax return. There are penalties for making a late return.

self-employment Being in business on one's own account. The self-employed include those who run their businesses, either alone or in partnership, and professional people such as doctors and lawyers. They may, in turn, employ other people.

self-employment retirement annuity A type of deferred annuity available before July 1988 and restricted to self-employed people, proprietors of and partners in business, and employed people who were not eligible for a joint pension scheme.

self-invested personal pension (SIPP) A type of personal pension scheme in which the investor make his or her own investment decisions. It is run by a professional manager.

self-liquidating asset An asset that has a predetermined lifetime and liquidates itself at the end of that period. For example, in the investment trust sector, a closed-end fund with a stock exchange listing is self-liquidating.

self-regulatory organization (SRO) Sometimes called a self-regulating organization, a non-governmental organization in the UK, set up under the Financial Services Act 1986, that governs a particular area of business activity, laying down codes of practice and protecting consumers and investors. There have been various mergers among the original SROs until there are currently four: the Financial Intermediaries, Managers and Brokers Regulatory Organization (FIMBRA), the Investment Management Regulatory Organization (IMRO), the Life Assurance and Unit Trust Regulatory Organization (LAUTRO) and the Securities and Futures Authority (SFA).

sell at best An instruction to a broker to sell shares or commodities at the best price possible. So if the broker is selling , he or she must find the highest selling price; or if buying, the lowest price.

sellers' market A market that is more favourable to sellers than to buyers. Such a market often arises (but generally for only a short time) when demand is greater than supply.

seller's option On the New York Stock Exchange, an option that enables the seller to deliver the relevant security at any time within a period of 6-60 days.

sellers over A market condition on a stock exchange where there are more sellers than buyers.

selling out If a person who agrees to buy shares cannot close the deal, the seller is entitled to sell the shares for the best price possible and then charge the person who made the original tender the difference between the selling price and the original tender price, plus any costs.

selling short The practice of making a bargain to sell securities or commodities that the seller does not own. The seller does this in the hope that before settlement is due, the price of the item will fall and he or she will be able to buy enough to cover the bargain at the lower price, thereby making a profit. It is also known as shorting or short selling.

sell-side The people who are on the market to sell, rather than to buy.

sen A subdivision (1/100) of the Malaysian ringgit, the Indonesian rupiah and the Japanese yen.

sene A subdivision (1/100) of the Western Samoan tala.

Senegal currency CFA franc (SNF); there is no subdivision.

senior debt The oldest existing debt owed by a person or company, hence the debt that should be paid first in normal circumstances.

seniti A subdivision (1/100) of the Tongan pa'anga.

sentimo A subdivision (1/100) of the Phillipines peso.

separate trading of registered interest and principal of securities (STRIPS) The act of separating a bond into its capital and its coupons. The capital can then be traded as a zero-coupon bond and the coupons as interest-only securities.

SERPS Abbreviation of *State Earnings-Related Pension Scheme*.

SES *See* **Singapore Stock Exchange**.

settlement date An alternative term for *account day*.

settlement day An alternative term for *account day*.

settlement price An alternative term for *official price* on the London Metal Exchange.

settlement risk The risk in securities trading that after one party to a deal delivers securities or pays cash while the other side delays payment or delivery.

seven-day money Funds that have been invested in the money market for seven days.

SFA Abbreviation of *Securities and Futures Authority*.

SFS Abbreviation of *summary financial statements*.

SGD (ISO) code Singapore – currency Singapore dollar.

shakeout When a market cannot support the number of suppliers it has attracted, many of the less profitable suppliers leave the market, with only the more healthy operators remaining. In the USA, this process of "natural selection" is known as a shakeout.

share broker A broker who charges commission on each share, rather than on a total transaction.

share *See shares*.

share capital The capital raised by a company through an issue of shares. *See also* **authorized capital; issued capital; uncalled capital**.

share certificate A document that proves a person's ownership of a company's shares.

shared currency option under tender (SCOUT) In situations where a foreign currency contract is under tender from several companies, SCOUT allows them to share a single hedge in the form of a currency option.

share exchange An alternative term for *stock exchange*.

share exchange scheme An arrangement by which investors can use an existing portfolio of shares (instead of cash) as an investment in an investment trust or unit trust.

shareholder A person who holds shares in a company (and is thereby one of its owners).

shareholders' equity The equity in a company held by shareholders rather than by the company itself.

share index An index that shows the average change in value of a

shark watcher 225

number of individual shares. Share indexes therefore give an overall guide to movements in the financial markets. Examples include the Financial Times Stock Exchange 100 Index (FOOTSIE), the Nikkei-Dow Average and the Dow Jones Industrial Average.

share issue A method of raising capital used by a limited company, which may issues shares valued at a fraction of the company's total value. The shares are generally placed on the market by a stockbroker acting on behalf of the company in question and may, in most cases, be purchased by financial institutions, other companies and members of the public.

share option A UK scheme that gives employees the option to buy shares in their company at attractive prices (normally well below market price) at a specific future date. It therefore constitutes a type of profit-sharing scheme.

share perk A benefit granted by a company to its shareholders (such as discounts off the price of its products).

share premium On a new issue of shares, a premium charged on the nominal value of the shares if it seems that the real value is likely to be much higher.

shares A form of security that represents the shareholder's stake in the ownership of a company. They may be bought and sold, usually on a stock exchange. Income from shares takes the form of a dividend rather than interest and is declared by the company depending on its performance over the financial year. In the USA shares are generally known as common stock.

share split A free bonus issue of shares to shareholders in some proportion to their existing holding, which has the effect of increasing the number of shares held but not the stake in the company. It is called a stock split in the USA.

share warrant A document issued by a company that certifies the shares to which the holder of the warrant is entitled.

shark An informal term for a person or company that may be preparing to make a take-over bid.

shark repellent An informal term for defensive tactics resorted to in the event of a take-over bid.

shark watcher A consultant who studies the buyers of a company's shares in an effort to identify possible *sharks*.

S

226 shelf registration

shelf registration A system whereby a large US company can file details of all planned security issues (undated) with the Securities and Exchange Commission (SEC), and when they want to make an issue to raise capital they can do it "off the shelf" without waiting for clearance from the SEC. The relevant SEC rule is Rule 415, and for this reason such issues are also sometimes known as Rule 415 issues.

shell company A company that does not produce anything in the usual sense, but exists only in name. Shell companies may be set up and sold to people who are unfamiliar with the procedure for doing this (for their convenience), or may be remnants of a defunct company that has been sold on to somebody else. They may also be set up for use at some future time, or to operate as the holder of shares.

shelter An investment instrument that gives little in the way of return but allows the investor to reduce income tax liabilities.

shilling The standard currency unit of Kenya, the Somali Republic, the United Republic of Tanzania and Uganda, all divided into 100 cents.

shogun bond A bond issued on the Japanese market by a non-resident and denominated in a foreign currency (i.e. not yen).

short See *selling short* and the following entries.

short bill A bill of exchange that is payable on demand or on sight, or in less than 10 days.

short bond A bond with less than five years to maturity.

short covering When a person is *selling short*, the purchase of the security concerned in order to cover the bargain.

short credit A loan that must be repaid over a short timescale.

short-dated gilt A gilt-edged security with a redemption term of less than five years.

short-dated security A fixed-interest security that has a redemption date of less than five years.

short end That part of the market that deals with securities with relatively little time to go before payment is due. The amount of time varies from a few days up to five years, depending on which security is being traded.

short hedge A hedge against a rise in interest rates on the futures market.

shorting An alternative term for *selling short*.

short interest The interest rate that is charged on loans over a period of three months or less.

short position A situation of having sold more commodities or securities than one owns. See *selling short*.

shorts An alternative term for *short-dated securities*.

short sale The sale of a security that the seller does not own, or any sale that is consummated by the delivery of a security borrowed by or for the account of the seller.

short-term Broadly, something (in the financial world, a security) with only a shirt time left before maturity. In the USA, short-term generally means something with less than a year to run. A US alternative is near-term.

short-term capital Capital raised for a short period (such as an overdraft), usually to cover temporary cashflow problems.

short-term deposit Funds deposited (e.g. with a bank, building society or finance house) that can be withdrawn at short notice, usually reflected in the comparatively low interest rate paid.

short-term investment An investment for a short period. In the City of London, it refers to an investment for a period of days; elsewhere, the period may be up to three months. Short-term investments are usually made in return for interest rates slightly lower than those available on long-term investments.

short-termism The policy of favouring short-term investments that yield immediate profit, rather than (possibly more secure) long-term investments.

short-term loan A loan that is repayable within three years.

show stopper An informal term for a court injunction initiated by the target company of a hostile take-over bid and taken against the raider, stopping it from taking action any further.

shunter A broker who deals on two different exchanges (usually a provincial exchange and a main exchange) in securities that are quoted on both.

SIB Abbreviation of *Securities and Investment Board*.

side-by-side trading The prohibited practice in the USA of trading a share option at the same time as trading the underlying security on the same exchange.

228 Sierra Leone currency

Sierre Leone currency leone (SLL), divided into 100 cents.

sight deposit Known in the USA as a demand deposit, it is money at call or money deposited overnight.

sight draft A bill of exchange payable on presentation (i.e. on sight).

silent partner A person who invests in an enterprise but takes no active part in its management; a *sleeping partner*.

SIMEX Abbreviation of *Singapore International Monetary Exchange*.

simple interest A rate of interest calculated by keeping interest that has already accrued separate from the capital sum. Thus, when calculating the next interest payment, the capital sum only (excluding the interest already accrued) enters the calculation. In mathematical terms, simple interest equals $Atr/100$, where A is the amount invested or borrowed, t is the time in years and r is the interest rate as a percentage per annum. *See also* **compound interest**.

simple reversionary bonus A type of *reversionary bonus* declared as a percentage of the sum assured only.

Singapore International Monetary Exchange (SIMEX) An exchange, founded in 1984, that deals in commodity, energy and financial futures.

Singapore Stock Exchange Formally the Stock Exchange of Singapore (SES), an organization established in 1973 by the separation of the joint Singapore and Malaysia stock exchange. An automated trading system modelled on NASDAQ was introduced in 1987.

single-life annuity/pension A type of annuity or pension that runs only until the death of the beneficiary (and not that of any surviving spouse).

single-premium assurance A type of life assurance in which the premium is paid as a single lump sum (rather than as a series of payments).

single-premium bond A type of bond in which the investor pays a lump sum to a life assurance company, which uses the money to invest in a unit-linked fund.

single-premium endowment policy A type of endowment policy in which the premium is paid as a single lump sum (rather than as a series of payments).

sinking fund A sum of money that is set aside for a specific purpose and invested so that it produces the required amount at the right time (usually for repaying a loan).

SIPP Abbreviation of *self-invested personal pension*.

six-month money Funds invested on the money market for six months.

skip day A US term for the settlement of a security purchase two days after the deal takes place.

sleeping partner A partner who invests capital in a firm but takes no active part in its management. He or she does, however, remain liable for the partnership's debts.

slippage The underperformance of a start-up company, which may lead to the need for additional capital It is also an alternative term for downward *fluctuation*.

Slovakia currency koruna, divided into 100 haleru.

Slovenia currency tolar.

slump A period of time during which the economy is poor, with high levels of unemployment and reduced economic activity.

small business investment company (SBIC) A US company established in 1958, using low-cost funds with tax advantages from the federal government, which invests in small businesses.

small cap stocks Shares in smaller companies quoted on the US stock markets (usually with a capitalization of less than $250 million).

smaller companies market (SCM) The Republic of Ireland's equivalent of the UK *alternative investment market*.

small company fund A fund that puts unit trusts or other collective investments in the shares of various small companies.

small loan company The US term for a *finance house* that provides funds for consumer credit.

small self-administered scheme (SSAS) A type of occupational pension scheme that is aimed at directors and gives its members control over investments. "Small" means fewer than 12 active members. Such schemes are subject to strict Inland Revenue rules, including the requirement for a pensioner trustee.

smart card A plastic card that incorporates a computer memory chip, which enables it to record financial transactions (debits and credits) without access to a central computer. For example it can be charged with a credit which is drawn down as the card is used as "plastic money".

smurfing A colloquial term for the practice of transferring into a single (often offshore) account many small sums of money from many different bank accounts. It may be a device for *money laundering*.

SNF (ISO) code Senegal – currency CFA franc.

Society for Worldwide Interbank Financial Telecommunications (SWIFT) A non-profit making communications system, established in Brussels in 1977, that enables its 1500 member banks to send funds and statements to each other.

SOFFEX Abbreviation of *Swiss Options and Financial Futures Exchange*.

soft arbitrage The movement of funds between the money market and bank deposits to benefit from the difference in interest rates.

soft commodity Also called softs, any commodity other than metals (though usually applied to agricultural products).

soft currency A currency of which there is a surplus on the market and which is therefore relatively cheap. Its exchange rate will tend to fall.

soft dollars Dollars traded on the foreign exchange markets for which demand is persistently low because of a US trade deficit. The value of soft dollars tends to fall.

soft loan A loan that carries an unusually low rate of interest, often advanced as a form of foreign aid.

softs Popular name for traded commodities other than metals (e.g. foodstuffs).

sole proprietor An alternative term for *sole trader*.

sole trader Also termed sole proprietor, a person who owns an unincorporated business. He or she may employ other people.

solvency The state of a person or company that is cash positive, and able to pay all bills as they fall due; i.e. its assets are more than its liabilities. Its converse is insolvency.

solvency ratio For any financial institution, its own funds divided by its liabilities. *See also* **gearing; liquidity**.

solvent Describing a person or company in a state of *solvency*.

som The standard currency unit of Kyrgystan.

Somali Republic currency Somali shilling (SOS), divided into 100 cents.

speculation 231

SOS (ISO) code Somali Republic – currency Somali shilling.

soum The standard currency unit of Uzbekistan.

South Africa currency rand (ZAR), divided into 100 cents.

sovereign risk An alternative term for political risk.

Spain currency peseta (ESP); there is no subdivision. The 1999 legacy conversion rate was 166.386 to the euro. It will fully change to the euro/cent from 2002

special bonus An additional benefit of some long-term endowment assurances, such as an extra percentage each year or a percentage of the accrued bonuses.

special deposits Interest-earning deposits that since 1961 UK commercial banks have to place with the Bank of England. It reduces the banks' level of deposits and their capacity for lending, thereby becoming effectively a method of monetary control.

special drawing rights (SDRs) A form of credit extended by the International Monetary Fund (IMF) to its member countries as an addition to the credit they already hold. SDRs do not represent actual money, they are simply a form of credit, but they do not have to be repaid to the IMF and thus form a permanent addition to the reserves of each member country. Originally they were allocated in proportion to a country's subscription to the IMF, but since then additional allocations have been made. At first SDRs were valued in relation to the value of gold, but have since been valued in relation to the member country's own currency. SDRs may be exchanged between member countries or between those countries and the IMF.

special endorsement An endorsement in the name of a particular person on a bill of exchange.

specialist A member of the New York Stock Exchange who buys all available stock of a number of companies and sells all that he is asked to sell.

special Lombard rate The interest rate charged by the German Bundesbank when lending against the *Lombard rate* is suspended.

speculation Broadly, in finance, the practice of making investments or going into a business that involves risk with the expectation that a profit can be made. The term is sometimes used with pejorative undertones to apply to investment for short-term gain and equates it with *gambling*. (It has even been said that the difference between speculation and gambling is in the expertise and experience of the speculator.) In certain markets, such as commodities and financial futures, speculation is clearly distinguished from transactions undertaken in the normal course of trading (physical buying or selling) or hedging (where the specific purpose is to minimize overall gains and losses arising from price movements).

split A marketing exercise in which a company issues more shares to existing shareholders in order to reduce the price per share. *See also* **bonus issue**.

split-level trust Also called a split-capital trust, a type of investment company or trust in which the capital is split into capital shares (which benefit from increases in the capital value of the investments) and income shares (which benefit from the income on the investments).

sponsor An alternative description of an *issuing house* for a new issue of securities.

spot Describing something that is carried out at once, on the spot. The term is most often used on futures markets, where its opposite is forward or highest (as in highest prices).

spot deal A deal for currency exchange that must be completed within two business days of signature (at the rate prevailing at that time).

spot market A market in which the items sold (commodities and financial instruments) are available for immediate delivery. It is also known as the non-contract market.

spot month The first month for which contracts are available for futures.

spot price A price quoted for goods available for immediate delivery, usually higher than the forward price because it takes into account all costs except delivery. It has various alternative names, such as actual price and physical price

spot rate The current *exchange rate*, as opposed to the forward rate.

spot transaction A deal for cash (rather than credit) or in futures.

spread Broadly, the difference between two (or sometimes more) prices, rates or values, such as the difference between a market-maker's bid and offer prices.

Sri Lanka currency Sri Lankan rupee (LKR), divided into 100 cents.

SRO Abbreviation of *self-regulatory organization*.

SSAS Abbreviation of *small self-administered scheme*.

SSE Abbreviation of *Stockholm Stock Exchange*.

stag A person who buys new issues of shares in the hope that he or she will be able to make a fast profit by selling them soon after trading opens on the stock exchange. It should not be confused with STAGS (sterling accruing government securities).

stagflation A US term for a combination of high inflation and economic stagnation.

stagging The practice of buying shares in a company flotation to make a fast profit by selling them on a stock exchange. See *stag*.

STAGS Abbreviation of *sterling accruing government securities*.

stakeholder pension A type of personal pension aimed at workers whose employer does not provide an occupational pension scheme. It is not earnings-related, and so is also available to people who do not work. Since 2001 in the UK, every company with five or more employees has to offer a pension scheme, and stakeholder pensions are often the preferred option for very small companies. The employer may or may not make contributions to the pension fund.

stale bull A dealer who has bought in the expectation that prices will rise but cannot then sell at a profit, either because prices have remained static or fallen, or because nobody wants to buy.

stamp duty An indirect tax levied by charging for stamps that have to be stuck on certain commercial and legal documents. The amount may be fixed or depend on the value of the transaction involved.

Standard and Poor's 500 (S & P 500) A US share index based on the weighted prices of 500 securities quoted on the New York Stock Exchange.

Standard and Poor's Ratings A classification of US securities in terms of risk, varying from AAA (Triple A), the highest, to DDD (in default).

standard life The typical average "life" as accepted for life assurance, which does not display evidence of ill health and is therefore acceptable at ordinary rates of premium.

standby letter of credit (LC) A contractual arrangement guaranteeing economic or financial performance involving three parties: the "issuer" (bank), "account party" (bank customer) and "beneficiary". The bank guarantees that the account party will perform on a contract between the account party and the beneficiary. See also **letter of credit**.

stand on velvet A colloquial term for making a profit from speculation in stocks.

standstill agreement When bidding for shares in a target company, an agreement that no more bids will be made for the time being.

start-up In normal use a company that is beginning from scratch. A start-up often needs venture capital financing to help it on its way.

State Earning-Related Pension Scheme (SERPS) A non-compulsory UK government scheme established in 1978 to provide a pension for every employed person (as well as the basic flat-rate state pension), funded from part of the National Insurance Contributions (NICs) paid by employers and employees. People contributing to a pension plan or occupational pension may opt out of SERPS.

state pension A pension paid by the UK government to people who have paid National Insurance Contributions (NICs) during their working lives (and the wives of men who have made such contributions). There are two categories of state pension : the basic pension (retirement pension) and the State Earnings-Related Pension (SERPS). *See also National Insurance Fund; old-age pension; pension.*

statute-barred Describing a debt that cannot be recovered through the courts because it is more than 6 years old.

sterling accruing government securities (STAGS) A type of *zero-coupon bond*, denominated in sterling and backed by Treasury stock.

sterling warrant into gilt-edged stock (SWING) An option to buy or sell a specific gilt-edged security (gilt), obtainable from an appointed dealer and first authorized by the Bank of England in 1987.

stock 1. A fixed-term security denominated in units of £100. 2. The raw materials or manufactured goods held by a manufacturer, wholesaler, retailer or end-user (also known as stock-in-trade or inventory). 3. Generally in the USA, and sometimes in the UK, *stock* is also an alternative term for ordinary share.

stock appreciation An increase in the worth of a company's stock (inventory), generally because of inflation.

stock appreciation right The right of a stock option holder to receive cash instead of exercising the option and receiving shares.

stockbroker Formal name agency broker, somebody who gives advice and buys and sells stocks and shares on a stock exchange on his or her own account or on behalf of clients.

stock dividend An issue of a company's stock instead of a dividend. See *scrip issue*.

stock exchange Essentially a place where securities, stocks and shares are bought and sold.

Stock Exchange Alternative Trading Service (SEATS) A service that displays quotations and orders for illiquid stock in which only one (or no) market maker is willing to trade.

Stock Exchange Automated Quotations System (SEAQ) An electronic system of the London Stock Exchange that displays in the offices of brokers and others up-to-date prices and information for all quoted securities. Only market-makers are permitted to quote prices on SEAQ, accepting certain obligations in return for the increased business that SEAQ offers.

Stock Exchange Automatic Execution Facility (SAEF) A computerized system on the London Stock Exchange that allows buying and selling of securities to be done at terminals in the broker's office.

Stock Exchange Council The governing body of the London Stock Exchange, a function it shares to some extent with the Securities and Futures Authority (SFA).

Stock Exchange Daily Official List See *Official List*.

Stock Exchange of Hong Kong (SEHK) An exchange established in 1986 by merging the four previous stock exchanges in Hong Kong. It produces the Hang Seng index of 33 leading shares.

Stockholm Stock Exchange (SSE) The main stock of exchange of Sweden, known locally as the Stockholm Fondbors. It became a limited liability company in 1993, with its shares available to the general public since 1994.

stock index future A future contract that is determined by share indexes.

stockjobber An alternative term for *jobber*.

stock market An organized market in securities, stocks and shares; a stock exchange.

stock option A UK term for an option to apply for or take a company's shares.

stocks See *stock*.

stock split A US term for a *share split*.

stop-loss Describing an automatic selling price assigned to a security that prevents any further losses to an investor.

stop-loss order An instruction given by a client to a stockbroker to sell securities should they fall below a certain price.

stop order An alternative term for *stop-loss order*.

stop rate In a *repurchase agreement* (REPO), the US term for the lowest rate of interest that is accepted.

store card A type of *credit card* issued by a retail outlet.

story A security that is being actively traded on the US market at the present time, but which may lack underlying value.

stotinki A subdivision (1/100) of the Bulgarian levi.

straddle The practice of simultaneously buying forward and selling forward a futures contract or an option in the same security in order to make a profit if the price of the security moves in either direction.

strangle The practice of buying out-of-the-money call and put options that are close to expiry at a relatively low premium. If the price of the underlying future rises or falls suddenly, the buyer makes a profit.

strap A combination of a put option with two call options at the same price (and for the same period). *See also* **strip**.

street name The name of a broker in which shares are registered and who retains them (the real owner not taking actual possession), making it easier to sell the securities later if required.

Street, The A popular name for the New York Stock Exchange, referring to its location, Wall Street.

strike price Also called the striking price, basis price and exercise price, the price at which an option for the purchase or sale of a security is exercised.

strip A combination of a call option with two put options at the same price (and for the same period). *See also* **strap**.

stripping The practice of taking US Treasury bonds, stripping the interest-bearing coupon and selling that and the principal separately. Such securities are said to have been stripped.

STRIPS Abbreviation of *separate trading of registered interest and principal of securities*. See also *stripping*.

strong bear hug During a take-over, a situation in which there is a high level of publicity surrounding the bid, putting pressure on the target company.

subject bid/offer A bid/offer that is subject to stated conditions; not a firm bid.

subordinated Describing a loan or security that has an inferior claim for repayment, sometimes called a junior debt (as opposed to a senior debt, which has priority).

subscriber capital An alternative term for *issued share capital*.

subscription A sum paid to a company for shares in a new issue.

subsidiary A company that has more than 50% of its voting shares owned by another company (which is known as the parent or holding company).

sucre The standard currency unit of Ecuador, divided into 100 centavos.

suicide pill A defensive tactic in the event of a take-over bid. If the raider manages to acquire a certain percentage of the target company's shares, the remaining shareholders are automatically entitled to exchange their shares for debt securities, thus exchanging the company's equity to debt and making it seem less attractive to the raider.

summary financial statements (SFS) A shortened form of a company's report and accounts that may be sent to shareholders instead of the full report (as long as certain conditions are complied with).

sunrise industry An industry that supplies a rapidly growing market (such as biotechnology and information technology).

sunset industry A declining industry that supplies less-needed products using obsolete technology.

superannuation An occupational pension paid to an employee (who makes contributions while working) who has to retire because of age, ill health or because of redundancy.

supermajority Among a company's shareholders, between 70% and 80%

of the voters. It is usual to demand a supermajority when deciding on such points as mergers or take-overs.

superstock A share issue in the USA that gives existing shareholders a large number of votes per share. Normally used as a defensive tactic during a hostile take-over bid, superstock must be held for a certain period of time before the extra votes are credited to the holder.

support The practice of actively buying securities or foreign exchange by an "official" in order to stop their market value from falling. This most often happens when the central bank buys its owns securities to stop the price falling and thus forestall a rise in interest rates.

surcharge An extra charge imposed on certain goods, such as an added tax on imported goods (when it may be referred to as surtax).

surety An alternative term for *guarantee*.

surrender value The value (realized on surrender) that certain kinds of life assurance policies may acquire after they have been in force for a certain period of time. Usually only whole-life and endowment policies accrue a surrender value, which can be little or nothing in the early years.

surtax A higher rate of income tax formerly levied in the UK on high incomes, abolished in 1973. See also *surcharge*.

sushi bond A bond denominated in a foreign currency and issued by a Japanese institution, when it then counts as a domestic bond.

suspension notice A notice published by a company that wants, for a defined period, to suspend the facility of converting *loan stock* into *share capital*.

swap 1. A financial transaction in which assets are exchanged by two people. See *bed-and-breakfast deal*. 2. The sale/purchase of foreign currency in the spot market against the simultaneous sale/purchase of the same amount of the same currency in the forward market.

swap rate The difference between a currency's forward rate of interest and its spot rate (expressed as a premium or discount on the spot rate).

SWIFT Abbreviation of *Society for Worldwide Interbank Financial Telecommunications.*

SWING Abbreviation of *sterling warrant into gilt-edged stock.*

Swiss Options and Financial Futures Exchange (SOFFEX) A futures and options market established in 1988 by five Swiss banks in conjunction with the stock exchanges in Basle, Geneva and Zurich.

Swiss stock exchanges The main exchanges are Zurich, Geneva and Basle (in order of size), which are grouped under the *Schweizer Borse*. In 1988 the *deuxième marché* (second tier) was established, with the *avant-borse* for pre-market trading.

switching The practice of transferring investment from one security to another (in a comparable class) in order to take advantage of price fluctuations or to improve a tax position.

switching discount A reduction in offer price or discount on a unit trust that is offered to people who have invested in other unit trusts of the same financial group.

syndicate 1. A group of people who jointly own a (material) investment, such as a yacht or racehorse. 2. A group of people who come together to work for a common aim, such as underwriting large risks for Lloyd's of London.

synergy Additional benefits that are to be gained by the combination of hitherto separate activities. It is sometimes colloquially expressed as "2 + 2 = 5", and cited to justify the take-over or merger of companies with complementary or mutually reinforcing activities or resources.

SYP (ISO) code Syria – currency Syrian pound.

Syria currency Syrian pound (SYP), divided into 100 piastres.

systemic risk A risk that difficulties in any one financial market or institution may spread and cause problems for the whole system.

SZL (ISO) code Swaziland – currency lilangeni (plural emalangeni).

T

tail-gating The action of a broker who recommends purchase of a stock to one client on the basis of another customer having expressed faith in it by making a purchase. The term also includes the personal trading in a share by a broker immediately after taking an instruction from a client to do the same.

tail swallowing The practice of selling enough of a deep-discounted rights issue (of company shares) to raise the money to buy the remainder at no cost.

tailspin A sudden plunge in market prices.

Taiwan currency Taiwanese dollar (TWD), divided into 100 cents.

Tajikstan currency rouble, divided into 100 tanga.

taka The standard currency unit of Bangladesh, divided into 100 paisa.

take back When a US company is sold, the take back is a situation in which the owner must accept payment in something other than cash.

take in To accept stocks as loan security in order to postpone a sale until the next settlement date.

take-over The act of buying of a proportion of another company's shares so that the purchaser gains control of the company or its assets. *See also merger.*

take-over bid An offer by one company to buy the shares of another, thereby gaining control of the target company. It is often shortened to "bid".

take-over panel A London Stock Exchange body responsible for seeing that the City Code on Take-overs and Mergers is observed by parties wishing to make a take-over bid.

take-over stock Shares that are bought by a raider during a take-over battle.

taker A person who purchases an option.

tala The standard currency unit of Western Samoa, divided into 100 sene.

tax avoidance

tambala A subdivision (1/100) of the Malawian kwacha.

TALISMAN Abbreviation of *Transfer Accounting, Lodgement for Investors, Stock Management for Jobbers*.

talon A slip of paper that is attached along with the coupons to a bearer bond. It is used when more coupons are needed.

tanga A subdivision (1/100) of the Tajikstan rouble.

tangible assets Literally, assets that may be touched, such as buildings or stock; also called tangibles. They may be contrasted with intangible (or invisible) assets, such as a company's goodwill or the expertise of its staff. *See also* **fixed asset**.

tangibles An alternative term for *tangible assets*.

Tanzania currency Tanzanian shilling (TZS), divided into 100 cents.

tap When the UK government makes a new issue on the gilt-edged security (gilt) market, it is very rarely fully subscribed. The remaining gilts in the issue are gradually released by the government broker and this action is known as a tap.

tap buying In certain circumstances, the government will buy back gilt-edged securities (gilts) before they have matured. This is known as tap buying.

tap issue An issue of government securities direct to government departments rather than onto the open market.

tap stock Gilt-edged stock released onto the market in a *tap*.

target A company that is the object of a take-over bid.

TAURUS Abbreviation of *Transfer and Automated Registration of Uncertified Stock*.

taxable income An income on which taxes are levied. It is calculated by deducting personal allowances (and any other tax-deductible expenses) from gross income.

tax allowance A deduction from gross income to give taxable income.

tax avoidance The legal avoidance of or reduction in income tax, achieved by arranging one's financial affairs so as to take advantage all possible concessions. Such a device is also termed a tax shelter in the USA. Tax avoidance should not be confused with tax evasion (which is illegal).

242 tax base

tax base The form of income upon which tax is calculated. For example, the tax base for income tax is a person's taxable income, for corporation tax a company's profits.

tax bracket The percentage of a person's income that he or she pays in tax depends on the level of income. Incomes are divided into brackets (ranges) for the purpose of calculating tax. The term is also applied to people in that bracket.

tax concession An allowance made by the Inland Revenue to taxpayers in certain categories, which means that these people or companies pay less tax than they would otherwise be liable for. For example, tax concessions are often used by government to induce companies to relocate in areas of high unemployment.

tax credit That part of a dividend payment on which a company has already paid tax, thus relieving the shareholder from the necessity of doing so.

tax-deductible Describing an amount that may be deducted from personal income or company profits to establish the tax liability.

tax deduction Money removed from a person's salary or wages to pay income tax. In the USA, however, the term means expenses that are deductible against tax.

tax deposit certificate A document that records the deposit with the UK Inland Revenue of interest-earning funds for the future payment of taxes.

tax evasion The evasion of tax liabilities by providing false information to the Inland Revenue. It is a criminal offence in the UK. *See also* ***tax avoidance***.

tax exemption Not having to pay tax. In the USA, however, the term describes the proportion of income upon which tax is not payable.

Tax-Exempt Special Savings Account (TESSA) A former type of tax-free investment, introduced in the UK in 1991 to encourage people to save. Up to £9000 could be invested, and interest was tax-free as long as no withdrawal was made for a period of five years. TESSAs lost their tax-free status in 1999, to encourage investors to transfer to ***Individual Savings Accounts*** (ISAs).

tax exile A person who lives abroad in order to minimize liability for tax.

tax-free Describing any income received without having had tax deducted.

tax haven A country (such as the Bahamas, the Cayman Islands, Liechtenstein and Monaco) that has liberal tax and banking regulations. In some instances it benefits companies to set up their registered offices in such a country, to avoid paying taxes in their own country.

tax holiday The period during which a start-up company need not pay taxes

tax liability The amount of money that is owed to the Inland Revenue for the payment of tax.

tax return A document that all people in the UK have to send to the Inland Revenue detailing their income (earned and unearned), capital gains and any allowances they can claim. See also *self-assessment*.

tax shelter An investment instrument that does not attract tax, such as an *individual savings account* (ISA), *personal equity plan* (PEP) or *tax-exempt special savings account* (TESSA). In the USA, the term is also used for *tax avoidance*. See also *tax haven*.

tax-sheltered account An account that pays interest tax-free.

tax year The period of 12 months, specified to start at any calendar month, for tax and accounting purposes. It is also known as the financial year. See also *fiscal year*.

T-bill See *Treasury bill*.

TCV Abbreviation of *total contract value*.

TDF (ISO) code Chad – currency CFA franc.

teaser A mainly US term for an initial low rate of interest offered on an adjustable rate mortgage (ARM), which may seem very attractive at the time of the arrangement, but which inevitably rises.

technical market analyst A person who studies the stock market and predicts changes on the basis of market trends and the state of the market as a whole. See also *fundamental market analyst*.

technical rally A sudden rise in the prices of commodities or shares for technical only reasons (perhaps a milestone level of a market index).

teddy bear hug A situation in which the target company approves of a take-over bid in principle but requires a higher price.

Ted spread The difference between the price of a US Treasury bill and the price of the Eurodollar.

244 teletext output price information computer

teletext output price information computer (TOPIC) A computerized system that provides stock dealers with up-to-the-minute information on market prices, sometimes called a quote machine.

temporary annuity An annuity that begins immediately and makes annual payments for a specified number of years.

tenancy Either an agreement whereby a person is entitled to occupy a property, usually in return for rent, or the length of time agreed for such occupancy.

tenancy at will A tenancy that can be terminated at any time by either the landlord or the tenant.

tenancy in common In principle, a situation in which two or more people are entitled to tenancy of the same property and may do as each wishes with their part of it. If one tenant dies, his or her share of the property is passed to the heir, rather than to the other tenant(s). Now, however, tenancy in common applies only to groups of four or more people. *See joint tenancy.*

tenant A person who occupies a property under some form of tenancy agreement.

tenant at sufferance A tenant who remains in occupation of a property after the tenancy agreement has been terminated (a "squatter").

tender Generally, an offer to supply goods or services at a certain price and under certain conditions. A tender is usually submitted in response to an invitation to do so, normally in competition with other potential suppliers.

tender bill A Treasury bill, issued by the UK government each week to cover short-term finance. Tenders for these bills are made by discount houses and financial institutions. It is also termed a tender issue. *See also tap.*

tender issue An alternative term for a *tender bill*.

tender offer An offer for sale by tender. In the USA, it is an offer made to the shareholders of a public company to buy their holding at a certain price, normally above the current market price. This may be done by a company in order to effect a take-over.

tenge The standard currency unit of Kazakhstan.

TEP Abbreviation of *traded endowment policy*.

term assurance A life assurance policy whereby a premium is paid to provide a policy that pays the sum assured on death within the specified term. If the assured survives the term, then nothing is paid on the policy. It can be used as surety for a loan. It is also known as temporary assurance.

terminable annuity An annuity that stops after a certain time, or on an agreed date, or on the death of the beneficiary.

terminal bonus A bonus paid to with-profits insurance policyholders as a lump sum on death or maturity of a participatory policy. It is not guaranteed.

terminal date Also called terminate date, the date of expiry of a futures contract.

terminal market The financial market in futures.

terminate date An alternative term for *terminal date*.

term loan A fixed loan made for a specified number of years at a fixed rate of interest, unlike a demand loan which a borrower may be asked to repay at any time.

term shares Funds deposited with a building society for a stated number of years, to earn higher than usual interest.

TESSA Abbreviation of *Tax-Exempt Special Savings Account*.

Texas hedge A transaction in derivatives that increases risk; i.e. the opposite of a proper hedge.

TGF (ISO) code Togo Republic – currency CFA franc.

TGRs Abbreviation of *Treasury investment growth receipts*.

Thailand currency baht (THB), divided into 100 satang.

THB (ISO) code Thailand – currency baht.

thebe A subdivision (1/100) of the Botswana pula.

The Opening The call-over at the start of each trading session on some exchanges. The term is also used to mean opening price.

thin bid A take-over bid backed by an aggressor who holds only a small number of shares. It is also known as a skinny bid.

thin market Describing shares that are only rarely traded.

third-class paper A corporate debt issued by companies with a low credit rating. It can be a hazardous investment.

Third Market A London Stock Exchange market introduced in January 1987, with less stringent entry requirements than the unlisted securities market (USM), which was abolished at the end of 1990. It is also known as the third tier.

thrift and loans Financial institutions in the USA that are backed by an insurance fund and oriented towards the customer. They are also known as industrial banks.

thrift institution 1. A UK organization that encourages people to save (and use their savings in a sensible way). They range from small loan clubs to large building societies. 2. The usual US term for a savings bank.

thrifts A general US term for non-bank organizations that take deposits and make loans.

tick The minimum allowable price movement on a financial futures contract.

ticket day Also called name day, the day on the Stock Exchange when brokers give sellers the names of buyers so that deals can be settled (the names are written on slips of paper called tickets).

tigers A colloquial name for *Treasury investment growth receipts*.

tighten Describing what happens to the market price of a bond whose interest yield is lower than that at which it was issued.

tight money A US term for *dear money*.

time deposit Cash deposited in a bank and earning interest (as opposed to a non-interest earning demand deposit).

time draft A draft that matures a particular number of days after the date on it or a particular number of days after it is accepted.

time sharing An arrangement whereby people buy time during which they are entitled to use a property (such as a two-week time share in a holiday villa abroad).

time value The amount by which an option premium is greater than its intrinsic worth.

time value of money A theory which postulates that one's money is more valuable now than at any time in the future, whether it be in a hour's time, next week or next year. For example, the earlier money is received the sooner it can be invested to earn interest, and the later it is paid out the longer it will earn interest.

TND (ISO) code Tunisia – currency Tunisian dinar.

toea A subdivision (1/100) of the Papuan New Guinea kina.

toehold purchase The first acquisition of up to 5% of a target company's shares in an attempted take-over bid.

Togo Republic currency CFA franc (TGF); there is no subdivision.

Tokyo Stock Exchange (TSE) The second largest stock exchange in the world (after New York), which handles with 80% of share dealings in Japan (there are 1200 listed companies including, since 1986, non-Japanese companies). There is still a trading floor, although most deals are computerized.

tolar The standard currency unit of Slovenia.

toman 1 toman = 10 Iranian rials.

tombstone An informal term for an advertisement, placed in the press, giving details of those involved in a securities issue. A tombstone is not normally an offer of sale.

Tonga currency pa'anga, divided into 100 seniti.

tontine A type of annuity where a group of people contribute a lump sum to a fund, a sort of cooperative insurance (popular in the 11th century). When somebody dies, his or her money is shared among the other members. It ends when the last member dies.

top-hat pension An extra pension provided to a senior important employee, taken out by his or her employer.

TOPIC Abbreviation of *teletext output price information computer*.

Topix An index of the 1200 shares quoted on the Japanese stock markets, forming the basis for the Tokyo Stock Exchange futures contracts.

top up To improve the benefits gained from an existing arrangement, for example by increasing contributions to a pension or assurance scheme.

top-up loan An alternative term for a *margin loan*.

Toronto Stock Exchange (TSE) An exchange established in 1878 that today handles three-quarters of the deals done in Canada. It is regulated by the Ontario Securities Commission and since 1996 has produced the TSE 100 share index.

total assets The total of all of a company's assets (as opposed to net assets).

total asset turnover An *accounting ratio* equal to a company's sales divided by its average total assets, express as a ratio to 1.

total contract value (TCV) A figure applied to futures markets calculated by multiplying the size of the contract (e.g. 10 tons of cocoa) by the market price (e.g. £1000 per ton) to give the value of the contract (£10,000).

touch For any security, the difference between the best bid price of one market-maker and the best offer price of another. See also *spread*.

tracker An investment fund that tracks a share index, such as the FTSE 100 Index (FOOTSIE).

tracker bond A lump-sum account invested in equities that guarantees the capital and often guarantees also a minimum return.

trade bill A bill of exchange between traders. The value and acceptability of a trade bill depends on the standing of the accepting trader.

traded endowment policy (TEP) An endowment policy that can be bought and sold on the open market before maturity.

traded months The months for which futures markets quote deliveries of commodities. Each market generally uses standard months in the year.

traded option An option, and not the contract to which it relates, that is bought or sold before its expiry date.

trade investment A company investment in capital goods relating to another (usually associated) existing business, or in a new business in an established sector.

trading crowd A colloquial term for a group of traders interested in a particular security.

trading day A day on which trading takes place on a stock exchange, i.e. all days except *non-trading days*.

trading floor The area within an exchange building where trading takes place.

trading halt A temporary stoppage of trading on a securities or options market.

trading partnership The relationship that exists between two or more people running a business in order to make a profit. See *partnership*.

trading post On the trading floor of the New York Stock Exchange, an area where dealers congregate to trade.

trading risk Also called transaction risk, in a deal denominated in a foreign currency the risk that unfavourable changes in exchange rates may affect amounts of income or expenditure in the home currency.

traditional option A non-transferable option that has been available on a market for over a century, written on a variety of shares listed on the exchange. Each time a dealer wishes to buy a traditional option, the terms are rewritten.

tranche A slice or portion; an instalment. In general, one of a series of payments which when put together add up to the total agreed.

tranchette A small block of gilt-edged securities issued to the market, as an addition to stock already on the market.

transaction charge A charge payable to the London International Financial Futures Exchange on each transaction made.

transaction risk An alternative term for *trading risk*.

transferable credit A type of trade credit in which a letter of credit is opened by an importer in favour of an agent, who then transfers it to the exporter.

Transfer Accounting, Lodgement for Investors, Stock Management for Jobbers (TALISMAN) A settlement and clearing system for equities on the London Stock Exchange. Shares sold by market-makers are transferred into SEPON (Stock Exchange Pool Nominees) and buying orders are met from the same central pool. It was replaced by **CREST** in 1997.

transfer agent An organization that transfers shares from one owner to another on behalf of the issuing company, and keeps records of shareholders' names.

Transfer and Automated Registration of Uncertified Stock (TAURUS) A computerized share settlement system on the London Stock Exchange, but discontinued in 1993 in favour of **CREST** (established in 1996).

transfer deed A document that proves the sale of a property or registered stock. The make the transfer official, the seller must sign the deed. In the case of registered stock, the document is also known as a stock transfer deed or transfer form.

250 transfer stamp duty

transfer stamp duty A duty levied on the transfer of securities on the stock exchange; it is therefore a form of capital transfer tax. It is not imposed on government stocks, nor on securities bought and sold within one account.

transfer value In a pension plan, the amount available instead of preserved benefits, and able to be transferred to an alternative pension arrangement.

transmission of shares The automatic transfer of shares that does not involve a *transfer deed* but through the operation of law (as when executors of a will become registered shareholders after probate.

traveller's cheques A safer and more convenient way of carrying money abroad than taking cash. They are issued by banks, building societies and travel agents in round-number denominations in major international currencies. They are guaranteed against loss or theft. The purchaser signs the cheques when they are bought, and overseas countersigns a cheque in the presence of the person to whom it is being paid; usually proof of identity (such as a passport) is also required. They may be exchanged for foreign currency or used to pay for goods and services. A commission is usually charged when they are issued and when they are cashed.

Treasury bill In the UK, a government bill of exchange issued in £5,000 denominations to discount houses at a discount on its face value and repayable on a certain date (usually 91 days hence). In the USA, often abbreviated to T-bill, it is short-term bill of exchange issued by the US Treasury in $10,000 denominations.

Treasury bill rate The interest rate that applies to Treasury bills bought in the money market.

Treasury bill tender The Bank of England's weekly (every Friday) offer for sale of Treasury bills.

Treasury bond 1. An alternative term for a *government bond*. 2. A bond issued by the US treasury.

Treasury investment growth receipts (TGRs, or **tigers)** A form of US *zero-coupon bond* in dollar denominations.

trickle-down theory A theory according to which the money put into the pockets of those who are already rich through government policy is thought to seep down into the hands of those who are less well off. Trickle-down is thought to be a more effective method of redistributing wealth than are *transfer payments*.

trigger point The point at which a take-over bid becomes mandatory because of the percentage of shares obtained by another company or person, or the percentage of shares held by one person that must be disclosed to the company (3 per cent of the voting rights).

triple-A In the rating of US stocks and bonds, the highest rating a stock may achieve.

triple witching hour A colloquial expression for the time when expiry dates of US stock index futures contracts, options on the contracts and options on individual stocks coincide.

TRL (ISO) code Turkey – currency Turkish lira.

trust 1. A group of companies that join forces to create a cartel, or in some cases a monopoly. In the later sense it is more often used in the USA, e.g. in the term anti-trust law. 2. A sum of money or property places in the care of a group of trustees, to be managed (although not necessarily invested) for the benefit of an individual or organization such as a charity. 3. In the securities industry, an investment operation that is managed by a group of trustees on behalf of other people, such as a unit trust.

trust assurance A life assurance policy that is placed into trust for the benefit of somebody other than the assured.

trustbusting US government action taken to prevents trusts (in the US sense) forming, and to break them up if they are already in operation in an apparent effort to stimulate competition.

trust corporation A company (corporate body) legally authorized to act as trustee.

trust deed A legal document that transfers property into the hands of trustees and sets out the terms of the trust. It takes the place of a mortgage deed in some parts of the USA.

trustee A person (usually with others) who manages a trust.

trustee investment An investment that can legally be bought a trust.

Trustee Savings Bank (TSB) An organization founded in 1910 in Scotland as a savings bank for low-income small investors. It grew to become a network of banks which went public in 1986. It later merged with Lloyds Bank as part of Lloyds TSB.

trustee status Describing trustees authorized under the UK Trustee Investments Act 1961 to invest in ordinary shares (not previously permitted).

252 TSB

TSB Abbreviation of *Trustee Savings Bank*.

TSE Abbreviation of *Tokyo Stock Exchange* and *Toronto Stock Exchange*.

tughrik The standard currency unit of Mongolia, divided into 100 moengoe.

Tunisia currency Tunisian dinar (TND), divided into 1000 millimes.

Turkey currency Turkish lira (TRL), divided into 100 kurus.

Turkish Republic of North Cyprus currency Turkish lira (TRL), divided into 100 kurus.

Turkmenistan currency manat.

turn The difference between the price at which a security is bought and the price at which it is sold. It is thus the profit on the transaction.

turnover The gross value of all sales made by a company during an accounting period; total sales revenue. The term is also used for the rate at which stock or some other asset is turned over (the turnover rate).

turnover rate *See turnover*.

turn-round rate On a commodity transaction, a charge consisting of the sum of the clearing fee and the broker's commission.

two-way market A market in securities in which brokers are as willing to sell at the quoted selling price as they are to buy at the quoted buying price.

TWD (ISO) code Taiwan – currency Taiwanese dollar.

TZS (ISO) code United Republic of Tanzania – currency Tanzanian shilling.

U

UA (ISO) code Ukraine – currency hryvna.

UCITS Abbreviation of *Undertakings for Collective Investment in Transferable Securities*.

Uganda currency Ugandan shilling (UGS), divided into 100 cents.

UGS (ISO) code Uganda – currency Ugandan shilling.

Ukraine currency hryvna (plural hryvni) (UA).

ultra vires Latin for "beyond the power of", a phrase that denotes an act that goes beyond or against the acting company's objectives as defined in its articles of association.

umbrella fund An offshore fund of funds that is invested in various other offshore funds.

unappropriated profits The part of a company's profits that are not distributed as dividends or set aside for a particular use.

unbundling Colloquial term for *asset stripping*.

uncalled capital Money owed to a company on partly-paid shares. It exists as a reserve to be called upon at any time by the directors of a company.

uncertified units In unit trusts, the dividends from the trust may be reinvested, to form new units. In most cases the dividends are too small to justify the issuing of a new certificate and so uncertified units are held on behalf of the investor until the units are surrendered.

undated security An irredeemable UK government security that has no option or redemption date, also called an irredeemable security.

under-average life In life assurance, an insured person who has a physical defect or disability. It is also known as an impaired life.

undercapitalization The financial situation of a company that does not have enough capital to take it through the initial burn-out period immediately after start-up.

underlying security The security that is the subject of an options contract.

Undertakings for Collective Investment in Transferable Securities (UCITS) Unit trusts that may be traded in any of the EU countries.

undervalued currency A currency that has been oversold, i.e. its value has fallen below market value, usually because of government intervention to make its country's export prices more competitive.

underwater A colloquial term to describe shares that drop in value after the initial public offering.

underwater option A stock option offered to US employees. The shares are normally offered at a discount on the market rate, but when the market price falls below the grant price, the option goes underwater.

underwriter A person or institution that agrees to take up a proportion of the risk of something, for example an underwriter may take up the shares of an issue that are not taken up by the public, in return for a commission (known as an underwriting commission). For the issuer, the underwriter represents a guarantee that the whole issue will be subscribed. An insurance underwriter assesses a risk and decides whether to accept or not and, if so, at what premium rate.

underwritten Describing a euronote or other note that is backed by a bank, which guarantees to buy any unsold notes.

undistributed profits An alternative term for *retained earnings*.

unearned income Personal income that is not received as wages or salary for work done (employment), such as dividends, interest on investments and rents.

unearned increment A rise in an asset's value resulting from increased demand (rather than in any intrinsic improvement in the asset itself).

unfunded pension scheme A government scheme in which employed people make contributions to provide funds for paying pensions.

uniform business rate See *business rates*.

unincorporated Describing a business that is not legally a company (such as a partnership or a sole proprietorship).

United Arab Emirates currency dirham (AED), divided into 100 fils.

United Kingdom currency pound sterling (GBP), divided into 100 pence.

United States of America currency US dollar (USD), divided into 100 cents.

unitization The act of converting an investment trust into a unit trust.

unit-linked assurance A type of life assurance for which the premiums purchase units in a fund of the policyholder's choice. The value of the policy is directly linked to the performance of the underlying investments in that fund.

unit-linked personal pension A type of personal pension plan in which contributions are invested in unit trusts to provide funds for paying the pension. The commonest type of personal pension, it can be purchased with a lump sum or by means of regular payments (with a maximum allowable investment of £6000 per year).

unit trust A trust into which investors may buy by acquiring units. The capital thus collected is invested in various securities in a wide range of markets. Contributors to unit trusts benefit from the diverse nature of the portfolio built up, and from the expertise of the *fund manager*. It is called a mutual fund or a unit investment trust (UIT) in the USA.

universal whole-life policy A unit-linked whole-life assurance contract that offers flexibility in terms of varying the sum assured, and added benefits such as waiver of premium or permanent health insurance.

unlimited company A company that consists of members who are all liable for the total of the company's debts. See *limited company*.

unlimited liability The open-ended liability of the members of an unlimited company, or of the general partners in a partnership, or of the sole proprietor of a sole proprietorship. See *limited liability*.

unlisted company Also called an unquoted company, a company whose shares are not traded on a major stock exchange.

unlisted securities Also called unquoted securities or investments, securities that are not listed on a major stock exchange.

Unlisted Securities Market (USM) The former market for shares that do not fulfil the requirements for a full quotation on the London Stock Exchange, or that do not wish to be quoted, but which do fulfil certain less stringent requirements. It closed in 1996 to be replaced by the *Alternative Investment Market*.

unloading The practice of putting on the market large quantities of certain shares at a low price.

unquoted Normally describing shares or debentures that are not quoted on a stock exchange.

unquoted company An alternative term for *unlisted company*.

unquoted investment An alternative term for *unlisted security*.

unsecured debenture A debenture (a loan to a company) that gives the holder no legal redress if full repayment has not been received by the specified repayment date. In such a case, the holder of the debenture must wait until the company is would up before claiming payment. For this reason, most debentures are secured against company property or financial assets. It is also known as a simple or naked debenture.

unsecured debt Also called an unsecured loan, a loan made without any security, such as a charge on the assets of the borrower.

unsecured loan An alternative term for *unsecured debt*.

unsecured loan stock An alternative term for *unsecured debenture*.

up-and-in call/put option An option that is valueless until the underlying security's price rises above a defined level.

up-and-out call/put option An option that becomes valueless when the underlying security's price rises above a defined level.

upstream A movement, for example of funds from a subsidiary company to its parent company. *See also* **downstream**.

uptick 1. Describing a transaction (such as a sale of shares) that is made at a higher price than one obtained immediately before. It is also known as a plus tick. 2. A short-lived rise in a price or value. *See also* **downtick**.

Uruguay currency peso Uruguayo (UYP), divided into 100 centesimos.

USD (ISO) code United States of America – currency US dollar.

USM Abbreviation of *Unlisted Securities Market*.

usury Moneylending at an excessive rate of interest, not in itself illegal.

utility stock Shares in a company that provides utilities such as water, electricity and gas.

UYP (ISO) code Uruguay – currency peso Uruguayo.

Uzbekistan currency soum.

V

valium picnic A colloquial term for a quiet day on the New York Stock Exchange.

valuation An estimate of what something is worth. More particularly, it is a summary of the value of a portfolio of investments at a given time.

value added The difference between the price a company or industry pays for its materials and the price at which it sells finished goods. For example, a used-car dealer may acquire a car, recondition the engine and repaint the body. When the dealer sells the car, the added value is the value of these operations as reflected in the new (higher) selling price of the car.

value added tax (VAT) A form of indirect taxation in which the producer, seller and consumer pay a percentage of the value added to the product or service. For example, if a manufacturer buys raw materials at £10 per unit and sells each unit of product for £20, the value added is £10. The manufacturer is required to pay a percentage of the £20 in VAT, and can claim back the VAT paid on the £10-worth of materials. VAT in the UK (introduced in 1973 to replace purchase tax) is currently set at a rate of 17.5 per cent for most things (since April 1991), although some goods and services are exempt and some are zero-rated.

value at par The face or nominal value of a share.

value broker A broker who charges a commission on a total transaction, rather than per share.

Vanuatu currency vatu.

variable interest rate An interest rate (on a loan or an investment) that varies up or down depending on the money market.

variable-rate mortgage A mortgage with a rate of interest that may be varied by the mortgagee to suit conditions on the money market.

variation margin When dealing in contracts on a futures market, the gain or loss at the end of a trading day that is recorded on a person's account. If the variation margin falls below the *initial margin* required, the trader is required to deposit more funds.

VAT Abbreviation of *value added tax*.

vatu The standard currency unit of Vanuatu.

VCTS Abbreviation of *Venture Capital Trust Scheme*.

VEB (ISO) code Venezuela – currency bolivar.

vehicle currency A currency used to make payments and quotations in international investment and trade, most often the US dollar.

vendor placing When a company issues shares in payment for another company, the practice of disposing of those shares (by the selling company) through a stockbroker (rather than selling them on the market, where a large block of shares may adversely affect the price).

Venezuela currency bolivar (VEB), divided into 100 centimos.

venture capital Also known as risk capital, capital invested in a venture (usually a young or start-up company, often in high-technology areas) that presents a risk to the investor.

Venture Capital Trust Scheme (VCTS) A UK scheme established in 1993 that gives incentives (such as tax-free dividends) to corporate investors in unquoted companies.

verbal contract Also called an oral contract, a contract representing a verbal agreement between two parties, not written down nor signed by them. Most verbal contracts are enforceable by law, if they can be proved.

vertical diversification The diversification into industries or businesses at different stages of production to the diversifying company. *See also horizontal diversification.*

vertical integration An amalgamation of companies involved in different stages of production in the same industry, for example to form one company capable of extracting raw materials, using them to produce goods and then distributing and selling the manufactured product.

Vienna Stock Exchange (VSX) One of the world's oldest exchanges, established in 1771, it now handles about half of all Austrian share trading using an electronic dealing system.

Vietnam currency dong, divided into 100 xu.

volatility A measure of the stability of a particular financial instrument. If, say, a share price or a market index moves often and oscillates wildly, it is said to be volatile.

VSX Abbreviation of *Vienna Stock Exchange*.

vulture capitalism A pejorative view of *venture capitalism*, whereby investors lure talented people away from established companies, encourage them to set up on their own, work hard and be ingenious, and then face a demand for a high return on the investment.

W

WACC Abbreviation of *weighted average cost of capital*.

wager A bet. Essentially, a wager is a contract between two parties that one will give the other something of value depending on the outcome of some unpredictable future event. Such a contract is not, however, recognized in English law and for this reason gambling debts cannot be resolved through the courts. *See* **gambling**.

waiter A person on the London Stock Exchange or at Lloyd's who runs errands, takes messages and looks after the day-to-day running of the exchange. Historically, the original waiters were those in the coffee houses at which dealings first took place.

wallflower A colloquial name for a slow-moving share that is not in favour with stock market investors.

Wall Street A brief name for the New York Stock Exchange (which is located in Wall Street, Manhattan). Sometimes the name is further abbreviated to The Street.

Wall Street Journal A daily US business newspaper published by the Dow Jones company, which produces the main share index the New York Stock Exchange.

warrant (WT) 1. A long-dated option. 2. A security of a specific market value that may be exchanged for a certain share at a predetermined price. The warrant's value lies in the difference between the predetermined conversion price and the current market price of the share.

wash sale A US term for the sale and then simultaneous repurchase by a single investor of a block of securities, perhaps to give a false impression of active trading in that security. It is illegal if done between two brokers in order to avoid paying tax.

wasting asset An asset that has a limited useful life (such as a natural resource that becomes depleted as it is consumed).

watered stock Stock that has become a smaller percentage of a company's total share capital because of a subsequent share issue.

wealth tax A tax that is levied annually on wealth (which is notoriously difficult to define). It is used in some European countries but not in the UK.

weekend effect The theory that the prices of stocks and shares do better on a Friday than on a Monday, because of such influences as the way in which dealers time their settlement of purchases, etc.

weighted average cost of capital (WACC) A way of determining a company's cost of capital by assigning a required rate of return to each source of funds on its balance sheet. The size of the source is then used to weight the required return and the WACC expressed as a percentage by dividing the total return by the total weights.

weighted ballot A ballot (for shares) that is in some way biased towards a certain type of investor (e.g. an institutional investor or a small investor).

Western Samoa currency tala, divided into 100 sene.

whipsaw A colloquial term for a violent movement (or series of movements) in prices on any market.

whistle blowing A requirement under the Pensions Act 1995 that professional advisers notify the authorities if they become aware of any breach by an employer or trustee in connection with a pension scheme.

white knight When a company finds itself the target of a take-over bid, it may seek an alternative company or person to whom it offers to sell itself in preference to being taken over by the original bidder. This friendly company is known as a white knight and the tactic as a white knight defence.

white knight defence See *white knight*.

white squire defence When a company finds itself the target of a take-over bid, it may place a significant number of its shares with a friendly party in order to prevent the raider from acquiring them. This tactic is known as a white squire defence

whole-life policy A type of life assurance policy that pays out on the death of the assured whenever it occurs. He or she pays premiums until death or (sometimes) retirement.

widow's pension A government pension paid in the UK to a married woman after her husband's death.

will A legal document drawn up by a person (usually under the advice of a solicitor) giving instructions as to how the person's estate is to be distributed after his or her death. The signature on a will has to be witnessed by two people, neither of whom is a beneficiary but can be an executor.

windbill An alternative name for an *accommodation bill*.

windfall A one-off gain from an investment that cannot be relied on to recur.

winding-up The cessation of a company's business activity and the start-up of its liquidation. See *administration*.

windmill An alternative name for an *accommodation bill*.

window The normally short time for which particular funds are available, as with special lending by a central bank.

wire house An informal US term for a large stockbroking firm.

without-profits policy A type of life assurance policy whereby the policyholder does not share in the assurance company's profits. It is also referred to as non-profit insurance.

without recourse A note on a bill of exchange indicating that in the event of non-payment of the bill, the current holder may not blame the person from whom he or she bought it. It is also sometimes written in French as sans recours.

with-profits policy A type of life assurance policy whereby the policyholder receives a share of the assurance company's profits as annual bonuses during the term of the policy, and a terminal bonus on death or maturity.

won The standard currency unit of North Korea, divided into 100 zeuns; and South Korea, divided into 100 chon.

working assets All of the assets of a company except its *capital assets*; current assets less current liabilities. They include outstanding debts, stocks of raw materials, work in progress, stocks of finished goods and cash in hand.

working capital The capital available for the day-to-day running of a company, used to pay such expenses as salaries, purchases, and so on.

working-capital ratio An alternative term for *current assets ratio*.

working men's club A type of *friendly society*.

workout loan A loan that is not being repaid according to the terms of its contract (e.g. payments may be overdue).

write down To decrease an asset's book value.

write off Known as charge off in the USA, to delete an asset from the accounts because it has depreciated (or been written down) so far that it no longer has any book value.

writing off See *abandonment*.

World Trade Organization (WTO) A free trade organization encompassing more than 100 countries which superseded the *General Agreement on Tariffs and Trade*.

write down To take the cost of an asset and deduct the amount by which it has depreciated in capital terms. This gives its written-down or book value. See also **depreciation**.

write off To charge the whole of the value of an asset to expenses or loss (i.e., assign it zero value on the balance sheet). It is also known as charge off in the USA. **Bad debts** may also be written off.

writer A person who issues (sells) an option.

write up To increase the value of an asset without recording any spend on it (i.e., there is no corresponding transaction).

WT Abbreviation of *warrant*.

WTO Abbreviation of *World Trade Organization*.

X

XD Abbreviation of ex dividend, denoting a share that has been sold without the right to receive the next dividend.

XEU (ISO) code European Monetary Cooperative Fund – currency ecu.

xu A subdivision (1/100) of the Vietnamese dong.

Y

yankee A colloquial term on the London Stock Exchange for a US security.

yankee bond A bond that is written in dollar denominations to attract US investors.

yearling bond A UK fixed-interest security that has a life of less than five years. Such bonds are issued through banks and stockbrokers on a weekly basis.

yen The standard currency unit of Japan, divided into 100 sen.

YER (ISO) code Republic of Yemen – currency Yemeni rial.

yield The return on an investment, taking into account the annual income and the capital value of the investment, usually expressed as a percentage. There are also various other methods of calculating yield.

yield curve The usual tendency for a security's yield to rise with increasing maturity.

yield gap The difference in average yield between investments in ordinary shares and in gilt-edged securities.

yield to maturity An alternative term for *redemption yield*.

yuan The standard currency unit of China, divided into 10 jiaos.

YUD (ISO) code Yugoslavia – currency Yugoslavian new dinar.

Yugoslavia currency Yugoslavian new dinar (YUD), divided into 100 para.

Z

Zaire Republic currency zaire (ZRZ).

zaire The standard currency unit of the Zaire Republic, divided into 100 makuta.

Zambia currency Zambian kwacha (ZMK), divided into 100 ngwee.

ZAR (ISO) code South Africa – currency rand.

zebra A form of *zero-coupon bond* for which the accrued income is taxed annually (rather than at maturity).

zero Shorthand for *zero-coupon bond*.

zero-coupon bond Also termed a non-interest-bearing note, a US *bearer bond* that pays no dividend, but is issued at a substantial discount. A capital gain is made by the bearer when the bond matures, and so tax on the proceeds is paid at a lower rate that if they were in the form of dividends.

zeun A subdivision (1/100) of the North Korean won.

Zimbabwe currency Zimbabwean dollar (ZWD), divided into 100 cents.

zloty The standard currency unit of Poland, divided into 100 groszy.

ZMK (ISO) code Zambia – currency Zambian kwacha.

ZRZ (ISO) code Zaire Republic – currency zaire.

ZWD (ISO) code Zimbabwe – currency Zimbabwean dollar.